Entrepreneur
MAGAZINE'S

2nd EDITION

Interviews
with Top
Credit
Experts!

DIRTY LITTLE SECRETS

What the
CREDIT REPORTING
AGENCIES
Won't Tell You

Jason R. Rich

EP
Entrepreneur
PRESS®

Publisher: Entrepreneur Press
Cover Design: Beth Hansen-Winter
Production and Composition: Eliot House Productions

This publication is designed to provide accurate and authoritative information
in regard to the subject matter covered. It is sold with the understanding that the
publisher is not engaged in rendering legal, accounting, or other professional services. If legal advice or other expert assistance is required, the services of a competent professional person should be sought.

Library of Congress Cataloging-in-Publication Data
Rich, Jason
     Dirty little secrets : what the credit reporting agencies won't tell you / by
Jason R. Rich.—2nd Edition.
     p.   cm.
ISBN-10: 1-59918-499-0 (alk. paper)
ISBN-13: 978-1-59918-499-9 (alk. paper)
     1. Credit bureaus—United States. 2. Consumer credit—United States.
I. Title.
HG3751.7.R53 2013
332.7—dc23   2012034552

Printed in the United States of America

17 16 15 14 13   10 9 8 7 6 5 4 3 2 1

Contents

CHAPTER 6
How to Update or Fix Your Credit Report 109

CHAPTER 7
Ten Strategies for Improving Your Credit Rating . . 139

CHAPTER 8

Credit Card Management Strategies 171

Dirty Little Secrets

Dirty Little Secrets

CHAPTER 14

Managing Your Finances:
There's an App For That 301

Dirty Little Secrets

Acknowledgments

*T*hanks to Leanne Harvey, Randy Ladenheim-Gil, and Ronald Young at Entrepreneur Press for inviting me to work on this project. Thanks also to Karen Billipp at Eliot House Productions for her help in editing and designing this book.

I'd also like to thank my family and close friends for their ongoing love and support, and express my gratitude to you, the reader, for picking up and reading a copy of this book.

To visit my website, point your web browser to www.JasonRich.com, or you can follow me on Twitter @JasonRich7.

Discover Why Your Credit Rating Is So Important

We're living in challenging financial times. It's harder than ever for someone, even with average credit and a steady job, to get approved for a mortgage, or even receive a good deal when applying for a new credit card or car loan.

As a result, it's become essential that Americans take a proactive role when it comes to responsibly managing and protecting their credit rating. This is not something that the credit reporting agencies (credit bureaus), banks, financial institutions, credit card issuers, the government, or even your own accountant will do for you or on your behalf.

Yet, few people truly understand how to properly manage and protect their credit rating. Even fewer people comprehend exactly how essential it is to build and maintain above-average credit scores.

The information within your credit reports that are compiled by the three credit reporting agencies (credit bureaus)—Equifax, Experian, and TransUnion—combined with your numeric credit scores (which are calculated based on the information published within your credit reports) have a direct impact on almost every aspect of your financial life.

For example, your credit scores directly impact:

■ Your ability to obtain a mortgage or refinance your mortgage, as well as get approved for any type of home equity loan (or home improvement loan)

■ A landlord's application approval decision if you're looking to rent a home or apartment

■ Your chances of being approved for an auto loan

■ Your ability to get an application approved for any type of credit card

■ Whether or not you'll be able to obtain student loans for yourself or your children

■ Whether or not you'll be approved for many types of insurance policies

■ A potential employer's decision to hire you

If you do get approved for any type of credit or loan, your credit scores (and the information within your credit reports) will impact what interest rate you pay and how much you'll pay in fees to that creditor or lender over time. As a general rule, the lower your credit scores, the greater risk you pose to a potential lender. Thus, you'll wind up paying significantly higher interest rates and fees, if you're even granted credit or approved for a loan, than someone with above-average or excellent credit scores. In the case of credit cards, you'll also be offered a lower credit limit and fewer cardholder benefits.

Earning a credit rating that's classified as below average could easily cost you hundreds, perhaps thousands of dollars every month in interest charges and fees when you add up how much extra you're paying your lenders and creditors for your mortgage, car loan(s), credit card(s), student loans, etc.

Building and maintaining above-average credit scores will save you money, plus make it significantly easier to get approved for the credit and loans you want or need in the future. Contrary to popular belief, building and maintaining high credit scores and protecting your credit rating isn't difficult or terribly time consuming once you understand

Dirty Little Secrets

exactly how the process works (which is something you'll learn from this book).

Yet, going through your adult life being oblivious to how the credit reporting agencies, credit reports, and credit score systems work will most likely result in costly mistakes that will impact your financial well-being for many years in the future.

Are you aware that a mistake you make (or an irresponsible financial behavior you practice) that leads to a negative impact to your credit rating will most likely remain on your credit reports and continue to negatively impact your credit scores for seven to 10 years?

Knowing what the credit reporting agencies do, how they work, and what goes into calculating your credit scores, for example, is the first step toward building, maintaining, and protecting your credit rating.

Plus, cleaning up the credit mistakes you've already made, practicing responsible spending habits moving forward, and properly utilizing your existing credit on an ongoing basis will help to ensure an above-average credit rating now and in the future.

Dirty Little Secrets offers easy-to-understand advice and information about:

- Credit reports and how they're compiled
- Credit scores and how they're calculated
- How the credit reporting agencies work (and their relationship to your creditors, lenders, insurance companies, employer, and banks)
- Working with lenders and creditors without overpaying interest charges and fees
- Successfully working with collection agencies, creditors, and lenders to pay off debts and overcome past mistakes (without further destroying your credit rating or becoming a victim of harassing phone calls from collection agencies)
- Overcoming past credit and financial mistakes to rebuild your credit rating

■ Maintaining and protecting your credit scores and overall credit rating

■ Understanding the relationship between your credit scores, your credit reports, and your ability to obtain credit and loans (including mortgages, car loans, student loans, home equity loans, credit cards, etc.)

■ How to get approved for the loans and credit you want and need

■ Building and improving your overall credit rating and credit scores

■ Using computer software and online banking, plus easy-to-use apps on your tablet or smartphone (such as an iPhone) to help you better manage your finances, credit cards, spending, and bill-paying schedule

■ Working with a legitimate credit counseling agency if you've already run into serious trouble and need assistance rebuilding your credit and getting yourself out of significant debt

Regardless of who you are, how much money you earn, what you do for a living, where you live, your marital status, or your ability to save money, it's absolutely essential that you develop a thorough understanding of how to build, improve, maintain, and protect your credit rating. This includes the information that's published within your credit reports and paying close attention to your corresponding numeric credit scores.

As you'll discover from this book, you don't have to become a financial guru or a wiz at math to improve your overall credit rating or boost your credit scores. This book is chock full of advice, tips, strategies, and easy-to-understand information that you can start applying immediately in order to rebuild, improve, protect, and/or maintain your overall credit rating.

By reading this book, you'll discover secrets for saving money, starting immediately—on your existing loans and credit cards, for example—plus you'll learn how to save a fortune in the future by being more

Dirty Little Secrets

credit savvy. You'll also learn to avoid the most common financial and credit-related mistakes that millions of Americans make that lead to destroying their credit rating and wind up costing them a fortune.

If you're in the process of shopping around for a mortgage (to purchase a new home), or you're looking to refinance your existing mortgage, your credit scores and the information within your credit reports will have a huge impact on your ability to obtain an approval from a lender, plus directly impact how much you'll pay in fees and interest charges.

Not only does this book teach you how to find and work with a reputable mortgage broker/lender in order to save money, it offers proven strategies for saving money when acquiring or refinancing a mortgage by first working to improve your credit scores and overall credit rating before you start the application process.

Dirty Little Secrets will also help you avoid the many "credit repair" and credit score boosting scams that are out there. Regardless of what some ads for credit repair services tell you, if you've managed to destroy your credit rating, it could realistically take you three, six or 12 months (perhaps several years) to legally rebuild your credit rating and dramatically improve your credit scores. This is not something that can be done quickly and it requires effort on your part.

While this book will teach you how to repair and improve your overall credit rating and credit scores as quickly as possible, it offers no overnight solutions, especially if you've already made serious financial or credit-related mistakes that you first have to recover from. Thus, it's important that you approach your credit repair efforts with realistic expectations.

No matter what financial or credit situation you're currently facing, this book will help you improve it, plus teach you how to save money and become more responsible with your credit management practices. But, as you learn the financial and credit management secrets and strategies that are revealed, it's essential that you begin applying them in a well-organized and consistent manner in order to generate the best results in the shortest amount of time possible.

Dirty Little Secrets

Your ongoing commitment will be required if you want to achieve success and enjoy an above-average credit rating and the money-saving perks and benefits that go along with this status.

Understanding How Credit Works Can Save You Money

*I*f you examine current statistics relating to American consumers' reliance on credit cards, the number of home foreclosures taking place every month, and the percentage of people who are being forced into bankruptcy due to poor financial management or circumstances (such as job loss) that are beyond their control, the country's economic situation looks bleak.

The Federal Reserve Bank reports that 40 percent of American families currently spend more than they earn. Are you one of these people? Have you gotten yourself in over your head financially? Obviously, nobody wants to be known among their creditors and lenders as a deadbeat. Few people intentionally set out to accumulate so much debt that it becomes virtually impossible for them to eventually pay it off and get back on their feet financially. Yet, every year, millions of people find themselves experiencing dire financial problems.

These problems might be a result of your own irresponsible actions, or they could have occurred in whole or in part due to situations beyond your control (such as job loss due to downsizing, medical injury, long-term illness, divorce, death of a spouse, or being a victim of identity theft). Whatever the cause of your current financial problems, the end result will be the same.

While you may be feeling embarrassed or ashamed at your current predicament, it's important to understand that you are not alone, and that there are ways to remedy the situation over time. Furthermore, there are legitimate resources at your disposal that can provide affordable (sometimes free) guidance, if you make the effort to seek it out before it's too late.

As of March 2012, 46.7 percent of all American households maintained some type of balance on their credit cards. The average credit card balances in indebted households totaled $14,517 (versus $6,772 in average credit card debt in average American households). While this figure is actually an improvement from statistics from two years earlier, if you're one of those households juggling more than $14,500 in credit card debt, among your other debts, the amount of money you're paying in interest charges and fees is probably financially debilitating.

It's important to understand that while Americans are relying more and more on credit cards, the credit card issuers are generating record revenues as a result of fees and interest charges. In fact, the total amount of revolving credit card debit in America (as of March 2012) was $803.6 billion.

What Do You Believe About Your Debt?

Bankrate.com asked consumers a series of separate questions related to how credit works, and the results were somewhat alarming. According to Bankrate.com, "66 percent of Americans say debt is often the result of unfortunate circumstances beyond a person's control, while 60 percent say it is usually the result of bad decisions . . . . While 91 percent believe debt can be controlled by disciplined saving and spending, 72 percent also believe that debt is a part of modern life and difficult to avoid."

The number of people facing credit and financial problems is also on the rise, thanks to a generally poor economy, the troubled real estate market, rising gas prices, nationwide inflation, and carelessness when it comes to managing personal finances and credit. Lack of credit knowledge (something this book will help remedy) is also a key factor related to the cause of many people's financial woes.

Plenty of people simply mismanage their finances, can't control their spending, and choose to live beyond their financial means by over-utilizing credit cards until they're maxed out. Whatever the reason is for your financial woes, it's important to take the following steps in order to begin remedying your situation:

1. Carefully analyze your credit rating and overall financial situation so you know exactly where you stand right now.
2. Develop a comprehensive plan to begin fixing the problem.
3. Begin paying your bills on time, and simultaneously pay off past-due accounts to reduce your outstanding debt.
4. In the months and years ahead, stick to your plan to ensure a positive outcome.
5. Learn how to prevent a similar situation from happening again and take the necessary financial planning and budgeting steps to ensure you'll remain financially stable in the future.

As if experiencing financial problems isn't enough, it's important to understand how these problems can and ultimately will lead to credit problems over the long term. When you begin paying your bills late, skipping mortgage payments, and/or overutilizing your credit cards, for example, this information gets reported to the credit reporting agencies (formally known as credit bureaus). Negative information in turn gets added to your credit reports.

The information within your credit reports is then used by the credit reporting agencies and other parties to calculate your credit scores. To confuse the situation, a company previously called Fair Isaac Corporation and now called FICO calculates the FICO Score of

Dirty Little Secrets

Not Everyone In America Has Good Credit

According to CardHub.com, as of late 2011, 6.2 percent of all Americans with a credit rating had a FICO credit score between 300 and 499 (the lowest possible scores), 8.7 percent had a FICO credit score between 500 and 549, 47.4 percent had an "average" FICO credit score of between 550 and 749, 19.4 percent had a FICO credit score between 750 and 799, and only 18.3 percent of the population had the highest possible FICO credit scores (in the range of between 800 and 850).

all Americans with a credit history, while other third-party companies calculate credit scores as well. Each credit reporting agency also calculates its own credit score using proprietary formulas. You'll learn the difference between these different credit scores and how they impact your ability to obtain credit (in the form of a credit card, any type of loan, or a mortgage, for example) in Chapter 4. Your credit scores are ultimately utilized by your current and potential lenders and creditors to determine your credit worthiness.

People with excellent credit always get offered the very best credit card, loan, and financing offers with the lowest fees and interest rates associated with them. Those who have developed average or below-average credit wind up paying much higher fees and interest rates in order to obtain the same credit card and lending privileges as someone with excellent credit (someone with a history of paying all their bills on time and successfully managing their debt).

People who ultimately destroy their credit rating and earn below-average credit scores will wind up being denied credit and loans, which means obtaining credit cards, a mortgage, student loans, car loans, home equity loans, home improvement loans, store financing, or other types of credit becomes either impossible or extremely costly. Even if you have a mortgage, but wish to refinance, if your credit scores have

Dirty Little Secrets

dropped to "below average" or worse, you'll have an extremely difficult time getting approved these days.

Because we're living in a society that relies so heavily on the use of credit, it's vital that you learn how to properly manage the credit you have, protect your credit rating, build a positive credit history, and discover how to best utilize your available credit in the future.

If you've already made mistakes that have led to poor credit scores and negative information appearing on your credit reports, it's important to begin taking steps to fix the situation. The negative information currently listed on your credit reports could remain there for seven to ten years (or longer) and impact your future financial stability for many years to come.

From this book, you'll learn how to analyze and then improve upon your personal credit situation; discover the steps to take when preparing to apply for a mortgage (or refinance), car loan, or some type of major purchase; and you'll learn where to turn for help if your credit situation has gotten so far out of control that you don't have the knowledge or resources to turn the situation around yourself. You'll also discover how to utilize computer software, online banking, and apps on your tablet or smartphone to help you better manage your finances and protect your credit rating.

Finally, this book offers a handful of in-depth interviews with credit experts. From these people, you'll discover insider tips for managing your credit, improving the information listed within your credit reports, and strategies for boosting your credit scores over time.

Don't be fooled! Managing and, if necessary, rebuilding your credit can be a complex and sometimes confusing process. It's also something that can seldom be done quickly. This book will teach you exactly what to do to improve your credit situation and properly manage your credit, but if your credit scores have already dropped to a "below average" or "poor" classification, for example, it will realistically be many months or potentially several years before you can expect your credit scores to raise to an "above average" or "excellent" classification.

Dirty Little Secrets

Your Spending Habits Will Impact Your Credit Rating

The American Bankers Association published findings from a survey that concluded that less than half (48 percent) of all college upperclassmen believed their spending habits would impact their credit rating in the future—one of many misconceptions that often leads to low credit scores and a poor credit rating.

You've probably seen all kinds of ads for companies that can quickly "repair" your credit or have negative but accurate information permanently removed from your credit reports. The reality of the situation is these services are often scams or companies perpetuating some type of fraud. From this book, you will learn the process for having your credit reports modified, discover what information can be changed, and how to go about getting your credit reports corrected or updated by properly negotiating with your creditors and lenders, or by initiating legitimate disputes with the credit reporting agencies when it's appropriate.

From this book, you'll also learn the terminology you need to properly manage your credit, plus learn about a wide range of free and inexpensive resources available to you online that will help you discover even more about properly managing and rebuilding your credit.

The "Credit Tip" and "Warning" scattered throughout this book will help bring important money- and time-saving information to your attention, plus help you avoid common mistakes consumers make when dealing with credit-related issues.

What you won't learn from this book is how to manage your personal finances, balance your checkbook, manage your investments, or develop and implement a personal or family budget. This book exclusively focuses on building, rebuilding, and maintaining a good credit rating.

Dirty Little Secrets

Dirty Little Secrets was written to provide you with an introduction to the importance of credit and how credit fits into your financial life. This book will provide you with the core information you need, but it's only a start. As you'll discover, building, rebuilding, and/or maintaining good credit will require an ongoing effort and careful planning on your part. While there are many quick and easy strategies you can use to "fix" some credit-related problems, in order to ensure a good or excellent credit rating, you'll need to adopt a responsible approach to your spending, money management, and credit management techniques.

It's important to understand that changes are always happening in the credit industry and that the credit reporting agencies, creditors, lenders, banks, and other financial institutions are always adapting. Even the complex mathematical formulas used to calculate your credit scores are constantly being modified to reflect the latest consumer trends, economic conditions, and the needs of creditors and lenders.

We're living in tough economic times, which makes it much more difficult than ever for someone to get approved for any type of mortgage

Home Foreclosures Are Becoming Too Commonplace in the U.S.

In April 2012 alone, there were approximately 66,000 completed foreclosures nationwide. Nearly half (49.1 percent) of those foreclosures took place in California, Florida, Michigan, Texas, and Georgia. Meanwhile, there were 69,000 completed foreclosures in March 2012, and 66,000 completed foreclosures in February 2012.

Statistics show that approximately 1.4 million homes, which translates to about 3.4 percent of all homes with a mortgage, were in the national foreclosure inventory as of March 2012.

Dirty Little Secrets

or refinancing offer. Even credit cards, car loans, student loans, home equity loans, and other types of credit are now much more difficult to get approved for, even if your credit score is classified as "average" or better.

According to recent statistics, one out of every 622 homes in America is actively being foreclosed upon. The Mortgage Bankers Association reports that this translates to roughly 250,000 new families entering into foreclosure every three months. Just as alarming is that in a survey conducted by Freddie Mac/Roper, 6 out of 10 homeowners wished they understood the terms and details of their mortgage better.

There's no better time than the present to begin securing your financial future by building, rebuilding, and properly managing your credit. This book will show you exactly how this can be done, even if you don't consider yourself to be financially savvy and typically have trouble balancing your checkbook.

CHAPTER 1

Determining Your Current
Financial and Credit
Situation

What's in This Chapter

■ Understanding what debt is

■ Determine your current financial situation

■ Planning your short- and long-term financial goals and objectives

This book is all about understanding credit—how to obtain it, utilize it, manage it, and avoid getting financially devastated by it. To make the best use of credit, without overpaying for it, it's important to understand your relationship with creditors and lenders; the purpose of the three credit reporting agencies (formally known as credit bureaus); what credit reports are all about and what's contained within them; and the impact your numeric credit scores have on your overall credit rating, as well as your ability to acquire credit and get approved for loans.

Building a solid credit rating (and achieving high credit scores) takes time, yet it's possible to utterly destroy your credit rating (and see your credit scores nosedive) as a result of just one month's worth of financial indiscretions and mismanagement. Missing a mortgage payment, paying credit card bills late, or allowing any type of bill to get turned over to a collection agency will all have an almost immediate negative impact on your credit rating and credit scores.

Warning

Negative information that's placed on your credit reports will remain there for at least seven years and continue to negatively impact your credit scores and overall credit rating. However, as these negative items get older, they're weighed less heavily in your credit score calculation.

Information about you as a consumer, your relationships with your creditors and lenders, and your utilization of available credit is information that's maintained within your credit reports, which are compiled by Equifax, Experian, and TransUnion—the three credit reporting agencies that you'll be learning more about shortly.

Based on information that appears in your credit reports, which are constantly being updated based on new information being reported to the credit reporting agencies by your lenders and creditors, your credit scores are then calculated. Again, how this all works will be explained shortly.

What you need to understand right now, however, is that any negative information that appears in your credit reports stays there for at least seven to ten years. So, to fully understand your financial situation, you'll need to take a look at your past and present as you plan for your financial future.

This chapter will help you gather information about your financial past and determine how it's impacted your credit rating to date. Once you understand where you are right now from a financial standpoint, you can better make plans for your future by setting realistic goals.

Once you understand where you've been, where you are now, and where you want to be in the future from a financial standpoint, the next focus of *Dirty Little Secrets* is to help you understand how credit works, improve your credit situation, and fully utilize your available credit without overpaying for it. One of the major goals of this book is also to help you avoid the common mistakes people make when it comes to utilizing and managing their credit.

What Is Debt?

When you utilize credit or acquire a loan, you take on debt. Debt is simply borrowed money that eventually needs to be paid back (typically with interest). Whether the amount borrowed is secured or unsecured, or for a long or short term, when you borrow money for whatever reason from a creditor, lender, or even your best friends, you're acquiring debt.

There are many types of debt. When you acquire debt by borrowing money from a bank or financial institution, for example, there are always fees, interest charges, and/or finance charges associated with it. It's these fees that allow lenders, creditors, banks, and other financial institutions to earn money (and often huge profits).

Acquiring debt potentially allows you to spend more money than you currently have on hand (stored under your mattress or in your bank accounts) in order to purchase something you couldn't otherwise afford. In some cases, you can actually utilize debt to your advantage in order to leverage the money you already have, but more on that later.

Avoid Costly Payday Loans Whenever Possible

People who wind up with a poor credit rating are sometimes forced to utilize short-term "payday loans" to cover their living expenses. This is one of the most costly ways to borrow money.

A payday loan is a short-term loan, typically for a small amount of money, that is offered at an extremely high interest rate, and that typically has high fees associated with it. The way this process works is that the borrower writes a personal check to the lender, who agrees to hold onto it (without cashing the check) until the borrower's next payday (a period that typically ranges between one and four weeks).

The borrower receives cash immediately for the amount of the post-dated check they've written, but must pay a fee of $17.50 (or more) for every $100 borrowed. This can translate to an interest rate of 911 percent for a one-week loan, 456 percent for a two-week loan, or 212 percent for a one-month loan.

People who use payday loans are often already in serious debt and experiencing financial problems, and ultimately wind up having to take out additional payday loans to cover earlier ones, placing themselves in a faster downward spiral as they acquire significantly greater debt. As a result, it's very common for payday loan borrowers to wind up paying more in fees than they initially borrowed.

In some states payday loans are illegal. However, in other states, payday loan lenders are able to advertise heavily in order to attract desperate customers. If you're already experiencing financial problems, taking advantage of payday loans is one of the worst mistakes you can make.

Dirty Little Secrets

Avoid Costly Payday Loans, cont.

When payday loans are not available, consumers sometimes turn to credit card cash advances or utilize overdraft protection related to their bank account(s), but these methods for borrowing cash are also accompanied by high interest rates and high fees.

When you take out any type of loan and acquire debt, the amount of interest you pay and how long you have to pay the loan back is determined by how the loan is initially structured.

The interest rate associated with the loan or credit can be fixed (meaning it doesn't change for the life of the loan), or it can be variable (meaning it changes based on changes with the Prime Rate, for example). Interest you pay over the life of a loan, combined with the fees imposed by the creditor or lender, are considered the costs associated with borrowing money.

People with a proven track record of properly managing their finances, paying their bills on time, making timely payments toward loans and outstanding debts, and appropriately using their credit will ultimately receive the best deals from lenders and creditors and are ultimately charged the lowest fees when they acquire or utilize new loans on their available credit.

Beyond maintaining above-average credit scores, your ability to receive the best credit terms, financing deals, and loan terms from most creditors and lenders will depend on your ability to successfully shop around for the best deals and then fully understand how the credit or loan you're applying for actually works.

Before taking on a loan or utilizing credit (such as your credit cards), the most important question to ask is, "By borrowing this money, will I be able to achieve my financial goals and receive the financial benefits I desire, or am I paying interest charges and fees for a loan I don't want, don't really need, and/or can't afford to pay back?"

As you manage your finances, it's typically acceptable to borrow money and acquire debt for a variety of reasons. Your ability to properly manage your debt, keep it under control, pay off your debts, and ensure the costs of utilizing debt don't get out of control all relate to your ability to manage your personal finances and protect your credit rating.

Utilizing Loans or Credit Costs You Money

Every loan or type of credit you apply for will have costs associated with it. In addition to the interest, you'll be responsible for paying various fees and charges to your creditors or lenders. It's essential that you take both the interest charges and the fees into account when calculating the cost associated with utilizing credit or taking out any type of loan.

Even for the same type of credit or loan, the interest rates and fees/charges you'll be responsible for will vary greatly between lenders and creditors, which is why it's essential that you always shop around for the best deals.

The deals you'll be offered, however, will be impacted directly by your credit rating, the information published within your credit reports, and your credit scores. People with poor credit are considered much greater risks by creditors and lenders.

In Chapter 7, you'll discover strategies for improving your credit rating and boosting your credit score, which over time will allow you to qualify for much better loans and credit offers, and ultimately save money each and every month in interest charges and fees when you utilize credit or any type of loans.

Types of Debt

Throughout this book, you'll learn about a wide range of loans, credit, and financing opportunities, plus other ways to borrow money and acquire debt. You'll also discover how to save money and properly manage your finances as you take on these various types of debts.

Some of the most common types of credit and loans include:

- Automobile loans
- Business loans
- Credit cards
- Mortgages
- Other types of unsecured loans, including "payday loans" and borrowing money from friends and relatives
- Overdraft protection related to your checking account(s)
- Second mortgages, home equity loans, and home equity lines of credit
- Student loans

Determining Your Current Financial Situation

Before we start exploring all the different types of loans and credit opportunities, let's get a clear picture of your current financial situation. This will help you to determine whether or not taking on additional debt is the right decision for you at this time.

If you've already accrued a significant amount of debt, knowing exactly where you stand will help you create an organized and well-thought-out plan for paying it off and better managing it in the interim.

To evaluate your current financial situation, we'll look at several distinct areas of your financial life, including your:

- Income
- Savings and investments
- Current monthly living expenses

> ### ($) Credit Tip
>
> Your *credit utilization* is a percentage calculation related to how much of your overall available credit you're actually taking advantage of and using at any given time. This is just one of the things that's taken into account when your credit rating and credit scores are calculated.
>
> For example, if you have five credit cards with a total of $25,000 in available credit, but your total credit card balances are currently only $5,000, your credit utilization is much lower than if you've almost maxed out all of your credit cards and you're maintaining a $23,000 credit card balance between your five credit cards.

- Current (outstanding) debt
- Current available (but unutilized) credit

The following worksheets will help you analyze all aspects of your current personal financial situation. Later, we'll focus on what your short-term and long-term financial goals are, and get you started on achieving them through proper financial planning and better money management.

Begin by collecting your bank statements, pay stubs, W–2 forms, 1099 forms, receipts, bills, credit card statements, and other financial documents. This information will help you complete each of the following worksheets. These worksheets will then be used to help you examine your current financial situation.

Income

This simple worksheet in Figure 1–1 on page 9 will help you calculate your current income—how much you're earning. In this case, we'll refer to income as your net take-home pay *after* taxes. If you're married or you're part of a multiple income earning family, be sure to calculate your own earnings combined with your spouse's earnings.

FIGURE 1–1: **Worksheet 1: Income**
(Note: When calculating your income, be sure to focus on take-home pay (*after* state and federal taxes are paid.)

Current Salary (including tips, commissions, and bonuses, if applicable)	$
Spouse's Salary	$
Other Sources of Income (such as taxable interest, alimony, child support, investment dividends, etc.)	$
Total Average Monthly Income	$

Savings and Investments

The worksheet in Figure 1-2 will help you determine how much money you have available in cash or liquid assets, as well as other investments. Ideally, after you pay all of your monthly living expenses and cover your bills, you want to have extra money left over that can be put into savings or invested.

One of the first signs of financial trouble is when you must tap into your savings or investments (or worse yet, utilize your credit cards) in order to cover your everyday living expenses. If you find yourself having to do this more than once or twice, chances are you're quickly headed for serious financial problems and should take steps to address the situation immediately. Do not wait for the problems to fully manifest.

FIGURE 1–2: **Worksheet 2: Your Savings and Investments**

Checking Account Balance(s)	$
Investments (stocks, mutual funds, etc.)	$
Retirement Fund Contribution(s)	$
Savings Account Balance(s)	$
Other Savings	$
Total Savings	$

Monthly Living Expenses

Now that you know how much money you have coming in each month (your income) and how much money you have in savings and in investments, let's calculate how much you spend each month on your living expenses using the worksheet in Figure 1–3 on page 11.

Hopefully, your income is more than the total of your monthly living expenses. If not, with each passing month, you're acquiring additional debt and you're living beyond your means. To remedy this situation, you'll need to start changing your spending habits immediately. Unless you're retired, never rely on your savings, investments, credit cards, and other types of loans to pay your ongoing living expenses. This starts a negative financial cycle that is extremely difficult to break away and recover from, plus it almost always leads to serious financial troubles.

Your Current Debts

Your current debt represents how much money you owe to other people, in addition to the amount of interest and loan/credit-related fees you're paying each month. Your debt can take on many different forms.

Let's start off by looking at your largest debt—your mortgage and other loans that are secured by your home and property, such as your home equity line of credit (HELOC) and/or home equity loan. You'll record this information in the worksheet in Figure 1–4 on page 13.

A mortgage is a loan where the home is used as collateral. Failure to make the monthly payments associated with the mortgage could result in the lender foreclosing on the property or, at the very least, additional late-payment fees and penalties.

In the past, a traditional mortgage was available from a bank, credit union, or savings & loan and had a fixed interest rate for 15, 20, 25, or 30 years. This was referred to as a fixed-rate mortgage.

To quality for a fixed-rate mortgage, a borrower needed to have a high credit score, be employed, have enough money to cover a

FIGURE 1–3: **Worksheet 3: Personal or Family Expenses**

Expense Type	Priority (1 = Mandatory) (2 = Important) (3 = Optional)	Monthly Amount ($)	Annual Amount ($)
AAA (or other Automobile Club) Membership			
Alimony & Child Support Payments			
Babysitting / Childcare			
Cable TV, DVR Service Fees and/ or Satellite Radio Fees			
Car Insurance			
Car Maintenance Fees			
Car Payment			
Cell Phone			
Cigarettes / Tobacco			
Clothing			
Coffee and Snacks			
Cosmetics			
Credit Card Payment(s)) (including store credit cards)			
Dining Out / Restaurant Expenses			
Entertainment Expenses			
Food & Groceries			
Garbage pickup and disposal			
Gas (for your car)			
Gifts			
Gym / Health Club Membership			
Health Insurance			
Home Telephone & Fax			

Dirty Little Secrets

FIGURE 1–3: **Worksheet 3: Personal or Family Expenses,** cont.

Expense Type	Priority (1 = Mandatory) (2 = Important) (3 = Optional)	Monthly Amount ($)	Annual Amount ($)
Homeowner's or Renter's Insurance			
Household Items			
Housekeeper			
Internet Access			
Landscaper			
Life Insurance Premium(s)			
Magazine subscriptions			
Membership Fees or Dues			
Other Insurance			
Pet Grooming & Daycare			
Postage			
Prescriptions			
Real Estate Taxes			
Rent or Mortgage Payment			
Student Loan Payments			
Tolls & Parking Fees			
Travel Expenses			
Utilities–Electricity			
Utilities–Gas			
Utilities–Water			
Vet Bills & Pet Insurance			
Other			
Other			
Other			
Other			
Total Expenses:		$	$

FIGURE 1–4: **Worksheet 4: Home Mortgages and Lines of Credit**

Current Mortgage, Second Mortgage, HELOC and/or Home Equity Loan

Lender	Loan Description (Example: 15-Year, Fixed-Rate)	Interest Rate (%)	Monthly Payment	Duration	Number of Months/ Years Remaining
Total Monthly Payment				$	
Interest Paid This Month				$	

20-percent down payment (based on the property's sale price), and meet a variety of other criteria. Today, there are many different mortgage products available, and the qualification requirements are dramatically different than they were just a few years ago.

A home equity line of credit (HELOC) is a type of second mortgage. It provides the borrower with a firm commitment from the lender to make a pre-determined amount of funds available to the borrower for a pre-set amount of time.

The equity in the borrower's home is used as collateral. The difference between a HELOC and home equity loan is that with a HELOC, the borrower can borrow any amount of money, up to their credit limit, pay the outstanding balance back over time, and potentially re-borrow the money during the term of the loan agreement.

Thus, while there is a pre-set limit as to how much the homeowner can borrow, it's up to the borrower to determine how much they wish to borrow and when. Another difference is that HELOCs are adjustable-rate loans, not fixed-rate loans, so the amount of interest to be paid on the loan will change. Once established, a HELOC has an annual fee.

This type of loan can be used as a financial safety net for homeowners that can be tapped only when and if it's needed.

A home equity loan is a loan (in addition to your mortgage) that allows you to obtain one lump sum of money, then pay it back over a pre-determined period of time, with a fixed interest rate. Like a fixed-rate mortgage, your monthly payment on a home equity loan remains the same. Your home is used as collateral for this type of loan. Interest rates on a home equity loan are typically higher than a mortgage, but lower than other types of loans, such as credit cards or car loans.

Understand the Loans You Take On and What Their Long-Term Costs Are

For every type of loan listed, you're paying interest each and every month, based on the terms of the loan. Once you improve your credit scores, chances are you'll be able to refinance some or all of these loans at a lower interest rate and save money each month. This could wind up saving you a fortune over the life of the loans. Even if you lower your interest rate by just a quarter or half of a percentage point on your loan, your savings will be significant.

The free online mortgage refinance calculator found at Bankrate.com (www.bankrate.com/calculators/mortgages/refinance-calculator.aspx), for example, can help you calculate your potential savings by refinancing your mortgage. If your credit score isn't in the above-average or excellent range, however, you'll first need to improve it before you will qualify for the very best loan rates available from banks, financial institutions, mortgage brokers, or other lenders.

Current Car Loan Information

Now, let's take a look at your debt as it relates to automobile financing in the worksheet presented in Figure 1-5.

FIGURE 1–5: **Worksheet 5: Automobile Loans**

Car Loans

Lender	Loan Description	Interest Rate (%)	Monthly Payment	Duration	Number of Months/ Years Remaining
Total Monthly Payment					$
Interest Paid This Month					$

You Should Know . . .

When you take on an auto loan, you're paying a pre-determined amount of interest each and every month, based on the terms of the loan. Once you improve your credit score, chances are you'll be able to refinance the loan at a lower interest rate and save money each month.

The free online auto loan calculator found at Bankrate.com (www.bank-rate.com/calculators/auto/auto-loan-calculator.aspx), for example, can help you calculate your potential savings by refinancing your auto loan. Typically, credit unions offer excellent deals on auto loan refinancing, compared to traditional banks or the financing departments of major car manufacturers.

Dirty Little Secrets

Current Student Loan(s)

In this section, we'll examine your outstanding debt related to your student loans using the worksheet in Figure 1-6. Based on the type of student loan(s) you possess and how much is owed, you might save money by consolidating these loans into a single loan with a lower interest rate.

FIGURE 1–6: **Worksheet 6: Student Loans**

Student Loans

Lender	Loan Description	Interest Rate (%)	Monthly Payment	Duration	Number of Months/ Years Remaining
Total Monthly Payment:					$
Interest Paid This Month:					$

Current Credit and Charge Card Balances and Information

For many Americans, relying on credit cards has become a way of life. Unfortunately, most people don't use their credit cards responsibly and wind up racking up tremendous debt as a result of interest charges and the many different types of fees and penalties associated with these cards. Let's evaluate your credit card situation right now.

As you complete this worksheet in Figure 1-7 on page 17, focus on your Visa, MasterCard, American Express, and Discover Card accounts. In the next worksheet in Figure 1-8, page 17, you'll summarize your

FIGURE 1–7: **Worksheet 7: Major Credit Cards**

Major Credit Cards

Credit Card Name	Credit Limit	Interest Rate (%)	Minimum Monthly Payment	Actual Monthly Payment	Annual Fees and Other Charges	Current Balance
Total Monthly Payment						$
Interest Paid This Month						$

debt relating to store credit cards, gas station credit cards, and other types of credit and charge cards.

FIGURE 1–8: **Worksheet 8: Store and Gas Credit Cards**

Other Revolving Credit (such as Store Credit Cards, Gas Station Cards, etc.)

Credit Card Name	Credit Limit	Interest Rate (%)	Minimum Monthly Payment	Actual Monthly Payment	Annual Fees and Other Charges	Current Balance
Total Monthly Payment						$
Interest Paid This Month						$

Dirty Little Secrets

Store Credit Cards Are Often More Expensive to Use than Traditional Credit Cards

Did you know that the interest rates and fees associated with most store credit cards are significantly higher than, for example, many Visa or MasterCard credit cards? In general, a store credit card will have a higher interest rate and offer a lower credit limit than a traditional credit card, plus it offers an added spending temptation.

Before applying for and using a store credit card, read the fine print carefully. Don't just rely on a promotional headline that says, "Pay No Interest for X Months" or "Receive 10 Percent Off Your Purchase When You Use Your [Insert Store Name] Credit Card."

Often, if you take advantage of a "pay no interest for x months" offer, after that initial period, you will have a balance on your store credit card; all of the interest you would have accrued to date (from the day of your purchase) will be automatically added to your outstanding balance.

Most store credit cards have APRs (Annual Percentage Rate of interest) of 20 percent or higher. If you're someone with average or better credit, you're often better off applying for and using a traditional credit card that has a lower APR of between 10.90 and 12.90 percent for your purchases.

In July 2012, if you were to apply for a store credit card from consumer electronics superstore Best Buy, for example, the APR for purchases was between 25.24 percent and 27.99 percent, depending on the applicant's credit worthiness. For consumers who are late with payments, the penalty APR rate associated with the Best Buy credit card was 29.99 percent.

Dirty Little Secrets

Store Credit Cards, cont.

The APR for purchases if you were to apply for a Sears credit card in July 2012 was 25.24 percent, while the APR for purchases using a Macy's store credit card was 24.50 percent.

If a store is offering a significant discount on a purchase if you use their store credit card, have a plan in place to immediately pay off that balance. Also, determine how applying for the additional credit card will impact your credit scores and overall credit utilization, which are topics we'll cover a bit later.

For many consumers, credit card debt winds up getting out of control and costing them a fortune, not just in interest charges, but in all of the different fees associated with credit cards. Starting immediately, you can develop an understanding of these fees and when they kick in so that you can avoid them.

Annual fees, late payment fees, cash advance fees, balance transfer fees, and over credit limit fees can wind up adding $50 to $200 or more per month to each of your credit card bills, not including interest charges that will automatically increase to the "default" rates (25 percent or higher) if you don't adhere to the terms listed in your cardholder's agreement.

Chapter 8 focuses specifically on managing credit cards. However, for now, figure out how much in interest and fees you're paying each month on your existing credit cards. Later, you'll discover ways to lower these rates by transferring your balances to other cards, using a debt consolidation loan, or renegotiating your credit terms with each credit card issuer.

The free online calculators related to credit cards that are offered by Bankrate.com (www.bankrate.com/calculators/index-of-credit-card-calculators.aspx) will help you determine how much maintaining a balance on each of your credit cards is costing you in interest. Be sure to add in all of the other fees and charges imposed by your credit card issuers to calculate your total costs, however.

Other Outstanding Debts

Using this worksheet in Figure 1-9, include all of your other outstanding debt, including unsecured loans, medical bills, alimony payments, and money you've borrowed from friends or relatives, etc.

FIGURE 1–9: **Worksheet 9: Other Debt You Owe**

Other Debt

Type of Debt	Creditor/ Lender	Amount Owed	Interest Rate	Monthly Payment
Total Monthly Payment				$
Interest Paid This Month				$

Summary of Current Debt and Debt-Related Expenses

This worksheet in Figure 1-10, page 21, will help you summarize all of your debt. Take the totals from the previous worksheets and add up all of their totals here.

So, Where Do You Stand Financially?

You will be referring back to these worksheets as you read this book. Right now, however, let's do a simple mathematical calculation to determine where you stand financially.

Are you currently living beyond your means? Here's an easy way to find out:

Dirty Little Secrets

FIGURE 1-10: **Worksheet 10: Summary of All You Owe**

Debt Summary

Type of Debt	Monthly Payment	Total Debt
Mortgage Worksheet 4 Total	$	$
Car Loan(s) Worksheet 5 Total	$	$
Student Loans Worksheet 6 Total	$	$
Major Credit Cards Worksheet 7 Total	$	$
Other Revolving Credit Worksheet 8 Total	$	$
Other Debt Worksheet 9	$	$
Totals:	$	

1. Add together the total monthly expenses/payments from Worksheet 3, page 12 and Worksheet 10.
2. Subtract that total from the total of Worksheet 1 on page 9.

If you wind up with a positive number, this means you're able to cover all of your monthly expenses, plus you have some left over, disposable income that can be used for savings and investments or for making frivolous or non-critical purchases.

If, however, you wind up with a negative number, this means you're spending more money than you're earning each month and need to take steps to remedy the situation by paying down your outstanding debts and better managing your money (spending).

Let's now take a look at Worksheet 2 on page 9. Is the money you have in checking, savings, and investment accounts being used to its utmost potential? Are your investments earning as much as they could be if they were being better managed or if you were to explore more lucrative investment opportunities? If you have money sitting in a generic savings account, could you shop around for a bank or financial institution that pays a higher interest rate, or would your money serve you better if it were being invested in a money market account, mutual fund, or other type of investment? Perhaps this extra money should be used immediately to pay off high-interest loans.

Identifying Credit Mistakes You've Made in the Past

By looking carefully at your current overall financial picture, you should be able to identify money or credit management mistakes you've made in the past. If you can't pinpoint these problems already, you'll learn how to identify many of them as you continue reading this book.

It's important to learn from your past and most costly mistakes and discover strategies to avoid repeating them. Once you understand what triggered dramatic drops in your credit scores in the past, or why your credit card companies are charging you maximum fees and interest rates when you utilize your credit cards (or maintain a balance), for example, you'll be in a better position to start saving money and better manage your credit.

Unless you already have credit scores categorized as "above average" or "excellent," chances are you've done something in your past to lower those scores, which in turn have impacted the fees and interest rates you're now paying on virtually all of your loans and credit cards.

As you analyze your current financial situation, be on the lookout for two things:

1. *Mistakes you've made in terms of mismanaging your credit.* Have you taken on too much debt, missed monthly payments, been late making your monthly payments, racked up charges by constantly exceeding your credit card limits, applied for too many loans or credit cards in a short period of time, or allowed

delinquent accounts to be turned over to collection agencies, for example?

2. *Ways you've mismanaged your spending on a day-to-day or month-to-month basis.* Are you spending too much on frivolous purchases or living beyond your means based on your income and your current monthly expenses? Have you constantly racked up extra fees from your bank or financial institution for overdrafts on your checking account? In any given month, are you spending significantly more than you're earning?

Chances are, if you've run into financial problems, you've made mistakes in the past that relate to these two areas, which, as you'll soon discover, interrelate rather closely.

Setting Your Financial Goals and Objectives in Today's Economy

Everyone has goals and dreams: things they'd like to achieve, items they'd like to buy, people they'd enjoy meeting, relationships they'd like to have, and career objectives they'd like to realize. Well, in most cases, to achieve one's goals and dreams requires a detailed plan of action, hard work, plus plenty of dedication. Hoping, wishing, and even praying seldom works, unless accompanied by a plan, hard work, and dedication.

The same is true for someone who'd like to establish, improve, or repair their credit or better manage their personal finances. After all, achieving some goals and dreams, like buying a home or a new car, for example, will require money and good credit.

After completing the various worksheets in this chapter, hopefully you developed a good understanding about the current status of your personal finances, plus you've identified costly mistakes you've made in the past. If you had trouble doing this yourself, sit down with a personal financial planner or accountant and ask for their assistance in analyzing your current financial situation.

This section focuses on what you're hoping to achieve in the future in terms of your credit rating and personal finances. By establishing goals now, you'll be in a better position to develop detailed plans of action for achieving them.

Your Financial Goals

While it's impossible to predict when emergencies will happen, you can prepare for them financially by building up an emergency savings fund over time and acquiring insurance to protect yourself and your assets. In terms of planning, however, by looking at your short-term and long-term goals, you can determine when large sums of money will be needed to make various purchases and then plan accordingly.

You may already know that in the next three to five years, you plan to buy a home and will need a mortgage. In the next six months to one year, perhaps you'll need to finance the purchase of a car. Sometime in the next two years, maybe you'll need to invest in a new home computer, or a washing machine and dryer set. If you have young children, you also know that in a pre-determined number of years, you'll need money to pay for their college tuition. And what about your own retirement plans?

Take a few minutes to think about what your financial needs will be. Then, as you read this book, consider how you'll start addressing those needs now, whether it's by building up your savings, improving your credit scores, increasing your income, or making sure you'll be able to afford the monthly payments and fees associated with taking on new types of loans.

Short-Term Goals (Immediate to One Year)

What major purchases do you plan to make in the next few months up to one year (car, major appliance, vacation, home improvements, etc.)? How do you plan to finance these purchases? Will you use a credit card? Acquire some type of loan? Tap into your savings? Use the worksheet in Figure 1–11 on page 25 to outline your plans.

Dirty Little Secrets

FIGURE 1–11: **Short-Term Goals Worksheet**

Short-Term Goals

List your short-term financial goals here.

Short-Term Goal #1: _____

Approximate Amount of Money Required: $ _____

Financing/Payment Method to Be Used: _____

Anticipated Interest Rate & Fees: $ _____

Anticipated Financing Term: _____

Short-Term Goal #2: _____

Approximate Amount of Money Required: $ _____

Financing/Payment Method to Be Used: _____

Anticipated Interest Rate & Fees: $ _____

Anticipated Financing Term: _____

Short-Term Goal #3: _____

Approximate Amount of Money Required: $ _____

Financing/Payment Method to Be Used: _____

Anticipated Interest Rate & Fees: $ _____

Anticipated Financing Term: _____

Dirty Little Secrets

FIGURE 1–11: **Short-Term Goals Worksheet,** cont.

Short-Term Goal #4: _____

Approximate Amount of Money Required: $ _____

Financing/Payment Method to Be Used: _____

Anticipated Interest Rate & Fees: $ _____

Anticipated Financing Term: _____

Short-Term Goal #5: _____

Approximate Amount of Money Required: $ _____

Financing/Payment Method to Be Used: _____

Anticipated Interest Rate & Fees: $ _____

Anticipated Financing Term: _____

Long-Term Goals (One or More Years in the Future)

What major purchases do you plan to make in the one year, two years, five years, or 10 years from now (new home, school loans, new car, home improvements, wedding, honeymoon, etc.)? How do you plan to finance these purchases? Will you use a credit card? Acquire some type of loan? Tap into your savings? List your long-term financial goals in the worksheet in Figure 1-12 on page 27.

Now that you have a general idea of what your major purchases or financial requirements will be over the next few years, utilize the rest of the information within this book to ensure that when and if you need to take on new debts, loans, or credit, that your credit rating will be strong enough not only to get yourself approved for the credit and loans you need, but also that you can obtain approvals at the best

FIGURE 1–12: **Long-Term Financial Goals Worksheet**

Long-Term Financial Goals

Long-Term Goal #1:_____

Approximate Amount of Money Required: $ _____

Financing/Payment Method to Be Used: _____

Anticipated Interest Rate & Fees: $ _____

Anticipated Financing Term: _____

Long-Term Goal #2:_____

Approximate Amount of Money Required: $ _____

Financing/Payment Method to Be Used: _____

Anticipated Interest Rate & Fees: $ _____

Anticipated Financing Term: _____

Long-Term Goal #3:_____

Approximate Amount of Money Required: $ _____

Financing/Payment Method to Be Used: _____

Anticipated Interest Rate & Fees: $ _____

Anticipated Financing Term: _____

FIGURE 1–12: **Long-Term Financial Goals Worksheet,** cont.

Long-Term Goal #4:_____

Approximate Amount of Money Required: $ _____

Financing/Payment Method to Be Used: _____

Anticipated Interest Rate & Fees: $ _____

Anticipated Financing Term: _____

Long-Term Goal #5:_____

Approximate Amount of Money Required: $ _____

Financing/Payment Method to Be Used: _____

Anticipated Interest Rate & Fees: $ _____

Anticipated Financing Term: _____

possible rates in order to save thousands of dollars in fees and interest charges.

What's Next?

Before you can successfully create, build, repair, or protect your credit rating, it's important to understand which companies gather the information that ultimately gets included within your credit reports (which are, in turn, used to calculate your credit scores). This is the responsibility of the credit reporting agencies Equifax, Experian, and TransUnion. You'll learn more about these organizations in the next chapter.

CHAPTER 2

The Credit Reporting Agencies
Who They Are and What They Do

What's in This Chapter

- An introduction to the credit reporting agencies Experian, Equifax, and TransUnion

- "Credit reporting agency" versus "Credit Bureau": What's the difference?

- The credit reporting agencies describe themselves, in their own words

What Is a Credit Reporting Agency, Anyway?

Being a money lender is a risky business. After all, some people pay off their debts on time, while others don't. When someone doesn't pay back a loan or is late with their payments, it becomes costly for the lender and represents a financial loss.

So, to be successful as a lender or a company that offers any type of credit to an individual or company, that lender needs to make intelligent approval or rejection decisions when evaluating a loan or credit application. Obviously, the lender/creditor only wants to issue loans or credit to someone who is apt to pay it back, with interest, in a timely manner.

Helping creditors and lenders make intelligent decisions about a person's credit worthiness is a service offered by credit reporting agencies. These agencies collect details about a person's current debt-paying practices and past credit history in order to provide an overall credit rating and ultimately help lenders weed out the deadbeats.

As a consumer, you may have heard the names Experian, Equifax, and TransUnion, and you've probably heard them referred to as credit bureaus. While you might know of these companies, few people truly understand what they do and how much impact they directly and indirectly have on your credit reports, credit scores, and overall credit rating.

Before we explore what a credit report is (which is the main focus of Chapter 3), it's important to understand who is compiling the data that gets listed within your credit reports. After all, it's the content of your credit reports that impacts your credit scores, which are in turn used by potential creditors and lenders to make their approval or rejection decisions when you apply for any type of loan or credit.

The first thing you should understand about Experian, Equifax, and TransUnion is that in today's financial world, the term "credit bureau" is outdated. These days, the terms "credit reporting agency" or "credit reporting company (CRC)" are more accurate. Thus, Experian, Equifax, and TransUnion are referred to as "credit reporting agencies" (not "credit bureaus") throughout this book.

Credit bureaus was a term used in the past, when the companies that collected and reported financial data about consumers were regionalized and actually had many offices around the country (referred to as bureaus). These days, Experian, Equifax, and TransUnion maintain vast databases and work on an international scale using centralized databases. The local "bureaus" or offices no longer exist.

In fact, the three major credit reporting agencies combined collect and report more than 4.5 billion pieces of credit-related data each and every month. The information that's collected is used within the credit report that each credit reporting agency compiles about all consumers.

So, you now know that Experian, Equifax, and TransUnion are credit reporting agencies that maintain detailed information about every American's credit history. This information is gathered through a voluntary system in conjunction with all of your creditors and lenders, who make regular monthly reports to the credit reporting agencies about each of their customers/clients (that probably includes you).

You Now Have the Legal Right To Know Why You Have Been Denied Credit

According to the HowStuffWorks.com website (http://money.howstuffworks.com/personal-finance/debt-management/credit-reporting-agency.htm), "For decades, the information collected by credit reporting agencies was hidden from consumers. Individuals had no idea why they were denied credit or whether or not their reports contained mistakes. Beginning with the Fair Credit Reporting Act in 1971, and continuing with recent legislation, U.S. citizens have free access to their credit reports and credit scores from each of the three national credit reporting agencies: Experian, TransUnion, and Equifax. Citizens also have the right to know exactly why their credit was denied."

Dirty Little Secrets

The credit reporting agencies are global companies that have multiple purposes and offer many different services to industry and consumers. As far as what consumers like you need to understand, Experian, Equifax, and TransUnion are in the information gathering and reporting business. They do their jobs well, and what they do directly impacts virtually every aspect of your financial life.

Credit reporting agencies do not make approval or denial decisions when you apply for any type of loan or credit. These companies simply provide timely data pertaining to your credit history and credit rating. This information allows creditors and lenders to make their own intelligent decisions about to whom to grant credit.

Here's how the process works. All of the creditors and lenders you already do business with maintain detailed records about you as a client or customer. This includes facts about who you are, how much you owe, the terms of your loan/credit, and your payment history. This data is typically updated monthly, based on whether you pay your bills on time, you're late paying your bills, or you skip payments altogether, for example.

Each of your creditors and lenders report this information to one, two, or all three of the credit reporting agencies on a monthly basis. Experian, Equifax, and TransUnion then take this data and update their credit report for every consumer, based on the data provided by your creditors and lenders (as well as certain government agencies). Thus, every consumer has three separate credit reports, which are updated monthly, and that are compiled by Experian, Equifax, and TransUnion.

The credit reporting agencies make their individual credit reports, which profile individual consumers, available to any creditor or lender that pays for the data. So, when you apply for any type of new loan or credit and complete an application for a new credit card, mortgage, car loan, or student loan, for example, the potential lender or creditor will contact Experian, Equifax, and/or TransUnion and pay to obtain an up-to-date copy of your credit report(s).

Using the information listed within one, two, or all three of your credit reports, potential lenders and creditors can quickly learn about you as a consumer and determine whether or not you pay your bills on time and what your past payment history has been like. Just by reviewing the content of your credit reports, someone can see who your past and current creditors and lenders are, how much credit you have available, and how much credit you're utilizing.

Additional information, such as whether or not you have any legal judgments against you, who your employer is, and your current address, for example, are among the other pieces of information available from your credit reports, but more about that later.

Utilizing data from your credit report, an added service offered by Experian, Equifax, and TransUnion, as well as other companies, including FICO (previously called Fair Isaac Corporation), is the ability to quickly calculate a consumer's credit score. A credit score allows potential lenders and creditors to save additional time when evaluating someone's credit history by making it possible to automate many credit/loan approval decisions.

What consumers need to understand is that many different formulas can be used to calculate credit scores. While the credit reporting agencies each calculate their own credit scores based on data from a consumer's credit report, third-party companies, like FICO, also calculate credit scores. FICO makes FICO Scores available to both consumers and lenders. Plus, individual creditors and lenders also use their own proprietary formulas (or modified formulas licensed from credit reporting agencies or another company) to calculate their own credit score(s) related to a consumer's credit reports.

From Chapter 4, you'll discover that as a consumer, you can have multiple credit scores associated with your credit reports, based on who is calculating the score and why. Thus, any credit score you purchase to review yourself may or may not be the same score your potential lender or creditor is looking at to make their approval decision.

Dirty Little Secrets

So, while you want to understand what your credit scores are and the scale or range they're being evaluated upon, you also want to determine whether your overall credit rating is being categorized as "poor," "below average," "average," "above average," or "excellent," as this will play a huge factor in the approval process for all new loans and credit you apply for.

As their name suggests, the credit reporting agencies are in charge of collecting, formatting, and reporting financial and credit data in the form of credit reports. Again, contrary to popular belief, Experian, Equifax, and TransUnion do not make credit or loan approval decisions, nor do they determine how individual pieces of information (called trade lines) within your credit reports are listed or what specific facts they contain; this is determined by your past and existing creditors and lenders who submit data on a monthly basis to the credit reporting agencies.

In Their Own Words . . .

The credit reporting agencies are not government agencies. They are *for-profit* corporations. In fact, Experian, for example, has more than 17,000 employees worldwide (including 6,000 people in North America), and for the year ended on March 31, 2011, the company earned $4.2 billion. (Yes, being a credit reporting agency and having consumers rely on their credit reports and credit scores to obtain credit is an incredibly profitable business.)

According to their respective websites, here's how each of the credit reporting agencies describe themselves and the work they do.

Experian's Description

"Experian is a global leader in providing value-added information solutions to organizations and consumers. Experian provides information, analytics, decision-making solutions and processing services. Using its comprehensive understanding of individuals, markets and economies, it helps organizations to find, develop and manage customer relationships to make their businesses more profitable.

Experian promotes greater financial health and opportunity among consumers by enabling them to understand, manage and protect their personal information." (Source: www.experian.com/corporate.)

The company's website also reports the following statistics:

- Experian's North America databases contain more than 1.5 peta-bytes of data. (To help you understand how much data this really is, consider that 1.5 petabytes is equivalent to about 300 million four-drawer filing cabinets filled with individual pages of text.)
- Experian maintains credit information on approximately 220 million U.S. consumers.
- Experian maintains demographic information on approximately 235 million consumers in 117 million living units across the United States.

Equifax's Description

"Equifax empowers businesses and consumers with information they can trust. A global leader in information solutions, we leverage one of the largest sources of consumer and commercial data, along with advanced analytics and proprietary technology, to create customized insights that enrich both the performance of businesses and the lives of consumers.

"Customers have trusted Equifax for over 100 years to deliver innovative solutions with the highest integrity and reliability. Businesses—large and small—rely on us for consumer and business credit intelligence, portfolio management, fraud detection, decisioning technology, marketing tools, and much more. We empower individual consumers to manage their personal credit information, protect their identity, and maximize their financial well-being.

"Headquartered in Atlanta, Georgia, Equifax Inc. employs approximately 7,000 people in 15 countries through North America, Latin America and Europe. Equifax is a member of Standard & Poor's (S&P) 500® Index. Our common stock is traded on the New York Stock

Exchange under the symbol EFX . . . . Going far beyond self-reported data, we integrate trade credit history, financial payment history, business demographics and organizational insight. Access to better information sheds new light on credit worthiness, business viability, potential prospects and more." (Source: www.equifax.com/about_equifax.)

TransUnion's Description

"TransUnion is a global leader in credit information and information management services. For more than 40 years, we have worked with businesses and consumers to gather, analyze and deliver the critical information needed to build strong economies throughout the world. The result is two-fold:

1. Businesses can better manage risk and customer relationships
2. Consumers can better understand and manage credit to achieve their financial goals

"Our dedicated associates provide solutions to approximately 45,000 businesses and approximately 500 million consumers worldwide." (Source: www.transunion.com/corporate/about-transunion/who-we-are.page.)

Included within TransUnion website's "Public Policies" section is the following text: "The existence of an individual's updated credit file makes it possible for businesses to make nearly instantaneous credit and insurance decisions that are objective and well informed. Processes that used to take days or weeks can now be completed in minutes without personal prejudice or subjective judgment."

What's Next?

Now that you understand who the three major credit reporting agencies are and grasp the basics of what they do, let's take a closer look at the credit reports they generate and how the content of those credit reports are a true measure of your credit worthiness and summarize your overall credit rating. That's the focus of Chapter 3.

Credit Reports
101

What's in This Chapter

- An introduction to what credit reports are and what information is included within them

- Details about where the information listed within your credit report comes from, who puts it there, and how long it stays

- How your credit reports impact your financial life

It's impossible to watch TV, listen to the radio, or read newspapers and magazines and not see and hear advertisements promoting incredible financing deals for mortgages, car loans, consumer electronics, or major appliances. The ads make statements like:

- "This weekend only, receive one year of interest-free financing on all new major appliance purchases."
- "Lease a new car today for less than $400 per month, with no money down."
- "Receive an introductory rate of zero percent financing for six months when you apply for a new credit card today."
- "Enjoy miles of possibilities. Earn up to 40,000 bonus miles." [Typically, 25,000 frequent flier miles is enough to earn a free round-trip ticket.]
- "4% back in rewards. Pay over time with special financing on storewide purchases. Enjoy exclusive discounts and events."

These deals all sound enticing. However, there's always fine print that states that these amazing offers are only available to qualified consumers with excellent credit. Someone with a less than stellar credit rating, but who is still credit worthy, can expect to pay higher interest rates and extra fees. For people with poor credit or no credit history, these amazing offers simply don't exist.

We're living in a society that relies heavily on the need to have above average credit. Unless you pay for absolutely everything you buy using cash, chances are at least periodically you will utilize some form of credit. For example, to book a hotel room, make an airline reservation, or to rent a car, you almost always need a major credit card (not necessarily a debit card) in your name.

Credit is the process of borrowing money from a lender (or creditor), then paying back what you owe over time, typically with interest. There are also typically fees and charges associated with acquiring and using credit. Most people have credit cards, one or more car loans, a mortgage, a home equity loan, student loans, and/or pay for big-ticket items (like major appliances, consumer electronics, or furniture) using credit offered by retail stores.

Some credit is secured with your property or other assets that are used as collateral, whereas other credit, like credit cards, is unsecured (meaning no collateral is needed). Unsecured credit allows you to obtain credit based on your credit history (your credit rating). People use their credit cards to pay for everyday items, like gas, groceries, clothing, and meals. In fact, it's extremely difficult for people to exist in today's society without utilizing credit.

If you use credit cards, you're certainly not alone. Learning how to properly manage your credit and finances will help you protect your credit rating, which over time will save you thousands or even tens of thousands of dollars.

"Credit" Defined

When someone borrows money with the understanding it will be repaid, that person is given credit. Obtaining credit from a creditor has costs associated with it. The cost is incurred based on the interest rate and fees you'll be required to pay over time, in addition to the principal.

Although the interest rate you qualify for can be pre-set and be fixed or variable, how much you ultimately pay will also be determined by the amount of time it takes you to fully repay the loan, whether it's a mortgage, credit card, car loan, or any other type of loan. As you'll learn from this book, there are many forms of loans and credit, and each works slightly differently. Yet, any time you're granted credit by a bank, financial institution, creditor or lender, the information is recorded on your credit reports and it impacts your credit scores.

TransUnion defines credit as, "A consumer's ability to make purchases, obtain services, or borrow money based on his or her promise, ability, and demonstrated willingness to repay."

Dirty Little Secrets

Information about your credit rating or personal credit history is maintained and kept up-to-date (for creditors and lenders to access) within your credit reports. These credit reports are compiled by the three separate credit reporting agencies discussed in Chapter 2. Each of the three credit reporting agencies maintains a credit report for every consumer in America. Thus, the average person has three separate credit reports pertaining to them. From a credit report, a consumer's credit scores are calculated using one of many proprietary (and typically top-secret) formulas.

Every time you apply for credit or a loan, the creditor or lender will check your credit reports and obtain related credit scores. Based on the information that's uncovered, you're either granted or approved for the credit or loan, or denied it.

In many situations, your current credit worthiness, history, and credit scores directly determine the interest rates and fees you ultimately pay for the privilege of using credit. How much of a risk you represent to a creditor will help determine how much you ultimately pay for credit.

If you have an excellent credit rating and you apply for a $200,000, 30-year fixed rate mortgage, for example, you may be offered an interest rate somewhere around 3.62 percent (as of July 2012). If, however, your credit rating is below average and there is negative information published within your credit reports, for that same mortgage you could be offered an interest rate of 8.5 percent or higher. The extra interest alone (between paying 3.62 percent and 8.5 percent) will be extremely significant over the 30-year period. The same rules apply on a car loan, student loan, home equity loan, credit cards, and other types of loans or credit.

Understanding how credit works, what information is incorporated into your credit reports, and how credit scores are calculated will help you better manage your personal finances. As a consumer, you want your credit reports and credit scores to portray you in the best possible light, based on your credit worthiness. In today's uncertain economy, this has become more important than ever!

Dirty Little Secrets

A Credit Report Is Like a High School Report Card

Consider your credit reports to be like your high school report cards. Instead of listing each class, your credit reports lists each creditor and lender you've had or currently have a relationship with. As for your grades, your credit reports list your credit history and how responsible you've been with each creditor/lender.

The related credit scores you're given are like your grade point average. As a consumer, it's important to strive for an "A" or "B" average in order to be credit worthy and be able to receive the best credit offers and lowest interest rates. How credit scores are calculated and what they represent has become a somewhat confusing and convoluted concept that will be explored and explained within Chapter 4.

In today's economy, even the slightest mistake when it comes to managing your credit (such as missing a credit card payment, or being more than 30 days late on a mortgage payment) can have a huge and long-term negative impact on your credit rating and credit scores.

Overextending yourself financially, making late payments, and not properly dealing with all of your creditors will have a negative impact on your financial well-being and hurt your chances of obtaining credit in the future. Plus, it could cause your creditors or lenders to modify the terms of your existing credit cards or loans.

For example, if you're consistently late on your credit card payments, your credit card issuer can change your interest rate to its "default rate," which is significantly higher, plus charge you a variety of extra fees. This will immediately start costing you more money, even if you stop using the credit card altogether but take your time paying off the outstanding balance.

As you'll learn, information that's listed on your credit reports stays there for between seven and ten years (sometimes longer), depending on the type of information. Thus, defaulting on a loan, making late payments, or not paying your minimums on credit cards, for example, will have a long-term impact on your financial life.

It is Difficult if Not Impossible to Have Accurate But Negative Information Removed from a Credit Report

Although having inaccurate information removed from your credit reports is a straightforward process, having negative but accurate information deleted from your credit reports is extremely difficult (and often impossible), despite the ads you see from companies that offer "credit repair" services.

Warning

It's important to understand that when it comes to credit repair, there are no "dirty little secrets" that lead to quick fixes. Repairing credit is a long-term process that could take months or years, depending on the severity of the situation.

A Preview of How Credit Scores Work

Contrary to popular belief, there is not one single "credit score" that goes along with each consumer's credit report. There are, in fact, dozens of different scores that can be calculated and evaluated by potential lenders and creditors.

A credit score is calculated using a complex and often proprietary formula that's based on many criteria related to your current financial situation and credit history.

While most credit scores, regardless of who calculates them, range from 350 to 850, this is not always the case. Thus, what a score actually means in terms of your credit worthiness will vary based on the type of credit score you're looking at. Be sure to read Chapter 4 for a more comprehensive explanation of what credit scores are, how they're calculated, who calculates them, and what they're used for.

According to the Federal Trade Commission (FTC), "Most creditors use credit scoring to evaluate your credit record. This involves using your credit application and report to get information about you, such as your annual income, outstanding debt, bill paying history, and the number and types of accounts you have and how long you have had them. Potential lenders use your credit score to help predict whether you are a good risk to repay a loan and make payments on time."

TransUnion reports someone's credit score is "a mathematical calculation that reflects a consumer's credit worthiness. The score is an assessment of how likely a consumer is to pay his or her debts."

What Is a Credit Report?

The three credit reporting agencies each maintain credit reports on virtually everyone with a Social Security number who has some type of credit history.

You Should Know...

There are many "credit repair" and "credit counseling" services that boast they can repair anyone's credit, regardless of what's in your credit history and what negative information is listed within your credit reports. This is simply untrue!

As you'll discover, there are definitely legal and achievable ways to clean up your credit and boost your credit scores. However, doing this is rarely a quick and easy process. Chapters 6 and 7 offer strategies for improving the information that's included within your credit reports and ultimately boost your credit scores legally, while Chapter 12 offers information about reputable resources you can utilize if you need help fixing your financial and credit problems.

Someone's credit report becomes active once they're granted credit for the very first time, in the form of a credit card, charge card, student loan, or car loan, for example. Thus, many people begin to establish their credit histories around the age of 18, or in their early 20s. From that point forward, detailed and up-to-date personal and financial information is maintained by the credit reporting agencies and is made available to potential creditors and lenders in the form of credit reports. Every credit report gets updated monthly, based on new or updated information provided by creditors.

A credit report is a summary of your past and current relationships with your creditors and lenders. It lists facts and data that pertain to how and when you've paid your bills and how well you've met your financial obligations. Contrary to popular belief, a credit report offers absolutely no analysis of your financial situation or credit worthiness. Instead, creditors and lenders use the information found within your credit report to help them perform their own analysis and make predictions about your future potential.

💲 Credit Tip

Checking your credit report regularly (at least once every 12 months) can help you prevent identity theft and will allow you to better manage your personal financial situation. About six months before applying for credit, such as a mortgage, a car loan, or even a credit card, it's a good idea to review your credit report.

When you, as a consumer, acquire a copy of your credit report, it might contain an explanation or analysis of your overall credit situation, but this is a value-added service offered by the company you used to access your credit report. This is probably not an analysis your potential creditors or lenders will see.

 *Warning*

The FBI reports that identity theft is currently the fastest growing crime in the United States. Often, criminals who steal people's identities utilize information from illegally obtained Social Security numbers and credit reports.

One way to determine if you're a victim of identity theft is to check your credit reports regularly for irregularities. For example, look for credit cards that have been issued in your name but that were never applied for or received by you. Also, check your credit card and bank account statements each month for transactions that don't belong to you.

If you notice any problems, report them immediately to the appropriate financial institutions and law enforcement agencies. Identity theft can result in negative information being added to your credit reports that doesn't belong to you. If not recognized and dealt with quickly, being an identity theft victim can lead to huge credit-related problems. Chapter 13 deals with preventing and identifying identity theft. In that chapter, you'll also learn about a company called LifeLock (www.lifelock.com), which can help you avoid becoming an identity theft victim.

Information that appears within your credit reports is compiled legally from a variety of sources. According to Experian, "Details about your financial behavior and identification information are contained in your personal credit report. This consumer-friendly report is sometimes called a credit file or a credit history. The typical consumer credit report includes four types of information. By law, we cannot disclose certain medical information (relating to physical, mental, or behavioral health or condition)."

The Anatomy of Your Credit Report

Chapter 5 focuses on how to obtain free copies of your credit reports from each of the three major credit reporting agencies and will help you understand exactly what's listed on them, as well as the significance of that information.

To quickly view the information listed on your credit report from all three of the major credit reporting agencies (Equifax, Experian, and TransUnion), be able to compare the information, and then check for inaccuracies, consider purchasing a comprehensive 3-in-1 credit report, which can be done online. The process for doing this will be explained shortly.

Whether you request copies of your credit reports through the mail or obtain the reports online, the information will be the same, although the data might be formatted differently on the printed page (versus what's displayed on the computer screen) or read in a printed version that's mailed to you.

Information That's Included in Your Credit Report

Although the format of your credit reports will vary based on which credit reporting agency created it and how the report is obtained, the data should be basically the same. The four main categories of information included on every credit report are described in the following sections.

PUBLIC RECORD INFORMATION

Public record information includes bankruptcy information and unpaid tax liens, for example, as well as details about civil lawsuits, judgments, and other legal proceedings recorded by a court. Bankruptcy information can remain on your credit report for up to 10 years. Unpaid tax liens can remain on the report for up to 15 years. Other public record information can remain on the report for up to seven years. In some states, this could also include overdue child support.

Any information reported in this section of your credit reports will have a very negative impact on your credit scores. If the information is

Dirty Little Secrets

accurate, it can typically only be removed from your credit reports using a court order issued by a judge.

CREDIT INFORMATION

This includes details about all loans and credit you've been granted in the past. For each item, information on the report will include account specific details, such as the date opened, credit limit or loan amount, balance, monthly payment, and your payment pattern. The report also states whether anyone besides you (a joint account holder or cosigner, for example) is responsible for paying the account.

Active positive credit information can remain on your report indefinitely, whereas most negative information in this category remains on your report for up to seven years.

Credit cards, car loans, mortgages, student loans, home equity loans, charge cards, checking account overdraft protection accounts and other types of credits and loans will be listed individually within this section.

You Should Know . . .

Each piece of information provided by a creditor or lender that appears within your credit report is called a *trade line.*

All of the information found within this section of your credit report is provided directly by your creditors and lenders on a monthly basis. The credit reporting agencies simply format the provided information in a way that's easier to read and analyze by other creditors and lenders. The process of creditors and lenders providing timely information to the credit reporting agencies is voluntary.

Later in this book you'll discover how to read and understand what's published within your credit reports. However, for reference now, let's take a look at the information that can be obtained from each

Dirty Little Secrets

 **Warning**

While many of the companies you do business with do not regularly report to the credit reporting agencies, such as your doctor's offices, utility companies (gas, water, or electric), or your cell phone service provider, for example, if you fail to pay your bill and it gets turned over to a third-party collection agency, at that point the delinquent bill (regardless of the creditor) will be reported to the credit reporting agencies, and the negative information will appear on your credit reports and remain there for seven years.

To protect your credit rating, even if you can't pay a bill in full, or you know you're going to be late with various payments, take a proactive role and contact the companies you owe money to in order to work out a payment plan *before* the account is turned over to a collection agency.

trade line that appears within the "Account Information" section of your credit report. This trade line information includes:

- The lender's name
- Your account number
- The lender's address
- Your current balance
- Date updated
- High balance
- Past due
- Credit limit (if applicable)
- Last payment
- Pay status
- Account type
- Responsibility

- Terms
- Date opened
- Date closed (if applicable)
- Loan type
- Estimated month and year this item will be removed
- Number of late payments (during the past 48 months), including the number of payments that are 30 days late, 60 days late, and 90 days late

Each trade line also includes a color-coded table that depicts (graphically) your payment history for that account during the past 24 months.

REQUESTS BY OTHERS TO VIEW YOUR CREDIT HISTORY

This section of your credit report will display details about who has received information from your credit report in the recent past, as allowed by law. According to the Fair Credit Reporting Act, credit grantors with a permissible purpose may inquire about your credit information without your prior consent. This is referred to as a "soft inquiry" and has no impact on your credit scores or credit rating.

All inquires remain listed on your credit reports for up to two years. Hard inquiries, however, which are the ones initiated with your permission when you apply for a credit card, loan, or mortgage, for example, will negatively impact your credit scores by a small amount for between six months and one year, although they'll remain listed on your report for two years.

PERSONAL INFORMATION

This section of a credit report contains your personal details, including: your name, current and previous addresses, telephone number, your Social Security number, date of birth, and current and previous employers. Within the employment section of your credit reports, information about your position (job title) and length of employment are listed for current and past jobs.

It's important to understand that on most people's credit reports, multiple variations or misspellings of their name and/or past addresses, for example, will appear. This has no relevance, however, to how your credit score(s) are calculated or whether or not you're approved for credit or loans.

What's important, however, is that all of the information found within the other sections of your credit reports pertains to you and your accounts (and correspond with your Social Security number).

In other words, if your name is Robert Jones Smith, for example, within your credit reports, the names Robert Jones Smith, Rob Smith, Bobby J. Smith, or any other relevant variation may appear. Likewise, different variations of the same address might appear. Only be concerned if a totally false name, address, or employment data, for example, also appears within your credit reports.

You Should Know . . .

Information about your race, religious beliefs, medical history, personal lifestyle, political affiliation, friends, and your criminal record (if applicable) do not appear on your credit reports and have no impact on your credit scores. Other information that's not included on your credit reports includes: checking or savings account balances, bankruptcies that are more than ten years old, and charged-off or debts placed for collection that are more than seven years old.

How the Information on Your Credit Report Is Compiled

Every month, every creditor and collection agency you're actively involved with will report details about you to one, two, or all three of the major credit reporting agencies. Your credit reports will then be updated, so new credit scores can be calculated.

You Should Know . . .

Any creditor or lender you borrow money from has the ability to add information (positive or negative) to your credit reports, as long as that information is current and accurate.

Collection agencies that represent utilities (gas, electric, telephone service, cell phone service providers, cable TV, etc.); medical offices and hospitals; or any other type of company that you owe money to can also add negative information to your credit reports if you're late or negligent in paying, causing the account to be turned over to a collection agency.

Although it's possible that no new information will be added during any given month, older (preexisting) information remains on your credit reports for between seven and ten years (sometimes longer).

Warning

Many people don't realize that failure to pay a doctor's bill, for example, can eventually have a negative impact on your credit reports, credit scores, and overall credit rating, if that unpaid bill goes to collections (i.e., gets turned over to a third-party collection agency).

Likewise, although the utility companies or cell phone companies don't generally report to the credit reporting agencies, if a bill goes unpaid and gets transferred to a collection agency, that negative information will eventually appear on your credit reports and will dramatically lower your credit scores for up to seven years.

Dirty Little Secrets

As you'll learn, this preexisting information will continue to impact your credit scores for as long as it remains within your credit reports. However, older information (even if it's negative) is given less relevance and weight than newly reported information.

Thus, even during a seven-year period when negative but accurate information is listed within your credit reports, as time goes on, the negative impact of that information will be lessened, especially if you've had only positive information added to your credit reports since.

Who Can View My Credit Report?

According to the Office of the Attorney General of the United States, "Any business, individual, or government agency may request a credit report for its legitimate business needs involving a transaction with the consumer. Valid reasons for a company to review your credit reports and credit scores include: credit granting considerations; review or collection of an account; employment considerations; insurance underwriting; a potential partnership; security clearance; or lease. Reports may also be issued at the written request of the consumer or a court."

Listed here in alphabetical order are some of the companies, individuals, and organizations that can obtain a copy of your credit report (in order to make a credit worthiness or business-related decision pertaining to you):

- A company you hire to monitor your credit reports for signs of identity theft
- Any government agency
- Any state or local child support enforcement agency
- Anyone who has your written authorization to obtain your credit reports
- Companies that want to use the information within your credit reports (or a corresponding credit score) to pre-qualify you for a loan or credit card that you have not solicited. For example,

before a credit card company sends you a new credit card offer that states, "You've been pre-qualified!" chances are they've accessed your credit reports without your knowledge or permission to pre-qualify you.

- Current or potential landlords
- Employers and potential employers
- Groups considering your application for a government license or benefit
- Insurance companies
- Potential lenders (credit card companies, mortgage brokers, car dealerships, banks, financial institutions, etc.) after you have completed and submitted a loan or credit application, for example. (In other words, you've actively applied for new credit or a new loan.)
- Someone who uses your credit reports to provide a product or service you have requested

 Credit Tip

Certain types of inquiries that don't involve you applying for new credit or a loan are called "soft inquiries." Although these are listed on your credit reports, they do not impact your credit scores. A "soft inquiry" might come from a potential landlord, a government agency, an insurance company, a rental car company, or a credit card company or mortgage broker doing market research without your knowledge to "pre-qualify" you as a cardholder or potential borrower.

Why Your Credit Reports Are So Important

When you apply for a job; attempt to make a purchase using credit; buy a home; refinance your existing mortgage; rent an apartment; attempt to purchase or lease a car; apply for a student loan (for yourself or your children); apply for a credit or charge card; open a checking account with overdraft protection at a bank or financial institution; or apply for a new insurance policy, your credit report(s) and credit score(s) will be evaluated.

What someone finds listed within your credit report(s) will directly impact your ability to make a purchase using credit or to obtain a loan. Any company that's allowed to obtain and evaluate a copy of your credit report(s) can accomplish this in a matter of minutes and then make quick but intelligent business decisions based on your credit score(s). Depending on the type of loan or credit you're applying for, the creditor or lender will access one, two, or all three of your credit reports, plus access one or more of your credit scores that correspond to each credit report.

Because the information contained within your credit reports is so important when it comes to obtaining credit and loans, it's vital that you take the steps necessary to ensure the information on your credit reports, created by each of the three major credit reporting agencies, is up-to-date and accurate.

Furthermore, because having and being able to utilize credit has become such an important part of our culture (and it's become more difficult to acquire due to current economic conditions), it's more vital than ever that as a consumer, you take steps to ensure the information reported to the credit reporting agencies by your creditors and lenders is positive.

The easiest way to ensure the information listed within your credit reports is positive (which will help boost your credit scores) is simply to pay your bills on time on a monthly basis and to immediately begin paying off any old debt that's been negatively listed within your credit reports. As you'll discover, there are also many other things you can do to improve your credit rating over time.

Many people who apply for or attempt to refinance a mortgage, apply for a car loan, or who apply for a credit card, for example, are often surprised to learn that their credit scores (and their credit worthiness) have dropped considerably due to recent late or missed payments.

Credit Tip

Many Americans run into financial problems at various times in their lives. This is common. Instead of ignoring bills and skipping payments, however, it's important to at least make timely minimum monthly payments and stay in touch with your creditors, keeping them apprised of your financial situation if a problem arises.

If you can't meet your financial obligations for a few months, your creditors and lenders will often work with you if you show good faith, stay in contact, and are cooperative with them.

As you'll learn, even one late mortgage payment over a one- or two-year period will hamper your ability to obtain the best interest rate and overall deal when you attempt to refinance your mortgage or apply for a new mortgage if you're planning to move, for example. When it comes to refinancing a mortgage, even one late mortgage payment (by more than 30 days) within the previous 12-month period could result in your application being denied.

Once you understand the importance of your credit reports, credit scores and overall credit rating, it's important to carefully analyze your current financial situation using the worksheets in Chapter 1, then do whatever you can to improve or remove any negative information that could impact your ability to obtain credit in the future. This is particularly important if your future plans involve applying for a mortgage, a car loan, a home equity loan, a credit card, a student loan, or some other type of loan for a major purchase.

Never wait until the last minute to begin addressing potential problems within your credit reports, because fixing inaccuracies or having the report updated after overdue payments are made can take 30 to 90 days (sometimes longer).

What's Next?

Now that you understand the relevance of your credit reports and credit scores on your financial well-being, Chapter 4 focuses specifically on understanding the significance of your credit scores and how they're calculated.

Keep in mind, the actual numeric value of your credit score is not as important as what that number represents in terms of your credit rating and how a potential lender will categorize your credit rating based on your scores. Ideally, you want to be classified as having an "above average" or "excellent" credit rating, as opposed to an "average," "poor," or "below average" rating.

Each company that calculates credit scores uses a slightly different method and scale. Thus, a score of 680 calculated by one company may have a very different significance than the same score calculated by a different company. It's important to understand what your credit score is, but more important, what it means.

You Should Know . . .

When it comes to FICO credit scores, maintaining a score of 760 or higher (which translates to an "excellent" credit rating) out of a possible 850 score will allow you to qualify for the best rates when applying for credit or loans.

CHAPTER 4

Solving Credit Score
Mysteries

What's in This Chapter

- What are credit scores?

- How your credit scores are calculated

- The differences between credit scores

- The impact your credit scores have on your financial life

- The inside scoop on FICO® Scores from the company that calculates them

Prepare to Get a Bit Confused by Credit Scores

Credit scores are used by creditors and lenders, banks and financial institutions, insurance companies and employers, among other companies and organizations, to make a wide range of educated decisions about individual consumers based on their credit rating and information that appears within their credit reports.

The most important thing to understand from this chapter, and about credit scores in general, is that there are many different companies and organizations, including Experian, TransUnion, and Equifax, along with FICO (and others), that utilize information and data from one or more of your credit report(s) and then apply proprietary and complex formulas in order to calculate their own credit scores designed to help potential creditors and lenders, for example, make very specialized credit or loan approval decisions.

You Should Know . . .

In recent years, Fair Isaac Corporation, which is responsible for creating and calculating FICO credit scores, has changed its name and is now known as FICO.

Depending on which formula is used to calculate a specific credit score, which credit report(s) data is taken from, and when the score is calculated, the credit scores generated for you on any particular day by each organization can vary greatly.

If you access your three credit reports (from Experian, TransUnion, and Equifax) and pay to also access your corresponding credit scores, it's common to discover that each score will be different. In fact, because each credit report will often contain slightly different information, and different credit scoring formulas are used, you may find a score discrepancy of up to 50 points or more, depending on your situation.

In addition to the credit scores you're able to obtain as a consumer, your creditors and lenders, insurance companies, car financing company, or even a potential employer might use a different formula altogether (that you as a consumer don't have access to) in order to calculate a credit score that more accurately meets their decision-making needs in terms of whether or not you represent a good credit risk for a loan, mortgage, credit card, student loan, or insurance policy, for example.

So, before you get caught up in all of the hype surrounding credit scores, it's essential that you know what a particular score represents and how it's calculated before you can truly evaluate your credit rating and overall credit situation.

To make things just a bit more confusing, credit scores are scaled differently, depending on who calculates them. Some scores are based on a scale between 300 and 850, while others have different ranges and are evaluated differently.

Instead of focusing in on your specific numeric credit score, first obtain your credit scores, and then determine how each score fits into the system used to calculate that score, and develop an understanding of what that score means. In other words, a credit score of 650 from one company may signify an "average" credit rating, but when evaluated by another credit scoring model that same score (which was calculated using a different formula) could represent a "below average" credit rating.

This chapter explains the basic concepts you'll need to understand when it comes to obtaining your credit scores, discovering what they mean, and determining how they're used. Gone are the days when a consumer could obtain a single FICO Score (www.myfico.com), for example, and have total confidence that the score they received is the same score being reported to all of their (potential) creditors and lenders.

Today, for every consumer, many different credit scores can be calculated, and these scores can be used for a variety of purposes. As a consumer, your goal should always be to strive for the highest credit scores possible.

Remember, instead of focusing on individual numbers, it's more important to know if your credit score(s) puts you in the "poor," "below average," "average," "above average," or "excellent" credit category.

Reasons for Possible Discrepancies in Your Credit Scores

Some of the reasons why your credit scores will vary (sometimes dramatically) depend on a variety of criteria including:

- What credit scoring formula is used
- The credit report data to which the scoring formula is applied
- Information on your credit report changing as your creditors and lenders report new information. A credit score that's calculated on a Monday could change by Thursday or Friday if changes to your credit report have occurred.

If the same company applies a specific credit scoring formula to all three of your credit reports, the credit score you achieve that corresponds to each credit report will be different; likewise, two different credit-scoring formulas (such as a FICO and Vantage scoring model) used on the same credit report from the same credit reporting agency at the same time will result in different credit scores.

Understanding Credit Score Ranges

In the past, for a creditor to make an approval decision, it would require a person with specialized training to carefully analyze all of the information on someone's credit report manually, then make a determination about their credit worthiness. That was how things were done about two decades ago. Today, thanks to computers, the process is far more automated. A complex and proprietary mathematical algorithm is used to calculate a credit score based on a variety of criteria, each of which is weighted differently. The result is a three-digit number, often between 300 and 850 (or 350 and 900). Approval or rejection

Credit Tip

The FICO scoring system uses a range between 300 and 850.

decisions can be made in seconds, not in days or weeks, thanks to the introduction of credit scoring.

Using the FICO scoring system, a credit score in the 300s or 400s is given to someone who has a history of being an extremely high credit risk, while a score in the mid-600s to low 700s is considered a good credit risk.

Someone with a credit score in the mid-to-high 700s or in the 800s is considered an excellent credit risk. These are the people who get the best deals in terms of low interest rates, for example, when applying for loans and credit cards.

You Should Know . . .

It's important to remember that different lenders and creditors give different weight to these scores. Each of the credit reporting agencies (Experian, Equifax, and TransUnion) maintains a separate credit report for every consumer. In conjunction with this credit report, each has its own corresponding credit scores. The information on each credit report is often slightly different because not all creditors report data to all three credit bureaus.

When you apply for a major credit card or store credit card, for example, that creditor will typically check your credit history by reviewing your credit report obtained from just one of the credit reporting agencies. Which agency the credit card issuer uses (Experian, Equifax, or TransUnion) is their decision. In many cases, when you're offered a credit decision in less than five minutes, that decision was

Dirty Little Secrets

based exclusively on a credit score that was calculated using raw data within your credit report, not on the detailed content within the credit report itself. The quick approval or rejection was a completely automated decision.

When you apply for a more substantial loan, such as a mortgage, the mortgage broker or mortgage finance company will typically access all three of your credit reports, obtain credit scores from a specific source (or calculate their own scores using their own formula), and then use the middle credit score as a tool to help make an approval decision. If only two credit scores are available, which is not unusual, then the mortgage company will rely on the lower of the two credit scores.

Because the information on your credit report constantly changes, as creditors report new or updated data, and old data (over seven years old) drops off your credit report, your corresponding credit scores change. The information, however, is typically based exclusively on information found in a particular credit report.

Information Outside of Your Credit Reports Is Typically Not Used to Calculate Credit Scores

The calculation of credit scores does *not* take the following information into account:

- Personal information, such as your sex, race, religion, marital status, employment status, nationality, or sexual orientation
- Your current (or past) checking or savings account balances
- The value of your personal assets and/or investments (or your overall net worth)

In some cases, if a credit score is being calculated by an insurance company, for example, that company might incorporate data not found within your credit report (such as how many insurance claims you've made in the past) to calculate their own proprietary credit score.

Dirty Little Secrets

Most of the time, however, only data from your credit reports is used to calculate a credit score, although different types of lenders will put more or less emphasis on specific types of data from your credit reports, based on what is important to them.

For example, if you're being evaluated for a car loan, the lender might pay more attention to data pertaining to past car loans that appear within your credit report(s) and put more importance on that data than it does on your credit card payment history.

Likewise, a mortgage broker or lender will look at your past mortgage payment history and put the most emphasis on that as it calculates its own proprietary credit score. Even one late mortgage payment within the past 12-month period could dramatically hurt a credit score being calculated by a mortgage lender.

Credit Scores Are Considered a Reliable Indicator of Your Credit Worthiness

When used by lenders, credit scores are considered an extremely reliable indication of someone's credit worthiness. Thus, they can be used to make automated decisions quickly. A creditor or lender can obtain or calculate a credit score in a matter of seconds, then often make a loan or credit approval decision in just minutes, which is something that could not have been done before, without the use of credit scores as a decision-making tool.

Because credit scores are calculated by a computer, typically using only information that appears within your credit report, there is little or no room for human biases in the decision-making process. Thus, it's much harder for a lender or creditor to discriminate against someone based on their gender, race, religion, nationality, marital status, employment status, or sexual orientation.

Remember, not only will your credit scores help to determine whether you're granted credit or a loan, they also directly help to determine what interest rate and fees you will ultimately pay when using credit or taking out a loan.

Dirty Little Secrets

E = MC² Is a Complex Formula . . . Your Credit Score May Seem Just as Complex

A credit score is *not* an arbitrary number. It's a numerical score that's based on data from your credit report that is evaluated using a complex and periodically changed mathematical algorithm.

Using a proprietary mathematical formula that is modified as consumer trends change, your credit scores are usually calculated based on all of the following criteria:

- *Your payment history.* This takes into account your payment information on specific types of loans, including your mortgage, auto loan, credit cards, retail accounts, student loans, home equity loans, and so on. It also takes into account any negative information listed in the public records section of your credit report, such as a bankruptcy, judgments, lawsuits, liens, wage attachments, collection items, and so on. Within the calculation, not only is your score impacted based on how many late payments that are listed on your credit report, but the amount past due, and how late the payment(s) were, is also factored into the equation. On the positive side, your credit score will get a boost for each account (trade line) that's listed as "current" or "paid as agreed."
- *The amounts you owe.* This takes into account the amount of money you owe on accounts, the types of accounts, the number

(\$) Credit Tip

As payment history information is being utilized when calculating a credit score, the process will examine how many accounts you have that are current and paid as agreed, past due, and that are in collections and remain uncollected, for example. How long overdue payments are, and the amount of money that's owed (and late) for each will also be taken into account.

of accounts you have with outstanding balances, your current credit utilization (the portion or percentage of each available credit line that's being used), and the portion of installment loan amounts still owing.

■ *The length of your credit history.* This refers to the time since each account was first opened and the amount of time that has passed since the last activity on the account. The older accounts are, and the longer they've remained in good standing, the better this will reflect on you when credit scores are being calculated.

■ *New credit.* The number of newly opened accounts, the number of recent credit inquiries, the time that's passed since your last new accounts were opened, and the time since the most recent inquiries were made are all taken into account.

■ *Types of credit used.* The number and types of accounts listed on your credit report all play a role in the calculation of your credit scores. The number of accounts may include the number of car loans, mortgages, and credit cards.

All of this data is automatically lifted directly from your credit report and taken into account as a credit score is calculated. Depending on the creditor or lender and your overall credit profile, the amount of weight each piece of information or data is given will vary dramatically from person to person; however, your positive or negative payment history is typically weighted the heaviest when a credit score calculation is made.

Thus, late payments and other negative information will lower your score, while maintaining or re-establishing a positive track record over time (in terms of timely payments) will boost your score.

According to FICO, whose scores are commonly used by creditors and lenders, the amount of emphasis put on data from your credit report can be summarized as follows when calculating a credit score:

■ Payment history—35 percent
■ Amounts currently owed to creditors/lenders—30 percent

- Length of credit history—15 percent
- New credit—10 percent
- Types of credit used (or being utilized)—10 percent

A FICO Score (and most other types of credit scores) takes into account all of these elements (not just one or two of them), but each is weighed differently based on the overall information obtained from your credit report. Your income or current net worth, however, are not at all considered in the calculation of your credit scores.

($) Credit Tip

For more information about FICO Scores, or to obtain your own FICO score, visit www.MyFico.com.

When taking out any type of loan, you want to be aware of the direct correlation between your credit score and how much you'll pay in interest and fees. Visit the MyFICO website and use the free online Loan Savings Calculator (www.myfico.com/myfico/CreditCentral/LoanRates.aspx) to quickly determine potential savings based on improvements you're able to make to your credit score over time.

For example, if in July 2012, you were looking for a 36-month auto loan in the amount of $18,000 to purchase a new car, but you had a low FICO credit score (between 500 and 589), you'd most likely have been offered a loan with an APR of 17.174 percent. The monthly payment on the loan would be $643, and you'd wind up paying $5,159 in interest over the three-year period.

However, if your FICO credit score was between 690 and 719, for example, you would have been offered an APR for the same $18,000/36-month loan at 4.952 percent. This would put your monthly payment at $539 (not $643), and you'd wind up paying just $1,407 in interest (not $5,159) over the three-year period. This is just one example of how having a higher credit score will save you money immediately and over the long term.

You Should Know . . .

As of July 2012, the average FICO credit score in the United States was 689. In New York, the average FICO credit score was 701; in California it was 691; and in Texas it was 668.

Credit Score vs. FICO Score: What's the Difference?

Fair Isaac Corporation is the original name of the company that first created credit scores, now simply called FICO Scores. These scores (or variations of them) are used by 70 percent of all creditors and lenders.

Each of the three credit-reporting agencies, as well as certain creditors and lenders, also calculate their own version of each consumer's credit score based on information on your credit reports. These scores are simply called "credit scores," or they may have another fancy name given to them by the company that created them. These other credit scores, however, may or may not be the actual scores lenders and creditors use to make their decisions.

FICO licenses variations of its credit-scoring system to all three of the credit reporting agencies. Thus, a FICO Score issued by Equifax might be called a BEACON® Score. A FICO Score issued by Experian might be called an Experian/FICO Risk Model score. A FICO Score issued by TransUnion might be called an Empirica® score.

In addition to these variations of FICO Score, each credit reporting agency also offers its own proprietary credit scoring model and makes their own credit scores available to consumers as well as creditors and lenders. For example, a credit score calculated by Experian is called a

PLUS® Score. It uses a different formula than a FICO Score to calculate someone's credit score based on data found within an Experian credit report.

To determine your actual FICO Scores and be able to monitor them on an ongoing basis, you can purchase this information directly from FICO's website (www.myfico.com/Products/Products.aspx) for either $4.95 or $14.95 per month. The company offers its Score Watch and FICO Quarterly Monitoring subscription-based services, respectively. The Score Watch service, for example, continuously monitors your Equifax credit report and corresponding FICO Score, notifies you when you may qualify for better interest rates, emails you when changes to your FICO Score or credit report are detected, and informs you about how key positive and negative factors are impacting your personal score, based on information that is in your credit report. For $4.95 per month, the Score Watch program provides you just your current credit score, with little additional information.

The FICO Standard package (available for a one-time fee of $19.95 each) offers one-time access to your TransUnion or Equifax credit report (you can choose one, or pay $39.90 for both), along with your corresponding FICO Scores and details from FICO about factors that affected your score.

If you opt to purchase a subscription to the FICO Score Watch service, this is done online. A free 10-day trial is available for this service, or you can opt to pay on a monthly or slightly discounted annual basis. You'll need to provide your full name, physical and email addresses, as well as your gender, date of birth, and Social Security number. You'll then be prompted to create a user name and password for your new MyFico.com account, and also need to provide a credit or debit card number to pay for your purchase(s).

Within a minute or so, your FICO Score will be displayed on the main Score Watch screen, and you'll be able to set up your account to receive email or wireless text message alerts as your credit score changes over time. Under the "View Power Score Reports" heading, click on the

Dirty Little Secrets

"View" option to view your current credit report and related FICO Score information in more detail.

All three credit reporting agencies also offer online-based services and products for consumers that allow you to access your credit reports, see corresponding credit scores, and evaluate or monitor your credit rating on an ongoing basis. Each also offers the ability to purchase a three-in-one credit report (with or without corresponding credit scores). You'll learn more about these options in Chapter 5.

Before subscribing to any of these services or purchasing any of these products, however, determine what's included, what cost(s) are involved, whether or not there's a recurring monthly fee, what the cancellation policy for the service is, and what credit score data the service or product will provide.

As you'll learn from Chapter 5, individual credit reports, three-in-one credit reports, credit scores, and credit monitoring services are available from:

- Experian—www.experian.com/consumer-products/credit-report. html
- TransUnion—www.transunion.com
- Equifax—www.equifax.com

Warning

If you subscribe to a service that provides generic credit scores that are based on a proprietary formula that no creditors or lenders are using, the credit score(s) you receive will have little or no relevance to your situation or your ability to get approved for new credit or loans.

Dirty Little Secrets

What's a VantageScore 2.0?

As if the whole credit scoring system weren't complicated enough, in early 2006, yet another credit scoring system was implemented. The VantageScore system is designed to make the credit scores provided by the three credit reporting agencies more uniform for each consumer. Plus, to make this "generic" score easier to understand, it is accompanied by a letter grade (ranging from "A" to "F"), not just a number. More recently, the VantageScore 2.0 credit scoring system was introduced and implemented.

Until now, the information on a typical consumer's three credit reports varied, which translated to sometimes vastly different credit scores corresponding with each report. This new system is reported to reduce the discrepancy between scores by up to 30 percent. In order to calculate a VantageScore, the participating credit reporting agencies use a single methodology rather than slightly different formulas.

The VantageScore 2.0 system calculates credit scores based on a range between 501 and 990. Like the FICO Score system (which uses a range of 300 to 850), the higher your score, the better. The corresponding letter grades associated with each VantageScore 2.0 are as follows:

- 501 to 599 = "F" (very poor credit)
- 600 to 699 = "D"
- 700 to 799 = "C"
- 800 to 899 = "B"
- 900 to 990 = "A" (excellent credit)

If you access your VantageScore 2.0 credit score, use it as your own indicator in terms of how you might be seen by lenders. But don't confuse your VantageScore with a FICO Score, because a 700 FICO Score means something vastly different than a 700 VantageScore.

According to VantageScore Solutions, LLC, the company that developed the VantageScore and VantageScore 2.0 credit score system, "VantageScore leverages the collective experience of industry leading experts on credit data, credit risk modeling and analytics. The nation's three major credit reporting companies (CRCs)—Equifax, Experian and TransUnion—worked together to develop a generic credit scoring model that is regularly revalidated. VantageScore marks the first time that the three companies joined forces to produce a model that scores consumers consistently across all three companies...By utilizing cutting-edge, patent-pending analytic techniques, VantageScore provides lenders and consumers with a highly consistent, more predictive score that is easy to understand and apply."

To learn more about the VantageScore 2.0 credit scoring system, visit http://vantagescore.com/consumers/aboutyourscore or http://vantagescore.com/docs/vs_factsheet_1014_vs.pdf. However, to obtain your VantageScore credit scores, you'll need to go through one of the credit reporting agencies.

The Inside Scoop on FICO Scores from the Company that Calculates Them

Craig Watts is the public affairs manager for FICO. In this interview, Watts explains more about FICO Scores and how to improve yours using easy-to-follow strategies and advice.

FICO (NYSE: FIC) was founded in 1956 on the premise that data, used intelligently, can improve business decisions. Today, the company's solutions, software, and consulting services power more than 180 billion smarter business decisions each year for companies worldwide.

Many banks, creditors, lenders, and credit card issuers, for example, rely on FICO solutions, as do insurers, retailers, telecommunications providers, healthcare organizations, and government agencies. Through the www.MyFICO.com website, consumers use the company's FICO Scores to help manage their financial well-being.

When did FICO Scores first get introduced in the United States?

Craig Watts: "Automated credit reports were made available for the first time in the late 1970s. Using automated credit reports, the company developed the algorithm that calculates FICO Scores. The system was introduced in 1989 by Equifax. Our formula to calculate FICO Scores is now part of the operating system used by all three credit reporting agencies. Over 70 percent of all lenders and creditors rely on FICO Scores to help them make their lending or credit granting decisions. The three credit reporting agencies also calculate their own credit scores, plus many lenders and creditors have their own algorithms for calculating credit scores that are used in-house. In the mid-1990s, mortgage lenders began widely using credit scores as part of their approval process."

How is someone's FICO Score actually calculated?

Craig Watts: "There is a mathematical algorithm that we've created that's made available to the three credit reporting agencies, creditors, and lenders in the form of software. This formula is modified periodically, based on new or evolving consumer trends. Each algorithm used by the credit reporting agencies is also slightly different. Since 1989, we have never stopped redeveloping the algorithm that's used to calculate FICO Scores.

"FICO Scores look at someone's credit history, based on five categories. We put the greatest focus on how timely you pay your bills. If you've paid your bills late, we take into account how late bills were paid and whether or not accounts have been turned over to a collections agency. This represents about 35 percent of your FICO Score. We also put a lot of emphasis on the amount owed by a consumer. About 30 percent of your FICO Score is based on your credit utilization. The lower your utilization rates, the better. Again, we also look at the age of your various accounts and take this into consideration when calculating a FICO Score. The greater the length of your credit history, the better that is for your score. Your pursuit of new credit is also considered. On average, Americans open new credit accounts less than twice per year. It's to your advantage to be part of this group in terms of your FICO Score.

"Also, a mix of credit, handled well, is better for your FICO Score than multiple forms of the same type of credit. For example, having a student loan, car loan, and a credit card is a better combination than three credit cards, assuming they're all kept up-to-date and managed well."

What is the difference between FICO Scores and other "generic" credit scores?

Craig Watts: "There are several ways to answer this question. One is from a branding perspective. The other is from an algorithm perspective. What we call FICO Scores are based on the algorithm created by FICO. The three credit reporting agencies use our scoring model, but resell the scores under different names, like BEACON® Score and Empirica® Score.

"The credit reporting agencies, however, have also developed their own in-house versions of credit risk scores, which they sell to consumers, creditors, and lenders. These are different scores than FICO Scores. In some cases, the scores sold to consumers are meant for educational purposes only, and are not made available to lenders and creditors. Thus, our relationship with the credit reporting agencies has always been one of cooperation and competition.

"FICO Scores are widely used by lenders for decision-making purposes and they're readily available to consumers. This is not the case with other credit scores and any similarity these scores have to FICO Scores is coincidental.

"As far as the algorithm goes, our formula for calculating FICO Scores is a closely kept secret. We do not publicize what the formula is, but we do offer tips to consumers on how to better manage their credit, which in turn will improve their scores. In a public forum, there has not been a head-to-head comparison between the various credit scores available to consumers and how they're being used by lenders.

"Any credit score can be helpful in educating a consumer about their current credit situation. I equate this to going to the local pharmacy and using the free blood pressure machine to check your blood pressure. This will give you a general idea about what your blood pressure is, but your doctor will ultimately want to do their own tests using more advanced and specialized equipment before making any type of diagnosis. Ideally, as a consumer, you want to see the same credit scores that your creditors and lenders are seeing."

What are some of the recent trends used to calculate FICO Scores?

Craig Watts: "When Fair Isaac Corporation first developed the FICO Score system in the late 1980s, our research indicated that when people shopped around for car loans or mortgages, for example, they didn't have a lot of options, so they spent only about one week shopping for their best deals before making a decision. When we determined that people shopped for seven days, we modified the formula so that it ignored multiple inquiries from mortgage or car loan lenders within a seven-day period and counted them as just one hard inquiry.

"Over the years, our research has shown that people have begun spending more time researching and shopping around for their best options for mortgages and car loans. Thus, over the years, this seven-day window was expanded to 14 days in the late 1990s. It was later expanded again to 30 days. Most recently, we've expanded the window to 45 days, during which time someone can have multiple hard inquiries from a mortgage or car loan lender count as just one hard inquiry on their credit report.

"Also, in the past, if someone sought out credit counseling, it was reflected on their credit report, and their credit score was negatively impacted. This is no longer the case. We now encourage people to seek out credit counseling when it's needed. This will have no impact on their FICO Score."

Hard inquiries from lenders detract from someone's credit score. How long does inquiry information remain listed on a credit report and how much of a negative impact does it have?

Craig Watts: "Hard inquiries remain on credit reports for two years. However, in terms of our FICO Score calculation, we only look at the number and types of inquiries over the previous 12-month period. Beyond the national average of two hard inquiries per year, your FICO Score might take a five-point hit for each additional inquiry."

For a long time, people were told to close unused credit accounts in order to improve their credit scores. Is this still the case?

Craig Watts: "The FICO credit scores look at your available credit and the amount you owe. From this data, your credit utilization rate is calculated. The credit utilization rate determines how close you are to maxing out your credit accounts as a whole. Those unused accounts contribute to the total amount of credit you have available. If you were to close those unused accounts, your total amount of available credit would immediately decrease, but your current credit balances would remain the same, since you've done nothing to pay them down. With the lower available credit, the formula would raise your credit utilization rate, which would be detrimental to your credit score. This is why closing unused credit accounts with zero balances can hurt you."

What can someone do to improve their FICO Score?

Craig Watts: "The most obvious and common-sense answer is to always pay your bills on time. Never become late. The more late payments you have beyond 30 days, the worse off you'll be. If you have otherwise good credit, and one or two late payments suddenly appear on your credit report, that could cause your FICO Score to drop 50 to 100 points almost instantly. The higher your score is to begin with, the farther your score will tumble when negative information starts to appear on your credit reports. Just like your personal or professional reputation, it takes much longer to recover your credit score than it does to hurt it."

If your credit score has experienced a drop, what can be done to boost it up again?

Craig Watts: "The best thing you can do is get caught up with all of your creditors and then begin to once again pay all of your bills on time.

If you're able to do this, you'll notice your FICO Score will gradually rise. We've seen people with bankruptcies listed on their credit reports receive credit or be approved for prime-rate loans after three or four years of rebuilding their credit. That bankruptcy, however, will remain listed on their credit reports for ten years.

"When something negative impacts your credit score, the amount of negative impact will decrease over time. For example, a charge-off related to a credit card will be listed on your credit reports for seven years. However, the level your credit score is impacted by that negative information will become less relevant as time goes on. The older a negative item is, the less it will hurt your credit score, but it will continue to have at least some negative impact on your score for the full seven years or until that negative item is removed from your credit report altogether.

"FICO Scores look at negative information within your credit report in three different ways, which are timeliness, severity, and frequency. Timeliness refers to how recent the negative information is. Severity refers to how negative the information is. A 30-day late payment, for example, is better than an account being turned over to a collection agency, which is better than a bankruptcy. Finally, frequency refers to the number of accounts that are impacted. If five credit card accounts are all paid late, that's worse than just one account being reported as having a late payment. Or, if the same account is reported late multiple times, that's worse than the account being reported late just once."

What else can someone do to quickly boost their FICO Score?

Craig Watts: "Make sure your account balances on revolving accounts, such as credit cards, remain low compared to your credit limits. This will improve your score. Paying down your credit card debt will help your score, plus save you money. Ideally, you want to keep each credit card balance under 35 percent of your current limits. For the best impact on your credit score, pay off your credit card debt to zero.

"The reason why it's difficult to quickly raise your FICO Score is because this number is supposed to represent your credit reputation. If you have a history of being a credit risk, you need to show improvement over time in order to be rewarded with a higher credit score.

"The FICO Score is a summary of your entire credit history, not just what's happened in the past few weeks or months. If your score has dropped below 500, for example, it didn't happen by accident. The low score is a result of your ongoing actions when it comes to managing your debt, finances, and credit.

"One thing you can do to quickly improve your score, however, is to correct any errors on your credit report that could be keeping your score down. Corrections can be made in as little as 10 to 30 days, assuming the corrections you're seeking are legitimate. You cannot have accurate information that is negative removed from your credit report simply by initiating a dispute. When someone has a credit score over 800, it's because they've demonstrated good credit habits over many years."

If someone has a lot of negative information on their credit report, or if they've declared bankruptcy, how long will it take them to rebuild their credit score?

Craig Watts: "This will vary greatly from person to person, based on their unique situation. However, we have seen people who have declared bankruptcy be able to fully rebuild their credit in three to four years. In this situation, the best thing you can do is redevelop at least one line of credit that is being reported to the credit reporting agencies. You must be able to demonstrate that you can properly manage credit over a period of time. Unless you can do this and feed positive information to your credit reports, your score will not improve.

"Obtaining a secured credit card is one way someone can begin to reestablish and rebuild their credit. However, it's absolutely essential that you manage that new secured credit card account perfectly and pay your bills on time. Never be reported late paying a bill ever again. Also, keep your balances low based on its limit throughout the month. Simply paying off the credit card balance at the end of a month is not sufficient. Don't utilize too much of your available credit within a month. If you have a $5,000 credit limit on your credit card account and within a month, you utilize $4,500, but pay that off at the end of the month, it will still be reported to the credit reporting agencies that you utilized most of your available credit, and that hurts your credit score. Keep your revolving utilization of your credit low, but be sure to utilize at least some of your available credit.

"Once you start rebuilding your credit, don't open too many new accounts too quickly. Spread out the new accounts by at least six months each."

What is the bare minimum credit score someone should aim for in order to get good deals on loans and credit?

Craig Watts: "That's a difficult question, because every lender and creditor has its own criteria for approving loans or granting credit. Some lenders are very risk averse. Other lenders are much more willing to advance credit to higher risk borrowers. Asking this question is like asking what's the ideal SAT score to achieve in order to get into college. The answer is that every college and university has its own criteria for what it looks for.

"As a general rule, within the mortgage industry, having a FICO Score of 720 to 750 or above should allow you to qualify for the best prime-rate loans."

Why is someone's FICO Score from each credit reporting agency different, even if the three reports were accessed at the same time?

Craig Watts: "There are three reasons for this. First, different information is reported to different credit reporting agencies. For example, a mortgage or credit card company may only report data to one or two, not all three of the credit bureaus, and this will impact your score. Also, the algorithm used to calculate someone's FICO Score is slightly different with each credit reporting agency. Finally, the three credit reporting agencies have different search capabilities for finding and listing information in the 'Public Records' section of a credit report, which also impacts your credit score."

You Should Know . . .

From the MyFico.com website (www.myfico.com/Credit-Cards), you can quickly shop for credit card offers based on a wide range of criteria, including which credit cards you're most likely to get approved for based on your FICO credit score. You'll also find a variety of online calculators that can help you determine rates you qualify for as you shop for other types of loans, such as car loans, student loans, or mortgages.

What are some of the biggest misconceptions people have about FICO Scores?

Craig Watts: "One of the biggest misconceptions is that the FICO Score system takes into account someone's income and assets. This isn't true at all. The score is based on how you've handled credit in the past, not how much money you have in your checking or savings account. I have seen people at the poverty level have excellent credit scores, and multi-millionaires have very low credit scores, because they paid their bills late, and were not responsible with their credit or managing their loans.

"Another misconception is that creditors and lenders use someone's FICO Score exclusively to make decisions. This too is often false. Many creditors use someone's credit score as one tool. When you apply for a mortgage, for example, someone will evaluate all of the information actually listed on your credit reports, check your credit scores, and inquire about things like your employment history and your earning history before making a decision.

"One of the only times when a FICO Score alone is used to grant credit is when you apply for instant credit at a department store or retail store, or a financial institution offers instant approval for a credit card. In this case, a computer will look up your credit score, often your FICO Score, and make a decision using a fully automated process. If you're

Dirty Little Secrets

not immediately accepted, however, you can then complete a full credit application and have it reviewed. Credit scores are also used by credit card companies to provide pre-approved credit card offers to select groups of consumers who fit a specific credit profile."

Why don't the credit reporting agencies automatically provide a FICO Score or credit score when someone requests their annual free credit report?

Craig Watts: "This is a business decision made by the credit reporting agencies. The Fair Credit Reporting Act requires the credit reporting agencies to supply consumers with free copies of their credit reports upon request, at least once every 12 months, depending on the state where you live. Until this law was passed, the consumer had to pay for this information. Because the credit score is not actually part of the credit report, this is a piece of information that credit reporting agencies can still charge extra for."

How can a consumer know if they're receiving the right type of credit score?

Craig Watts: "The FICO Score is used by many lenders and creditors and it is also available to consumers. If the score you receive doesn't say it's a genuine FICO Score, chances are it's some other type of score that the lenders and creditors might not actually be using to make their decisions."

If someone has a charge-off or collection being reported on their credit report and they wind up paying off that debt, does this still negatively impact their credit score?

Craig Watts: "In terms of your FICO Score, yes, it does. Once your credit report reflects a negative piece of information, such as a charge-off, that will impact your credit score for seven years, even if the account is ultimately paid in full, thanks to the efforts of a collection agency or a legal judgment. The reasoning is pretty clear-cut. The FICO Score is designed to help creditors predict whether someone will become seriously late when paying off a debt. The fact that a charge-off, for example, happened is highly predictive of future behavior. The fact that the consumer made good on the debt later will ultimately look good on a credit report, but it has no positive advantage in terms of FICO Score calculations."

How much should someone obsess about their credit score?

Craig Watts: "My advice is to be concerned about protecting your credit rating by being a responsible consumer, but don't overly obsess about your credit score. If you are a responsible consumer with generally good credit, the time to get concerned about your credit score is starting about six months before you apply for a major loan or line of credit, such as a mortgage or car loan. If you find you need to improve your score and you begin checking it six months before a major purchase, that gives you plenty of time to pay down credit card balances, for example, which will boost your scores.

"In general, there are no legal ways to quickly boost your credit scores. You can trash your scores overnight, but to improve your scores is a slow process. Paying down credit card balances and keeping your balances low for a several-month or longer period of time is probably the quickest way to improve your credit scores. The other thing you can do is to have errors removed from your credit reports by filing disputes."

What's Next?

Now that you understand the basics about what information is contained within your credit reports (see Chapter 3) and what data is used to calculate your credit scores, the next chapter focuses on how to obtain copies of your credit reports and credit scores. You'll discover from Chapter 5 that the fastest and easiest way to obtain this information is online; however, you can also request this information by telephone or by mail.

Dirty Little Secrets

Obtaining Your Credit
Reports and Credit Scores

What's in This Chapter

- How to request a free copy of your credit report from each of the three credit reporting agencies once every 12 months (or more frequently, depending on the state in which you live)

- How to request a free copy of your credit report from each of the three credit reporting agencies once every 12 months through the Annual Credit Report website (www.annualcreditreport.com)

- The benefits of purchasing a three-in-one credit report with your corresponding credit scores

- Understanding what's on your credit report and how that information is presented

- Avoiding misleading "free credit report" offers

How to Request Free Copies of Your Credit Report Annually

While efforts have been made to streamline the ways in which consumers like you can request and obtain copies of their credit report from each of the credit reporting agencies, it's still ultimately necessary to contact Equifax, Experian, and TransUnion separately to obtain a copy of your credit report that's generated by each credit reporting agency.

Then, if corrections need to be made, it's necessary to contact each credit reporting agency separately and go through their respective processes for initiating a dispute. While the laws vary from state to state, in general, your credit report is available to you for free, from each credit reporting agency, once every 12 months.

At anytime, however, you can:

- Purchase a single copy of your credit report from one or more of the credit reporting agencies for a fee, with or without a corresponding credit score (which you'll pay a bit extra for).
- Request an additional free copy of your credit report if you get rejected by a lender or credit card issuer after applying for some type of credit or loan.
- Pay for a credit monitoring service that gives you continuous or monthly access to your credit report(s) from one or more of the credit reporting agencies. These subscription-based services typically provide you with one or more credit scores as well.

An alternative to requesting an individual credit report from each credit reporting agency is to purchase a comprehensive three-in-one credit report. This is a single report that compiles data and information from all three credit reporting agencies (and in some cases, includes a credit score that accompanies each report). It's necessary to purchase a three-in-one credit report or subscribe to a credit monitoring service that offers these reports as a benefit to members.

There are several ways to obtain a free copy of your credit report annually. As you'll discover, the fastest and easiest method is to initiate

Warning

When you request a free copy of your credit report, it will not include a credit score. For a fee, you can request a corresponding credit score from each credit reporting agency when you receive your report, or obtain a FICO Score from www.MyFico.com. Be sure, however, to read Chapter 4 carefully so you understand the significance of the credit score you receive.

the request online from the www.annualcreditreport.com website. In less than five minutes, you can be viewing copies of your credit report(s) on your computer screen, or print out the information in an easy-to-read format.

If you don't have internet access, it's possible to request copies of your credit reports by completing and mailing a single-page "Annual Credit Report Request Form," or by sending a letter to the Annual Credit Report Request Service. Yet another option is to call the toll-free phone number for the Annual Credit Report service to have copies of your credit report mailed to you.

Obtaining Your Credit Report Online

Using any computer with internet access, you can request and obtain a copy of your credit report from each of the three credit reporting agencies in under five minutes. Point your web browser to the official Annual Credit Report Request Service's website (www.annualcreditreport.com), select your home state, and complete the brief online form (see Figure 5-1 on page 86).

The Annual Credit Report Request Service is sponsored by all three credit reporting agencies and authorized by the Federal Trade Commission. It allows you to request one, two, or all three of your

FIGURE 5–1: **Request Your Free Credit Reports from the Annual Credit Report Website**

EQUIFAX®   experian®   TransUnion®

Annual Credit Report Request Form

You have the right to get a free copy of your credit file disclosure, commonly called a credit report, once every 12 months, from each of the nationwide consumer credit reporting companies - Equifax, Experian and TransUnion.

For instant access to your free credit report, visit www.annualcreditreport.com.

For more information on obtaining your free credit report, visit www.annualcreditreport.com or call 877-322-8228.

Use this form if you prefer to write to request your credit report from any, or all, of the nationwide consumer credit reporting companies. The following information is required to process your request. Omission of any information may delay your request.

Once complete, fold (do not staple or tape), place into a #10 envelope, affix required postage and mail to:

Annual Credit Report Request Service P.O. Box 105281 Atlanta, GA 30348-5281.

Please use a Black or Blue Pen and write your responses in PRINTED CAPITAL LETTERS without touching the sides of the boxes like the examples listed below:

A B C D E F G H I J K L M N O P Q R S T U V W X Y Z   0 1 2 3 4 5 6 7 8 9

Social Security Number:

Date of Birth: Month / Day / Year

First Name   M.I.

Last Name   JR, SR, III, etc.

Current Mailing Address:

House Number   Street Name

Apartment Number / Private Mailbox   For Puerto Rico Only: Print Urbanization Name

City   State   ZipCode

Previous Mailing Address (complete only if at current mailing address for less than two years):

House Number   Street Name

Fold Here   Fold Here

Apartment Number / Private Mailbox   For Puerto Rico Only: Print Urbanization Name

City   State   ZipCode

Shade Circle Like This → ●

Not Like This → ⊗ ∅

I want a credit report from (shade each that you would like to receive):
○ Equifax
○ Experian
○ TransUnion

○ Shade here if, for security reasons, you want your credit report to include no more than the last four digits of your Social Security Number.

If additional information is needed to process your request, the consumer credit reporting company will contact you by mail.

Your request will be processed within 15 days of receipt and then mailed to you.

Copyright 2004, Central Source LLC

31238

individual credit reports with a single request which ultimately get forwarded to the individual credit reporting agencies. This can be done by mail, phone, or via the internet. (Three-in-one credit reports, which are available for a fee, are not available from this service.)

Dirty Little Secrets

You'll be asked to provide your full name, date of birth, Social Security number, and current address. If you've lived at your current address for less than two years, you'll also be asked for your previous address. At the bottom of the on-screen questionnaire, you'll see a security code in a multi-colored box. At the appropriate prompt, reenter this security code and click the "Next" icon to continue.

You will now be prompted to select one or more of the credit reporting agencies from which you want to request your free credit report. Using your mouse, place an on-screen checkmark next to one, two, or all three of the available options, which include Experian, Equifax, and TransUnion (see Figure 5–2, page 88). When you've checked the desired options, click on the "Next" icon located near the lower-right corner of the screen.

At this point, you will be transferred to the official website of each credit reporting agency, one at a time, to obtain your free credit report. Upon accessing each separate website, you'll be asked several security questions that will help to confirm your identity.

Once you've obtained each report and printed it out, click on the "Return to AnnualCreditReport.com" option that's displayed near the top of the screen in order to return to the main AnnualCreditReport. com website. You'll then be redirected to the website of another credit reporting agency, if you've requested multiple reports.

You may be asked a question like, "According to your credit profile, you may have opened a mortgage loan in or around [insert month and year]. Please select the lender to whom you currently make your mortgage payments. If you do not have a mortgage, select 'NONE OF THE ABOVE/DOES NOT APPLY.'"

You'll then be provided with four or five possible options to choose from. Be prepared to answer three to five different security questions when visiting each of the credit reporting agencies websites as part of your credit report request.

Upon answering the security questions correctly, your credit report will promptly be displayed on the computer screen. Choose the "Print

FIGURE 5–2: **Choose Which of the Credit Reporting Agencies from Which You'd Like to Obtain Your Free Credit Report. Place a Checkmark Next to One, Two, or All Three Options.**

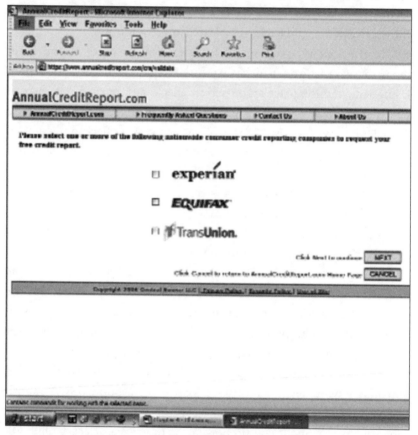

Your Report" option to view a printer-friendly version of your credit report.

The report printed will be current as of the date of your request. It will display only information from creditors and lenders that have submitted information to that particular credit reporting agency.

Keep in mind it is possible that as you review your three credit reports, slightly different information will appear on each report. This can be caused by a number of factors, including which of your creditors and lenders submitted information to a particular credit reporting agency and when that information was last reported or updated.

Every credit report you obtain will include a nine-digit file number that will be displayed on the report's first page. You will need this file number to re-access the same credit report online within a 90-day period, or to initiate a dispute.

Submitting Your Request by U.S. Mail

Once every 12 months, you can request free copies of your credit report from each of the credit reporting agencies by completing the Annual Credit Report Request Form (see Figure 5-3, page 90). The form is available from www.annualcreditreport.com or www.ftc.gov/freereports.

To complete the one-page Annual Credit Report Request Form, you'll need to provide the following information about yourself:

- Social Security number
- Date of birth
- First name

Warning

Many companies advertise that they will provide a free copy of your credit report. However, to obtain the free report, you'll need to subscribe to a credit monitoring service or purchase some other item or product. This typically involves an ongoing monthly fee of up to $40.00.

To obtain a truly free copy of your credit report with no strings attached, go to the Annual Credit Report Request Service (www.AnnualCreditReport.com), which is the only service authorized by the FTC. Beware of impostors and other companies that look or sound official.

Dirty Little Secrets

FIGURE 5–3: **Annual Credit Report Request Form**

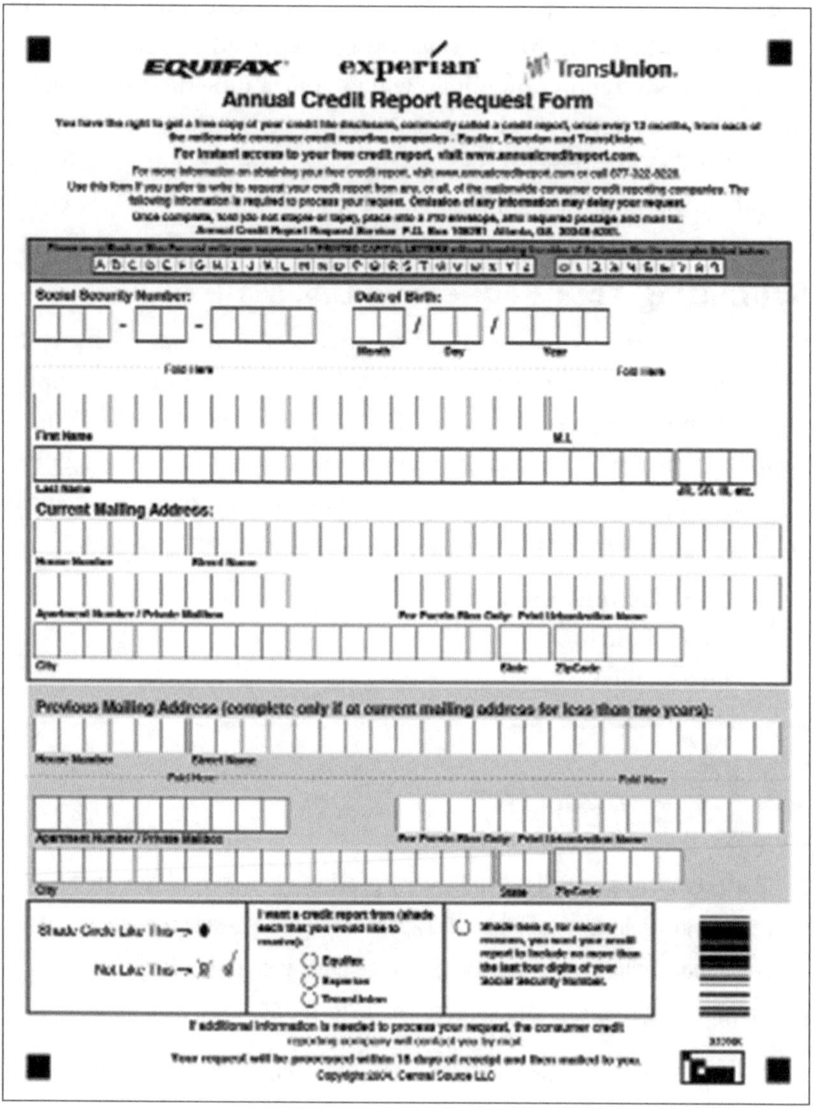

- Middle initial
- Last name
- Current address (If you've lived at your address for less than two years, you'll also need to provide your complete previous address.)
- At the bottom of the Annual Credit Report Request Form, you must request your credit report from each of the credit reporting agencies, or state specifically which report(s) you're interested in receiving.

To complete the written form, be sure to use black or blue ink and write in clear, block letters. All of the requested information must be provided to process your request. An alternative to completing the Annual Credit Report Request Form is to write a letter, addressed to the Annual Credit Report Request Service, containing all of the previously listed information.

The completed form or your letter should be sent in a standard #10 envelope to: Annual Credit Report Request Service, P.O. Box 105281,

You Should Know . . .

According to the FTC: Under federal law, you're entitled to an additional free report if a company takes adverse action against you, such as denying your application for credit, insurance, or employment, and you ask for your report within 60 days of receiving notice of the action. The notice will give you the name, address, and phone number of the consumer reporting company that provided the credit report that led to your being denied credit or rejected for a loan. You're also entitled to one free report a year if you're unemployed and plan to look for a job within 60 days; if you're on welfare; or if your report is inaccurate because of fraud, including identity theft. Otherwise, a credit reporting agency may charge you for additional copies of your report within a 12-month period.

Dirty Little Secrets

Atlanta, GA 30348-5281. It will take between two and three weeks for your request to be processed and for you to receive your credit report(s) in the mail. However, if you make your request online, you can view and print your credit reports within five minutes.

Requesting Your Free Credit Report by Telephone

By calling the Annual Credit Report Request Service toll-free at (877) 322-8228, you can follow the automated voice prompts and request that a copy of your current credit report from each of the three credit reporting agencies be mailed to you. Allow between two and three weeks to receive them by mail.

When placing this call, be prepared to provide your telephone number, Social Security number, date of birth, full name, and address. If you've lived at your current address for less than two years, you'll need to provide your previous address as well.

($) Credit Tip

Keep in mind, the content of your credit report changes constantly as your creditors and lenders report new information to the credit reporting agencies each month. To maintain an ongoing overview of what's being reported on their credit reports to potential lenders and creditors (and to help protect themselves against identity fraud), some people opt to request a copy of their credit report from just one credit reporting agency at a time, and spread their requests out by four months each. This allows you to see what's on your credit report for free throughout the year. However, if you'll be applying for a major loan, such as a mortgage or car loan, you'll want to see the contents of all three credit reports at once to ensure no erroneous information appears on any of them.

The Cost of Obtaining Additional or More Frequent Credit Reports

If you want to obtain copies of your credit reports more frequently than once every 12 months, there are several ways to do so. You can purchase single copies of your report from each of the credit reporting agencies, or you can subscribe to a credit monitoring service that includes unlimited access to your credit reports (and potentially your related credit scores) for a monthly fee.

To request single copies of your credit report (usually without a credit score) from each credit reporting agency separately, the fee will be up to $15 per report, depending on where you live. Different states have different rules about how frequently a credit report can be obtained and what the credit reporting agency is allowed to charge.

Use the following phone numbers or websites to purchase individual copies of your credit report from each credit reporting agency:

- Equifax, (800) 685-1111, www.equifax.com
- Experian, (888) 397-3742, www.experian.com
- TransUnion, (800) 916-8800, www.transunion.com

You Should Know . . .

If you're applying for a mortgage, working with a mortgage broker to refinance, or applying for a car loan, the lender you're working with will probably obtain a copy of your three-in-one credit report as part of their application evaluation and approval process. Feel free to request a copy of this current report from the lender at the time you submit your application. However, at least three months prior to applying for that major loan, obtain copies of your credit reports on your own and review them carefully.

The consumer division of each of these credit reporting agencies also offers online credit monitoring services (for a monthly fee) and the ability to purchase copies of your credit report with a corresponding credit score (again, for an additional fee).

For a higher one-time fee (usually around $30), you can obtain a three-in-one credit report (listing information from all three credit reporting agencies on a single report). Some of these three-in-one reports also include credit scores. However, as you learned in Chapter 4, it's important to understand the significance of the credit score you receive.

Three-in-one credit reports are sold by the individual credit reporting agencies, as well as independent and profit-oriented credit monitoring services and other companies.

What About Your Credit Score?

As you learned in Chapter 4, in addition to the credit report that's compiled by each of the three credit reporting agencies, creditors and lenders also evaluate corresponding credit scores, which are calculated based on information appearing within your credit reports.

Although you're entitled to free copies of your credit report every 12 months, the credit reporting agencies are not obligated to provide you with your corresponding credit score(s) for free. Instead, they charge you to obtain them.

At the time you request a free copy of your credit report, you may receive an offer to purchase your corresponding credit score and receive the report and score at the same time. For this, you'll be charged a flat fee (typically under $10) per score.

Before paying this fee, understand what type of credit score you're being offered. Also, don't be surprised if the credit scores relating to each of your credit reports are different. As you learned in Chapter 4, credit scores, how they're calculated, what they represent, and what type of score you can acquire is a rather confusing and convoluted topic.

Warning

Before purchasing an individual credit report or a three-in-one credit report online, make sure you're not inadvertently signing up for an ongoing credit monitoring service for which you'll be charged a monthly fee of between $14.95 and $49.95.

If you do wind up registering for one of these services, you can typically cancel the subscription at anytime. You will, however, continue being billed the monthly fee until you complete the credit monitoring service's subscription cancellation process.

Should you opt to use a credit monitoring service, be sure to carefully review the benefits and services it offers before subscribing. You'll find vast differences in what's offered at various monthly price points. Ideally, for the lowest possible monthly fee, you want unlimited online access to all three credit reports, corresponding credit scores, plus receive automated alerts when information on your credit reports changes.

You can also contact each of the three credit reporting agencies separately (see the contact information listed earlier in this chapter) to purchase a credit score in conjunction with a credit report or acquire just your credit score(s) separately.

The Benefits of a Three-in-One Credit Report

Many companies, including the three major credit reporting agencies, offer comprehensive, three-in-one credit reports. On one single report, you can receive detailed and current information from all three credit reporting agencies. This allows you to quickly review and compare content from all three reports at once, and will save you from having

> ## ⚠ *Warning*
>
> Before ordering a credit report, a three-in-one credit report, or subscribing to a credit monitoring service from a company that isn't one of the three major credit reporting agencies, make sure the company is legitimate.
>
> You will need to provide personal information, including your name, date of birth, address, and Social Security number, which is data that could easily be used for identity theft or other fraudulent purposes. For this reason, don't respond to online offers for these types of services that appear in pop-up ads or in your email's inbox. Instead, surf directly to the website of the company you want to acquire the report from.

to flip between the three separate reports as you analyze your current situation. The price you pay for a three-in-one report will vary, based on the company you use to retrieve it and whether some type of corresponding credit scores are included.

In general, a three-in-one credit report is easy to read and understand. Depending on what company you purchase this type of report from, it may come with a text analysis of your credit situation, based on information that appears within the report. This analysis can help you quickly pinpoint problem areas or trade lines that contain negative information that are negatively impacting your credit scores.

Ideally, when you purchase a three-in-one credit report, you'll want to print it out using a color printer. In addition to using specialized formatting to make these reports easier to read and understand, some of the content may be color-coded, with negative information displayed in red, for example.

For someone who is extremely interested in tracking their credit reports and credit scores on an ongoing basis, subscribing to a credit monitoring service is a worthwhile investment. For example, TransUnion is one of many companies that offer a fee-based credit monitoring service that provides unlimited access to your constantly updated three-in-one credit report (with corresponding credit scores) and notifies you anytime a change is made to your credit report.

Without subscribing to a credit monitoring service, expect to pay between $30 for a single three-in-one credit report around $40 for a three-in-one credit report with one or more corresponding credit scores.

The data provided within a three-in-one credit report will be identical to the data you'd receive by requesting separate credit reports from each of the three credit reporting agencies. The difference is in how the data is formatted and presented to you.

To see what a sample three-in-one credit report looks like (from TrueCredit.com, a service of TransUnion), visit www.truecredit.com/pdf/learnCenter/Reading_Your_Report.pdf. You can also visit Experian's website to see their sample (www.experian.com/consumer-products/3B3S_demo.html).

Credit Tip

Once you obtain your credit reports, write down or circle the date on which it was obtained and keep it with your financial records. As you work toward improving your credit rating, you'll want to refer back to older credit reports and compare them to newer versions in order to track your progress and see what changes have been made. You can typically re-access a credit report obtained online from one of the credit reporting agencies for up to 90 days, as long as you have the original file number that corresponds to the credit report.

Dirty Little Secrets

To see a free sample of a single credit report from a single credit reporting agency (in this case, Experian), point your web browser to: www.experian.com/credit_report_basics/pdf/samplecreditreport.pdf.

The following are just a few of the many online services that sell three-in-one credit reports, along with some type of credit scores, and an ongoing credit monitoring service that can be cancelled at anytime:

- Credit Report.com (www.creditreport.com)—Fee: $19.95 per month
- CreditScore.com (www.creditscore.com)—Fee: $12.95 per month.
- Equifax (www.equifax.com/3in1-credit-report-score)—One-time fee: $39.95 (for a three-in-one credit report with credit score), or $29.95 (for just a three-in-one credit report with no credit score)
- Experian (www.experian.com/consumer-products/experian-equifax-transunion-credit-report-and-score.html)—One-Time fee: $39.95 (for a three-in-one credit report with credit score)
- Privacy Guard (www.privacyguard.com)—Fee: $14.99 per month

You Have Your Credit Report, Now What?

The process for obtaining copies of your credit reports may sound a bit confusing, but it's actually relatively quick and simple, especially if you're obtaining free reports from the Annual Credit Report Request Service or purchasing reports from one of the three major credit reporting agencies.

After obtaining your report(s), the next step is to review the information included within each of them. Make sure all of the information is up-to-date and accurate. If you notice errors in any of the three reports, it's important to take the necessary steps to correct the error(s) as quickly as possible.

If the error involves information provided by a creditor or lender, you can begin by contacting the creditor/lender directly, or by submitting a *dispute* with the credit reporting agency. Each creditor's name and contact information should be listed within your credit report. The process for correcting inaccuracies in your credit report is described in Chapter 6.

If you find an error in the information listed within one or more of your credit reports, you have a right to initiate a dispute with each credit reporting agency. By law, a dispute must be investigated within 30 days. If the information is, in fact, inaccurate, it must then be corrected by the creditor/lender, causing your credit report and potentially your credit score to be revised. Keep in mind, erroneous information is different from negative but accurate information listed within your credit reports.

Errors in your credit report can be disputed online, by calling the credit reporting agencies, or in writing. For the quickest response, dispute errors online. Visit each credit reporting agency's website and follow the appropriate links.

 *Credit Tip*

Keep in mind, you will need to file separate disputes with all three credit reporting agencies for each item that is inaccurate.

- Equifax, www.equifax.com. From the website's home page, click on the "Dispute Info On Credit Report" option that's listed near the bottom of the page under the "Customer Service" heading. Follow the directions provided. You can also call (800) 685-1111 during business hours.
- Experian, www.experian.com/disputes/main.html. You can also call (800) 493-1058 during business hours.
- TransUnion, www.transunion.com/corporate/personal/credit-Disputes.page. You can also call (800) 916-8800 during business hours.

Before you can initiate a dispute, you must have accessed your credit report from that credit reporting agency within the past 90 days and have the report's file number in hand. You'll also need to confirm your identity by answering a series of security questions. The process for initiating a dispute takes between five to ten minutes, but you'll need to allow up to 30 days for the dispute to be reviewed and wait up to 60 days before inaccurate information is confirmed and removed from your credit report(s).

While you cannot dispute negative information that is accurate, you can dispute inaccurate information, such as incorrect balances, accounts that don't belong to you, or accounts that are being reported incorrectly. This might include your credit report showing late payments that were actually paid on time or an account that's been closed still being reported as active.

What Your Creditors Have to Say About Your Credit Report

All credit reports are divided into several sections, designed to make the reports easier to read and understand. The order in which these sections appear and their formats will vary, depending on the credit reporting agency and how the credit report was obtained.

All credit reports for consumers begin with a "Report Summary." This includes your name, the report number (file number), and the date the report was issued. You'll also find a short summary of the potentially negative and positive pieces of information found within the report.

Each credit or loan-related item listed on your credit report is called a "trade line," whether it's a mortgage, car loan, student loan, credit card, charge card, or other type of loan. For each trade line, you will see detailed information on your credit reports. The information listed is provided directly by your creditors and lenders. The credit reporting agencies do not alter this information in any way. While creditors and lenders can decide what information they wish to report, details pertaining to each trade line will typically include:

- *The creditor's name.* This will be the name of the creditor or collection agency that has reported the information to the credit reporting agency.

- *The creditor's address.* This is the mailing address of the creditor. Before sending money to the address listed, however, call the creditor first to confirm the mailing address.

- *The creditor's phone number.* This is the phone number you should use to contact the creditor to make a payment, to make a settlement offer, to initiate a dispute, or to get a question answered. If no phone number is listed for the creditor, contact the credit reporting agency directly or call directory assistance.

- *Account number.* This is the account number associated with your account or loan. Displayed here might be your loan number, credit card number, or other customer identification number. For security purposes, most creditors list only the first or last few digits of an account number or credit card number.

- *Status/remark.* This describes the current status of the account. It might read, "Open/Current," "Paid As Agreed," "Collection Account," "Paid, Closed/Never Late," "Account closed at consumer's request," "Paid in settlement," "Placed for collection," "Closed," or some variation that describes whether or not the account is active and in good standing. When you see "Open/Current" displayed as the status of an item listed in your credit report, it means the account is open, active, paid up-to-date, and is in good standing. This is the ideal status you want for each current listing on your credit reports.

- *Date opened.* This is the date the account was first opened.

- *Type.* Here, the type of account is listed. On your credit report, it might read, "Revolving," "Credit Card," "Collection,"

"Automobile," "Mortgage," or "Installment," for example. A revolving account typically refers to a credit card.

■ *Credit limit/original amount.* The amount of the original loan will be listed here, if the item is for some type of loan (such as a mortgage or car loan). The credit limit will be listed here if the account is related to a credit or charge card.

■ *Reported since.* This is the date that the credit reporting agency first started receiving information about the account.

■ *Terms.* Details about the loan, if applicable, will be displayed here. For example, for a mortgage, the monthly payment and length of the mortgage will be listed. In many situations, the "Terms" section may be blank or contain the letters "NA," meaning "Not Applicable."

■ *High balance.* This is the highest balance the consumer has put on the account. If it's a mortgage or car loan, for example, the original loan amount will be listed. For charge cards, the highest balance put on the card to date will be listed.

■ *Date of status.* This is the date on which the Status section was last updated.

■ *Monthly payment.* Depending on the type of account, the monthly payment the consumer is responsible for will be listed here.

■ *Recent balance.* Here you'll find the most recent balance owed on the account.

■ *Last reported.* This is the date the creditor last reported information about the account to the credit reporting agency. Creditors and lenders typically update information once per month.

■ *Responsibility.* This states whether it's an individual or joint account and who is responsible for it.

■ *Recent payment.* The amount of the last payment received is displayed. Depending on when a payment is received and processed, and when you requested a copy of your report, your most recent payment(s) may not yet be reflected on your credit report(s).

Understand What the Negative Information Means within Your Credit Report

As you review each credit report, look for a section with the heading "Adverse Accounts" or "Potentially Negative Items." Listed here will be creditors or lenders that are currently or have in the recent past (within the past seven years) reported negative information about you to that credit reporting agency. Any information listed within this section of your credit report is causing a negative impact on your credit scores and overall credit rating.

If you see information displayed under the "Adverse Account" or "Potentially Negative Items" heading, follow these steps:

1. Review the listing to determine its accuracy and that it actually belongs to you.
2. Determine the cause of the negative information.
3. Determine if you can improve the information being reported to the credit reporting agency by paying a late or outstanding bill, or lowering your outstanding balance, for example.

If the account has been turned over to a collection agency or has been "charged off" by the credit card issuer, for example, this negative information will remain on your credit report for seven years. However, by paying off the outstanding debt, or by entering into a settlement agreement (with the creditor, lender, or collection agency), you can slightly lessen the negative impact the information is having on your credit scores and overall credit rating.

The negative status for a trade line that says, "Paid in full, was a charge-off," means you were seriously delinquent to the point the credit card issuer closed the account and determined it was uncollectible, but you later paid off the outstanding debt in full. This status is better than "Charge off," which indicates you never paid your outstanding debt.

■ *Account history.* This section summarizes the account status on a month-by-month basis, typically over a several year period, if applicable. From this section of a trade line, you can determine how many times, if any, you have been late making payments (if applicable) and how late each payment was received. Having one or more late payments (or skipped payments) on any given account will have a negative impact on your credit score as well as your ability to get approved for a new loan or credit.

 Credit Tip

Each trade line listed within each of your credit reports will have a "Current Status" associated with it. Ideally, you want that status to read, "Paid or Paying Account as Agreed," or "Pays as Agreed," not "30 Days Past Due," "60 Days Past Due," "90 Days Past Due," "Charge Off" or "Account Closed By Creditor/Lender."

Figuring Out What Needs to Happen Next

The reason you requested a copy of your credit report will ultimately determine what happens next. If you notice any inaccuracies within any of your three credit reports, see Chapter 6. If you believe you're a victim of identity theft because you discover items on your credit report that don't belong to you, such as credit cards in your name that you never applied for and never received, it's important to take action quickly. In this situation, follow the directions offered in Chapter 13.

If you're like a huge percentage of the U.S. population, chances are you'll find some negative information listed on your credit reports. Determine if this negative information can be corrected or improved upon by contacting the creditor or lender, paying off an outstanding debt, or changing your spending habits so you'll be able to pay your bills on time in the future. Chapter 7 offers easy strategies you can begin implementing immediately to improve your credit scores and your overall credit rating.

Keep in mind replacing negative information that's displayed on your credit reports is a much more difficult and lengthy process than correcting legitimate errors. Negative but accurate information will typically remain on your credit reports for seven to ten years, although the older the negative information is, the less impact it will have on your credit scores. The best thing you can do as a consumer is to prevent negative information from ever appearing within your credit reports.

If you can't make your payment(s), call your creditors and lenders immediately, explain your situation, and work with them to develop a payment plan, for example, that will prevent negative information from being listed on your credit reports. Being proactive and dealing with potential problems before they happen, and communicating openly and honestly with your creditors and lenders is the best strategy for protecting your credit, even when experiencing difficult financial situations.

More often than not, your creditors and lenders will be eager to work with you and be understanding of your situation, assuming you approach them quickly and don't wait until after you've missed multiple payments, defaulted on a loan, or your account has been turned over to a collection agency.

 Credit Tip

On the day you review your credit report(s), make a note in your daily planner to review an updated credit report in 12 months. This is something you should get in the habit of doing, especially if you don't subscribe to a credit monitoring service.

Dirty Little Secrets

If you plan to apply for a mortgage, hope to refinance your current mortgage, apply for some other type of loan, or plan to apply for new credit cards, based on the information you discover within your credit reports and by evaluating your credit scores, you'll be in a better position to determine whether you'll qualify (and at what interest rates) based on your credit worthiness. This will allow you to take the appropriate steps to move your plans forward.

Misconceptions and Bad Information Can Lead to Costly Mistakes

For a variety of reasons, personal finances and credit can be extremely confusing topics. People have many misconceptions about credit that can ultimately lead to costly mistakes or problems.

Having the right information and acting appropriately based on the information you know is correct, and using your own common sense, will help you boost your credit score and overall credit rating, better manage your personal finances, avoid becoming a victim of identity theft, and ultimately save you a fortune.

Especially if you're planning to apply for a mortgage (or refinance your mortgage), or apply for some other type of significant loan or credit (such as a car loan, student loan, or home equity loan), never rely on information on a single credit report or a single credit score provided by just one credit reporting agency.

Instead, be sure to review all three of your credit reports. In general, the trade lines of all three of your reports should be identical or at least similar, but this isn't always the case. It's possible that by reviewing just one credit report, you will miss important information that potential creditors or lenders will have access to and that could impact their approval decision.

What's Next?

Now that you have a current copy of your credit report(s) in hand, you're in a much better position to analyze your credit rating, and if necessary, take steps to improve it. The next chapter focuses on strategies you can use to update and fix information contained within your credit report. You'll also discover information on how to better negotiate and deal with your lenders and creditors.

What your current and past creditors and lenders report to the credit reporting agencies (and how they report that information) directly impacts your credit scores, overall credit rating, and your ability to get approved for future loans and credit.

While it's very difficult, if not impossible, to get negative but accurate information removed from your credit reports altogether (despite what some fraudulent credit repair services advertise), by negotiating with your current and past creditors and lenders, you can often positively impact how they report negative information to the credit reporting agencies and thus improve your credit scores and overall credit rating. To do this, however, will require negotiation, plus that you make good on your past and current debts by settling or paying them off, for example.

CHAPTER 6

How to Update or
Fix Your Credit Report

What's in This Chapter

- Learn what information can legitimately be edited or removed from your credit reports.

- How to correct errors on your credit reports and initiate a dispute.

- How to get other information edited or changed on your credit reports, even if the information is negative, but accurately being reported.

Reviewing Your Credit Reports

By following the advice in Chapter 5, you should have no trouble acquiring copies of your credit reports from Experian, Equifax, and TransUnion by phone, mail, or within minutes online. With copies of each credit report in hand, or after purchasing a three-in-one credit report, you'll then need to spend time evaluating each trade line of each report.

During your evaluation, determine if the information being reported on each credit report is positive, negative, or inaccurate. If the information is positive, it's helping to boost your credit scores and it's based on the fact that you're up-to-date and in good standing with that creditor or lender. This will be reflected positively within the "Status" section of each trade line, which ideally should read something along the lines of "Paid As Agreed" or "Open/Current."

Warning

If you discover a trade line on your credit report that lists an account that does not belong to you, you could be a victim of identity theft. See Chapter 13 for details on how to deal with this situation.

If any information within your credit reports is negative, it could be there because of late or missed payments, or as a result of somehow mismanaging your credit. In this situation, you need to identify what the cause of the problem is, and then figure out the best way to rectify it. This might mean changing your habits and paying your bills on time in the future. It might mean making an effort to lower your outstanding balances. If the debt is long overdue or has been turned over to a collection agency, remedying the situation may require you to contact the creditor/lender or collection agency directly and then negotiate in order to achieve a mutually favorable solution.

As you already know, having negative information that's accurately being reported to the credit reporting agencies and that appears within your credit reports is difficult to remove within a seven-year period.

In some (albeit rare) circumstances, as part of a pay-off negotiation with a creditor or lender in which you're paying off your overdue balance in full, you can sometimes negotiate it so the related negative information gets removed from your credit reports, or you might be able to at least negotiate for the creditor/lender to improve how the account is being reported so your credit rating won't be negatively impacted as badly.

This negotiation tactic typically only works if you're paying off a past due debt in full, or in one or two installments. If you're negotiating a settlement offer (in which you're paying significantly less than the total amount due), or you're working out a long-term payment plan, the creditors, lenders, and collection agencies will typically not alter the negative information being reported to the credit reporting agencies. But, by paying off the debt, they'll stop harassing you with collection calls and lawsuit threats. On your credit report, the collections account that ultimately is paid off will be marked as "Paid" or "Settled," but this probably will not improve your credit scores.

Upon reviewing your credit reports and perhaps comparing the information to your current financial or credit-related statements, you may discover some errors. If these errors are in the personal information section of a credit report where your name, address, telephone number(s), Social Security number, date of birth, and employment information is listed, directly contact the credit reporting agency that provided you with the credit report containing the error. Errors in the personal information section of your credit report do not impact your credit scores, but they should still be corrected. You'll discover how to do this later in the chapter.

In the "Potentially Negative Items" or "Adverse Accounts" section of your credit report, you'll find trade lines that contain some type of negative data that is hurting your credit scores. The items listed in this section are the ones that potential creditors and lenders will look at carefully before making their future decisions about granting you loans or credit. From this information, a potential creditor or lender

What Is a Dispute?

When you notice an error in any of your credit reports, having it investigated and hopefully corrected by the credit reporting agencies starts with initiating a dispute.

Once a dispute is filed (either by phone, mail, or online), the credit reporting agency will immediately contact the creditor or lender and begin an investigation. The outcome of the investigation will typically be reflected on your credit report within 30 days.

If the error you disputed is, in fact, an error, it will be corrected and your credit report will be updated accordingly. Negative information that is being accurately reported, however, cannot typically be removed from your credit report by initiating a dispute.

When you find an error on a credit report, you must contact the credit reporting agency that issued that report (Experian, TransUnion, or Equifax). If the same error appears on multiple credit reports, you need to contact each credit reporting agency separately.

Initiating a dispute costs nothing and can be done quickly online. However, a dispute can also be initiated by telephone, or by sending a letter in the mail to the appropriate credit reporting agency. Before you can initiate a dispute, you'll need access to a copy of your credit report from the credit reporting agency you're contacting, and be able to provide the file or report number that's associated with it. The report must be less than 90 days old.

can easily determine the cause of the negative information, such as late payments, determine how late the payments are or have been, plus discover how much money you currently owe or that's past due.

As you review the information in this section, make sure it's accurate and up-to-date. Keep in mind, a payment you've made to the creditor or lender less than 30 to 45 days earlier might not yet have registered on your credit reports. Only if you discover inaccurate information should you initiate a dispute with the credit reporting agency that supplied the credit report. You cannot have negative but accurate information removed by contacting the credit reporting agencies directly.

After reviewing the "Potentially Negative" items section of your credit reports, continue to carefully review the remainder of each report, including the "Credit Items" section. This section lists all of your trade lines (individual accounts/loans) being reported to the credit reporting agency, as well as the "Accounts in Good Standing" section, which displays the information on your report that's favorable.

On a separate sheet of paper, as you're reviewing your credit reports, make a note of trade lines that contain negative information that you need to address, and create a list of inaccuracies on each report that need to be corrected.

$ Credit Tip

For additional help filing a dispute with one or more of the credit reporting agencies, access the FTC's website at www.ftc.gov/bcp/edu/pubs/consumer/credit/cre21.shtm.

The Types of Information That Can Be Removed from Your Credit Reports

Remember, only information that is inaccurate (erroneous) can be disputed and ultimately removed easily by initiating a dispute directly

Adding a Personal Statement to Your Credit Reports

If you have a legitimate reason for negative information appearing on your credit report (such as an illness, injury, loss of a job due to downsizing, etc.), you have the right to add a "Personal Statement" to each of your credit reports. This is a short text item you can add by contacting the credit reporting agencies. A personal statement can be used to share your side of the story. It will not impact your credit scores, but if a creditor/lender manually reviews your credit reports, the content of your personal statement can be taken into consideration.

A personal statement must be under 100 words in length. Make sure you have the personal statement removed after the situation described in your statement has been corrected or resolved. Otherwise, it could remain on your credit report indefinitely.

with the credit reporting agencies. If you want negative but accurate information removed from your credit report(s), you'll need to negotiate that with each creditor or lender separately (but this is typically an uphill battle).

How to Correct Errors Listed in Your Credit Reports

There are two basic ways to correct errors on your credit report:

1. Contact the creditor or lender directly via telephone or mail.
2. Initiate a dispute with the appropriate credit reporting agencies, based on which of your credit reports include the erroneous data.

If, however, you're trying to "fix" negative information that's accurately being reported to the credit reporting agencies, you'll need to negotiate with your creditors directly. The credit reporting agencies will only remove data from a credit report that's proven to be inaccurate.

Initiating Disputes with the Credit Reporting Agencies

Thanks to computers, initiating disputes with the credit reporting agencies is a relatively easy process. If the dispute is initiated online, you can typically have the issue resolved within about 10 days, although legally, the credit reporting agencies have up to 30 days to investigate your dispute.

 Credit Tip

Initiating disputes with the credit reporting agencies online will save you a lot of time. If the dispute is initiated via the mail, it will take longer for the investigation to get underway and be completed.

Filing a dispute will force the credit reporting agency to initiate an investigation, during which time the creditor or lender will be contacted and asked to provide proof that the information being reported is, in fact, accurate. If no proof is provided and the information on the credit report is really erroneous, it must be corrected within 30 days.

Follow these steps for initiating a dispute online:

1. Obtain a copy of your credit report from each credit reporting agency.
2. Make a note of the credit report number listed at the top of each report. If the credit report you received doesn't have a credit report number, you will need to obtain a new copy of your credit report directly from that credit reporting agency or from the Annual Credit Report (www.AnnualCreditReport.com) website.

Upon obtaining a credit report, the credit report number you receive will remain active for a period of 90 days.

3. Review each credit report carefully and identify errors you wish to dispute.
4. Point your web browser to the appropriate credit reporting agency's website.
   - Experian, www.experian.com/disputes/main.html
   - Equifax, www.equifax.com/CreditInvestigation
   - TransUnion, http://www.transunion.com/personal-credit/credit-disputes/credit-disputes.page
5. Click on the appropriate icon on the credit reporting agency's website to initiate an online dispute.
6. You'll be asked to enter your credit report number, plus additional information about yourself to verify your identity. This information may include your Social Security number, date of birth, the state where you live, and/or your ZIP code.
7. You will be asked to approve a terms and conditions statement from the credit reporting agency that appears on your computer screen.
8. Once you're looking at your credit report on the computer screen, click on the particular item(s) that you believe are inaccurate, then click on the "Dispute Item" option that's displayed.
9. You'll need to select a specific reason for the dispute and choose one of the options that explains why you believe the information is incorrect. Depending on the type of listing, options will include: "Payment never late," "No knowledge of account," "Account paid in full," "Account closed," "Unauthorized Charges," "Belonged to ex-spouse," "Balance incorrect," "Included in bankruptcy," "Belongs to primary account holder," "Corporate account," "Balance history inaccurate," or "Other reason." You can also add your own brief statement (up to 120 characters) explaining why the information is inaccurate.

Dirty Little Secrets

10. You will be asked to provide your email address so you can be contacted with the results of the investigation.
11. Upon completing this online dispute process, an investigation will immediately begin. You will be notified of the outcome within 30 days.
12. If your investigation concludes and the result is not in your favor, but you have evidence or information to substantiate your claim, initiate another dispute in writing and include copies of your information and evidence or contact the creditor directly.

To initiate a dispute in writing, you will first need to obtain a copy of your credit report containing a current credit report number. Next, determine what information is inaccurate. This information will need to be put in writing in the form of a letter addressed to the appropriate credit collection agency.

The letter should contain the following information:

- Your full name, address, and phone number
- Your date of birth
- Your Social Security number
- The credit report number
- A photocopy of your picture ID (such as a driver's license or passport), plus a copy of a recent utility bill that displays your name and address.
- A separate listing for each error and why you believe the information is incorrect. It's helpful to include a photocopy of your credit report or the trade lines that you're disputing.

A sample letter is shown in Figure 6–1 on page 118. Mail your letter, along with any additional information or evidence, to the appropriate credit reporting agency using the addresses in the following lists (you can also call each credit reporting agency to initiate a dispute using the following phone numbers):

Dirty Little Secrets

FIGURE 6–1: **Sample Letter to a Credit Reporting Agency Used to Initiate a Dispute**

Created by the FTC, the following is a sample letter you can use as a template when initiating a dispute. Be sure to fill in all of your own personal information and details, and include the pertinent documentation when submitting your letter via the mail.

Date

Your Name
Your Address
Your City, State, and ZIP Code
Your Social Security Number and Date of Birth

Credit Report Disputes Department
Name of Credit Reporting Agency
Address
City, State, ZIP Code

Dear Sir or Madam:

I am writing to dispute the following information in my file. I have circled the items I dispute on the attached copy of the credit report I received.

This item [identify item(s) disputed by name of source, such as creditors or tax court, and identify type of item, such as credit account, judgment, etc.] is [inaccurate or incomplete] because [describe what is inaccurate or incomplete and why]. I am requesting that the item be removed [or request another specific change] to correct the information.

Enclosed are copies of [use this sentence if applicable and describe any enclosed documentation, such as payment records and court documents supporting your position]. Please reinvestigate this (these) matter(s) and delete or correct the disputed item(s) as soon as possible.

Sincerely,

[Insert Signature]

[Insert Your Printed Name]

Enclosures: [List what you are enclosing.]

Experian
P.O. Box 2002
Allen, TX 75013
(888) 397-3742 or (800) 493-1058

Equifax Credit Information Services, Inc.
P.O. Box 740241
Atlanta, GA 30374
(800) 685-1111

TransUnion
P.O. Box 2000
Chester, PA 19022-2000
(800) 916-8800

Negotiating with Your Creditors

The process of creditors and lenders reporting information on an ongoing monthly basis to the credit reporting agencies is purely voluntary. Any information that a creditor or lender adds to your credit reports can theoretically be removed or modified to be less negative, if you can convince the creditor/lender to take this action.

If you're dealing with a collection agency working on behalf of a creditor, that agency's job is to collect the debt. Negotiating will be more difficult, but certainly isn't impossible, especially if the account is seriously past due and you're interested in negotiating a full payoff.

When a creditor or lender needs to report negative information about you to a credit reporting agency (information that will appear on your credit reports), they have some discretion about how negative that information actually is. So, depending on your financial and credit situation, if you take a proactive role in working with your creditors/lenders to pay off your debts, you can sometimes get them to work with you financially, plus get them to show mercy when recording information with the credit reporting agencies that won't have such a negative impact on your credit scores. This is something you'll need to negotiate, however. It's never something a creditor, lender, or collection agency will do automatically.

In terms of your financial obligations to your creditors and lenders, you have a wide range of options when negotiating with them. They may be willing to lower your monthly payments, defer one or more payments, waive late fees and penalties, lower your interest rate, or

---

You Should Know...

A collection agency that is working on behalf of a creditor is different from a collection agency that has purchased your debt outright from the original creditor or lender. If a collection agency or law firm has purchased the debt, which is something that would happen after it has been charged off or written off by the original creditor or lender, you must deal directly with that collection agency or law firm that now has full authority in regard to that debt. They'll often settle for a percentage of the total amount, since they paid just pennies on the dollar to purchase the debt and want to recoup their investment as quickly as possible.

Once negative information from a collection agency has begun appearing on your credit report(s), the damage is done in terms of the negative impact on your credit rating and credit scores. At this point, whether you agree to a settlement or pay off the debt in full, the negative impact will basically be the same, so do what's in your best financial interest. However, if you ignore the debt altogether, the collection agency can keep inflicting damage to your credit rating and then transfer your account to another collection agency that would start the process all over again. In other words, the outstanding debt will not simply disappear over time and you will just be prolonging the negative impact on your credit rating.

Dirty Little Secrets

somehow restructure the loan to make paying it off more achievable, based on your current financial situation.

As for actually making payments or paying off a debt, you might be able to schedule a long-term payment plan that you can afford, or settle the account for up to 50 percent less than the original debt. This will be based on your situation, how well you're able to negotiate, as well as your ability to pay off your debt(s) in a lump sum or via multiple payments.

Altering Your Payment Schedule vs. Making a Settlement Offer

An alternative to restructuring a payment schedule is to offer a settlement to the creditor. This is a legally binding agreement that allows you to renegotiate the amount owed. In many cases, this will stop interest, late fees, and other charges from accruing as you pay off the amount due, which can often be reduced.

The problem with negotiating a settlement and paying off less than the amount originally owed is that settlements are typically listed on your credit report for seven years and detract from your credit scores for that entire time, even after the account is paid and closed.

Settlements need to be negotiated with the creditor or collection agency. You need to negotiate how much is owed, how the repayment plan will be structured, and what the outcome on your credit reports will be once the debt is paid off. Ultimately, the creditor or lender should put all settlements in writing.

Typically, if you're offering to settle an account for significantly less than what's owed, the creditor, lender, or collection agency will insist that the entire negotiated amount be paid in full or in two installments. If you can come up with the lump sum, you'll potentially save a lot of money.

However, if you're looking for a long-term payment plan, you can often negotiate to pay a very low (and affordable) amount per month,

> ## (!) Warning
>
> If you set up a payment plan as part of your settlement, failure to meet your obligations on time could cause the original terms of the debt to be reinstated. This means interest, penalties, late fees, and legal fees could all be added to the amount due. It also increases the chances that the creditor or collection agency will take you to court or take whatever legal action allowable to collect the debt.

but you will be required to pay off the entire amount owed. In this situation, however, you can sometimes get them to waive late fees and/ or interest charges.

When negotiating with a creditor, lender, or collection agency, your ultimate objective is to convince them to list the account as "Paid as Agreed," "Current," or "Account Closed—Paid as Agreed" with each of the credit reporting agencies. Anything other than that will negatively impact your credit scores. Your willingness to negotiate and a demonstration of good faith with proper follow-through on your promises will help you achieve this objective. However, realistically you should be willing to settle for something a little less positive being reported to the credit reporting agencies.

If during the negotiation you're told that the person you're dealing with (who works for the creditor, lender, or collection agency) doesn't have the authority to change how the account is being reported to the credit reporting agencies, insist on speaking with someone who does have that authority, such as a supervisor.

Whether or not you pay off an account that's already gone to collections is irrelevant to your credit scores unless the account is reported to the credit collection agencies as "Paid as Agreed" or "Account Closed—Paid as Agreed."

Warning

When sending a letter to your creditor(s), be sure to use the correct address. The address you typically send payments to is almost always different from the creditor's business office or the address that's listed in your credit report.

Listings on your credit report to avoid include: "Paid," "Paid–Charge Off," "Settled," "Repossession," and "Paid–[insert number of days] Days Late." Any of these will have a negative impact on your credit scores for up to seven years and affect your ability to obtain credit in the future, even if the overdue amount is ultimately paid in full or you pay the amount agreed to as part of a settlement.

Some creditors will agree to alter how your account is being reported to the credit reporting agencies if the settlement involves you paying at least 70 percent of the amount due and you meet the obligations of the settlement with no further delays.

The decision to negotiate with a consumer and ultimately change how information is reported to the credit reporting agencies is made on a case-by-case basis and will depend on your ability to negotiate with the creditor, lender, or collection agency. It is *not* normal policy for a creditor or lender to delete negative information from a consumer's

Credit Tip

Especially when dealing with collection agencies, pay off your debts or make settlement payments using a money order or cashier's check. If you pay using a personal check, you'll be providing that agency with your checking account information, which may not be in your best interest.

Dirty Little Secrets

Warning

Anything you say could be held against you! When speaking or corresponding with a debt collector, creditor, or collection agency, your phone calls are typically recorded and anything you say could potentially be used in court. Always act professionally and refrain from lying or making threats.

credit report just because the debt is paid after it has been late or has gone to collections.

Quick Tips to Help Your Negotiations

When you're negotiating with creditors, their job is to collect the money you owe using tactics that are within the boundaries of the law. It's your job to protect your own interests, while at the same time living up to your financial and legal obligations. Someone who works for a collection agency, for example, does not have your best interests in mind, despite what they may say. They don't care about your problems. They just want to collect the money that's due to them or the company they represent.

Here are some tips to help you negotiate with a creditor or collection agency:

- If you make a request that is denied for whatever reason, ask to speak with a supervisor.
- Don't agree to pay more than you can afford when negotiating. Know in advance what your financial situation really is, then work within those confines. The last thing you want to do is negotiate a settlement or payment plan that you can't afford to adhere to.
- During your negotiating process, figure out what the creditor is willing to accept as a settlement. What's their absolute bottom line? If you're looking for a settlement, offering between 50 and

70 percent of what's owed, either as a lump sum or through a payment plan, isn't unreasonable. Achieving this settlement might take several rounds of negotiation, however.

- Try to avoid becoming intimidated by the person you're negotiating with, even if they make threats about lawsuits.
- Keep in mind, most successful negotiations require several rounds going back and forth with offers and counteroffers. The process could take days or weeks.
- If you can afford to settle an account by paying one lump sum (as opposed to using a payment plan), you'll have more negotiating leverage.
- The person you're negotiating with does this for a living and is a trained professional when it comes to debt collection. For them to use legal terminology during a conversation or in writing is a common tactic to confuse or intimidate you. Listen carefully to what's being said and make sure you understand exactly what you're committing to. Consult with a lawyer or credit counselor if you have questions.
- Make sure everything you ultimately agree to is put in writing, signed, and dated by both parties.

What to Negotiate for When Dealing with Creditors, Lenders, or Collection Agencies

As part of your negotiation, some of the things you could potentially ask for include:

- A lower interest rate
- For the interest accrued to be waived
- For the late fees, penalties, and/or legal fees to be waived
- For the loan to be extended or restructured, allowing you to skip one or more payments with no penalty
- A payment plan that would allow you to pay off the amount currently owed, but with no added interest or fees in the future

- A settlement that would include a significantly lower balance due (such as 50 to 75 percent of the total)
- Favorable reporting to the credit reporting agencies or the removal of negative information from your credit report pertaining to that account

Know Your Legal Rights as a Consumer

If creditors or collection agencies (or law firms representing them) are harassing you, you have some legal rights even if you owe the money. Be sure to review the federal Fair Debt Collection Practices Act so you know what your rights are. Collection agents cannot abuse, threaten, or harass you, provide you with false or misleading information, or use unfair practices to collect the monies due.

To read the Federal Fair Debt Collection Practices Act, point your web browser to: www.ftc.gov/os/statutes/fdcpa/fdcpact.htm or http://business.ftc.gov/documents/fair-debt-collection-practices-act. You can also learn more about debt collection practices by visiting the FTC's website at www.ftc.gov/bcp/conline/pubs/credit/fdc.htm.

According to the FTC, "A debt collector is any person who regularly collects debts owed to others. This includes attorneys who collect debts on a regular basis. A collector may contact you in person, by

You Should Know . . .

On February 22, 2010, the federal government released a new set of laws to govern credit card issuers and protect consumers, as well as to limit credit card-related fees that can be charged. To learn about these laws and how they benefit you, visit http://www.federalreserve.gov/consumer-info/wyntk_creditcardrules.htm.

mail, telephone, or fax. However, a debt collector may not contact you at inconvenient times or places, such as before 8 a.m. or after 9 p.m., unless you agree. A debt collector also may not contact you at work if the collector knows that your employer disapproves of such contacts."

Furthermore, according to the FTC, "You can stop a debt collector from contacting you by writing a letter to the collector telling them to stop. Once the collector receives your letter, they may not contact you again except to say there will be no further contact or to notify you that the debt collector or the creditor intends to take some specific action."

Sending such a letter to a collector does not make the debt magically disappear if you actually owe it. The debt collector or your original creditor could still sue you, which is a greater possibility if you demonstrate no interest in paying off or otherwise settling the debt.

The FTC reports, "If you have an attorney, the debt collector must contact the attorney, rather than you. If you do not have an attorney, a collector may contact other people, but only to find out where you live, what your phone number is, and where you work. Collectors usually are prohibited from contacting such third parties more than once. In most cases, the collector may not tell anyone other than you and your attorney that you owe money. Within five days after you are first contacted, the collector must send you a written notice telling you the amount of money you owe; the name of the creditor to whom you owe the money; and what action to take if you believe you do not owe the money."

By law, a debt collector may not harass, oppress, or abuse you. Thus, the use of threats of violence or harm; publishing a list of consumers who refuse to pay their debts (except to a credit reporting agency); the use of obscene or profane language; or repeatedly using the telephone to annoy someone is forbidden. It's also illegal for a debt collector to make false or misleading statements when attempting to collect a debt.

For example, the debt collector cannot falsely imply that he or she is an attorney or a government representative; imply that you have committed a crime; falsely represent that they operate or work for a

> **(!) Warning**
>
> All debt collectors know the law and are extremely familiar with the Fair Debt Collection Practices Act. However, some less reputable debt collectors will find ways to push the limits of the law in order to achieve their objectives. If you believe a debt collector has violated the law in its dealings with you, consider hiring an attorney or contact the FTC at (877) 382-4357.

credit reporting agency; misrepresent the amount of your debt; imply that papers that were sent to you are legal forms when they were not; or misrepresent that papers being sent to you are not legal forms when they are. These are all guidelines issued by the FTC that debt collectors must adhere to.

The FTC reports that some of the other things a debt collector may not do in an effort to collect money owed include:

- Giving false credit information about you to anyone, including a credit reporting or collection agency.
- Sending you anything that looks like an official document from a court or government agency when it is not.
- Contacting you via postcard (as opposed to a letter in a sealed envelope).
- Using a false name when contacting you.
- Collecting an amount greater than your debt, unless your state law permits such a charge. The additional charges could include legal fees incurred by the original lender, creditor, or debt collector.
- Depositing a post-dated check prematurely.
- Using deception to trick you into accepting costly collect calls.
- Taking or threatening to take your property unless this can be done legally.

Dirty Little Secrets

Communicating with Your Creditors in Writing

Any correspondence between you and your creditors or debt collectors, especially settlement or pay-off offers and agreements, should always be put in writing. Be sure to keep copies of all correspondence.

When sending your correspondence, use a method that will show proof of receipt. From the U.S. Postal Service, you can send a letter and add delivery confirmation, for example, or send the envelope via certified mail. In your letters, be sure your full name, address, phone number, and account number are listed. If you send a fax, follow it up by sending a hard copy of the fax via the mail or overnight courier.

Working with a Credit Counseling Company

Depending on your personal situation, you can initiate disputes and negotiate with creditors on your own behalf, or you could hire a professional credit counselor. For more information on credit counseling services, see Chapter 12.

Meet Collections Expert Michelle Dunn

Collection agents are trained professionals with a clearly defined business objective—to collect the money you owe to their creditors. They have a well-thought-out, highly organized and established process for doing their work. In other words, the actions a collection agent takes are not arbitrary. Most of the time, they will be within the legal parameters set forth by the Fair Debt Collection Practices Act and the state in which you live.

Based in Plymouth, New Hampshire, Michelle Dunn (www.MichelleDunn.com) is one of the nation's leading experts when it comes to credit and debt collection. She's published multiple books on this subject, and has more than 24 years' experience working as a debt collector. For debt collection professionals, she founded and operates the Credit and Collections blog (www.Credit-and-Collections.com), which professional collection agents use as a training and information resource.

In this interview, Dunn shares valuable insight into how collection agencies work and offers advice to consumers on how to negotiate and deal with them if they experience financial problems. If you're wondering how collection agencies really work and would like a few secrets revealed to help you deal with them, keep reading!

What exactly is a collection agency and when would a consumer have to deal with one?

Michelle Dunn: "A collection agency is a service business that helps business owners collect money that's owed to them. Most business owners don't know too much about credit and collections, and they don't understand all of the different laws that apply when trying to collect a debt, so they outsource this task over to experts who specialize in this type of service. In this situation, the collection agency only gets paid if they actually collect the debt. Most collection agencies work on a commission basis.

"Once hired by a client, the collection agency will contact the debtor and act as a mediator in an effort to collect the money that's owed on behalf of the client. The goal of the collection agency is to collect the full amount of the debt in a single payment. However, depending on the situation, they are often willing to negotiate in a variety of ways."

What is the biggest misconception consumers have about collection agencies?

Michelle Dunn: "People think collection agencies hire big tough men who will come to your door with a baseball bat and scare or beat you into paying your debt. Obviously, this is not at all what we do. Debt collectors, however, have a bad reputation and are feared by most consumers, which is why businesses opt to outsource their collection efforts to these companies.

"People get very defensive and uncomfortable when they're asked to pay a debt, especially if they're unable to pay it. In all of my years of working as a debt collector, I am amazed at how many people have been angry at me right from the start when I've called them and simply asked them to pay their debt. There's always a reason why people haven't paid their debt. A lot of time, people are frustrated or embarrassed that they haven't or can't pay. As a debt collector, I have always tried to show compassion and understanding to the people I've needed to call on behalf of my clients."

How should a consumer properly deal with a collection agency that starts to call them incessantly?

Michelle Dunn: "The very best thing you can do is to talk to the person calling you and open a dialogue. The very worst things you can do are hanging up on them or ignoring their calls. That will not make them go away. It will make them increase the number of calls they make trying to reach you.

"When you speak with a collection agent for the first time, explain why you have not paid your debt and what your current financial situation is. If you're not comfortable doing this over the telephone, send the collection agency a letter in writing.

"A lack of response on your part will always force the collection agency to increase their efforts to reach you by phone and mail."

What should someone do if, for whatever reason, they don't have the money to pay off a debt?

Michelle Dunn: "If you do owe the money, you can't just say, 'I don't have the money, go away.' If you don't have the money, you need to propose a realistic payment plan to pay off the debt, even if it involves paying only $25.00 per week or month. I've had people pay me just $5.00 per month until they could get back on their feet. But doing this kept me from calling them repeatedly and taking steps to further damage their credit rating.

"When you set up a payment plan, make sure you outline the plan in writing. If you follow through, week after week or month after

Dirty Little Secrets

month, and make the payments you've agreed to, you'll stop getting annoying collection calls and letters. It's that easy.

"If you don't believe you owe the money a collection agency is attempting to collect, you need to write a letter stating why you believe the collection agency is in error. Provide proof of payment, if available, or show any other relevant documentation. Be sure to ask the collection agency to offer proof you owe the money."

How in trouble is the consumer once a collection agency is put in charge of recovering their debt?

Michelle Dunn: "That depends on the creditor or lender. The longer you ignore your creditors or lenders, the greater actions a collection agency will typically take to recover the debt. Once any overdue bill or debt gets turned over to a collection agency, this is going to be reported to the credit reporting agencies and this negative information will appear on your credit reports and lower your credit scores. You can avoid this altogether simply by dealing with your creditors or lenders directly, before they deem it necessary to turn the account over to a collection agency. Most accounts are turned over to a collection agency as a last resort for the company trying to collect the money that's owed.

"If you suddenly lose your job, become ill, or get injured, and you know you won't be able to pay your credit card bills or car payment next month, call up your creditors and lenders as soon as you anticipate having a financial problem and make them aware of the situation. Before you even become late on a payment, the creditor might allow you to defer a few payments, or they might rework the loan to keep you out of financial trouble. They won't do this, however, if they must come after you to collect their money after you're long overdue with your payments."

How flexible are creditors, lenders, and collection agencies when it comes to negotiating a settlement or payment plan to repay a debt?

Michelle Dunn: "Every creditor, lender, and collection agency is different. When I was actively working as a debt collector, I had some clients tell me that they'd accept payment plans or that they'd take whatever money I could recover. Others made it clear they would not settle for anything less than the full amount due and authorized me to take whatever steps were necessary using the legal system to recover the debt.

"A collection agency does not have the authority to accept a settlement, knock off interest due, or remove late fees from a debt without permission from their client. The exception to this is if the collection agency has purchased the debt outright and is not representing the original lender or creditor. When a collection agency first contacts you in writing, they must make it clear if they represent another company."

Some collection agencies blur the line of what's legal when trying to collect a debt. What rights does a consumer have in this situation?

Michelle Dunn: "All collection agents must adhere to state laws and the laws outlined in the Fair Debt Collection Practices Act. You can learn more about this by visiting the FTC's website at www.ftc.gov. If a collection agent does something that is not within their rights, the consumer can and should report this violation to the FTC, plus hire an attorney to sue the collection agent for the violation. Doing this, however, does not excuse a consumer from paying their debt."

How does an account being turned over to a collection agency impact someone's credit reports and credit scores?

Michelle Dunn: "Again, this depends on your creditor or lender. Any debt that is reported by a collection agency to the credit reporting agencies will damage your credit rating and lower your credit scores. This is much worse than simply being late on a payment. On your credit reports, the phrase 'Placed for Collection,' will appear in the appropriate trade lines.

"What's worse than a 'Placed for Collection' message is a legal judgment, lien, or garnishment against you that appears in your credit reports. If, however, you pay the debt, the creditor or lender itself can change the credit report listing to 'Paid in Full' as opposed to 'Placed for Collection,' and/or 'Charged Off,' which will not impact your credit scores as badly. A collection agency cannot have the 'Placed for Collection' label removed from a trade line. Realistically, getting the negative item removed altogether from your credit reports is extremely difficult unless you have a court order from a judge or you're a proven victim of identity theft.

"If a 'Placed for Collections' message appears on your credit reports but you don't owe that money, in addition to writing a letter to the collection agency, also write letters to the credit reporting agencies and provide whatever documentation you have showing the error."

In situations when a collection agency has purchased a debt, does a consumer have more or less power to negotiate a settlement?

Michelle Dunn: "First, a consumer must determine if the collection agency owns the debt. In this case, the collection agency is not acting as a middleman for the original creditor or lender, so they have full authority to negotiate with you. They've also acquired the debt for pennies on the dollar, so they are typically more willing to negotiate a settlement offer for up to 50 percent less than the total amount due. The collection agency can settle for whatever they want in this situation.

"The very first letter a consumer receives from a collection agency will disclose whom the agency is working for, or if the agency has purchased the debt. Disclosing this information is a legal requirement.

"All debt that is purchased by a collection agency is very old. When you're contacted by a collection agency trying to collect an old debt, if you respond right away, you're more apt to achieve a better settlement deal for yourself, because that collection agency hasn't yet expended time and resources toward collecting the debt. It's important to understand, unpaid debt never goes away. Those old, uncollected debts will ultimately get sold five or six years down the road, and the consumer will once again start getting contacted about paying off that debt.

"If a collection agency has acquired an old debt and you acknowledge you're willing to pay it, offer to settle right away for half of what's owed, with the condition that the matter be closed immediately and reported to the credit reporting agencies as 'Paid in Full.' This will mean that your credit report will reflect the account was paid in full, not as a settlement or collection account, which is much better for your credit rating."

If a consumer starts receiving collection calls about an old debt they have no recollection of, what should they do?

Michelle Dunn: "Immediately ask that the collection agency provide written proof of the debt. This is your legal right, but you must make this request within 30 days of the collection agent's first contact. I recommend always putting this request in writing to create a paper trail."

What is the best negotiation tactic to adopt when trying to settle an account with a collection agency?

Michelle Dunn: "In the collection industry, it is common for the collection agent to always open a settlement negotiation asking for 80 percent of the amount due, to be paid in one or two lump sum payments. Your counteroffer can then be lower; however, whether or not your offer is accepted will depend on your circumstances and the creditor or lender the collection agency is working for. In some cases, consumers can negotiate a single payment of 50 percent lower than the original debt amount and it will be accepted. More often, however, making an offer of 60 to 70 percent of the outstanding debt has a better chance of getting accepted. A settlement offer must be realistic, and the consumer must be willing to make a lump sum payment.

"If you're looking for a payment plan, also getting the collection agency to agree to a lesser amount that's owed is a challenge. In some cases, you can get late fees or interest charges waived, however. Typically, a collection agency will either accept a payment plan or a settlement, not both. When I was working as a collection agent, I would sometimes allow a settlement to be made in two monthly payments, but most collection agencies will not accept this."

Dirty Little Secrets

Should the consumer always ask for interest charges, late fees, and other extra costs to be removed (or reduced) from their total balance owed to a creditor or lender as part of the negotiation process?

Michelle Dunn: "Yes. You need to ask for all of these things. No creditor, lender, or collection agency is going to offer to reduce the amount you owe, so you have to ask and negotiate for these fees to be waived. Always ask for extra fees, including annual fees and late charges, to be reduced. This is separate from negotiating a settlement amount to pay off the debt.

"American Express will never accept a settlement, but Visa and MasterCard almost always will, if you negotiate in good faith. You have to be the one to initiate the settlement offer, however."

Once a consumer agrees to a settlement or payment plan, what type of written agreement needs to be put into place to make the deal binding?

Michelle Dunn: "I recommend getting a letter in writing from the collection agency. If you don't receive something in writing, create a letter yourself outlining the agreement and send it to them via Certified Mail. Having a paper trail is essential. In most cases, a reputable collection agency will send you a letter outlining the agreement, and include payment envelopes. This letter should arrive before your first payment is made. Don't make any payments without a written agreement letter in hand.

"Your settlement letter should list the original amount that was due, the settlement amount that was agreed upon, the terms of the payments, and how the payments will be made. It should also state that once the settlement amount is paid, the account will reflect a zero balance."

What happens if the collection agency files court papers and begins the process of suing a consumer to collect a debt?

Michelle Dunn: "Even at this point, it's not too late to reach a settlement or pay off the debt, before going to court. Having a court judgment against you listed on your credit reports is much worse than having an account listed as 'Placed For Collection.' Plus, court judgments will remain on your credit reports and impact your credit scores for ten years, not seven years. As a consumer, making some type of payment right away will often prevent a court case from moving forward, because any payments made once legal papers are filed must be reported to the court."

Is there a statute of limitations for getting out of paying old debts?

Michelle Dunn: "A lot of people think that if a debt is very old, say more than seven years, they don't have to pay it. In reality, the debt may not be legally enforceable after seven years, depending on what type of debt it is, but that debt can still be placed with a collection attorney, who will attempt to collect the debt for as many years as they want. After seven years, the debt collector cannot sue you or take the matter to court, but they can still take other steps to collect the debt, regardless of its age."

If you personally were to start getting harassed by a debt collector over an overdue account, with all of your knowledge and expertise, how would you handle the situation?

Michelle Dunn: "I have actually had this happen to me. My husband lost his job, and for a while, we experienced financial problems. I took the initiative and called all of my creditors to explain the situation. I had to close my credit card accounts, but they took off all of the late fees and interest charges. They also allowed me to set up a $20.00 per month payment plan for six months, until my husband found a new job and we were able to increase our monthly payments and get back on our feet. I did the same thing with my phone company. Instead of having them turn off the service, because I needed a phone, I was able to keep basic service, with no long distance calling, and pay just that bill. When we got back on our feet, I paid off the outstanding balance and reinstituted our full service. During this time, none of my accounts went to collection and we salvaged our credit."

What's Next?

This chapter focused on how to clean up errors within your credit reports and negotiate with creditors, lenders, and collection agencies to help fix the credit-related mistakes you've already made. The next chapter, however, discusses strategies you can use to prevent problems in the future and effectively rebuild your credit rating over time.

CHAPTER 7

Ten Strategies for
Improving Your
Credit Rating

What's in This Chapter

- Strategies you can begin implementing immediately to start cleaning up your own credit rating and improving your credit scores

- Avoiding popular credit repair scams and credit repair mistakes

- An in-depth interview with an experienced credit counselor

Your Actions Always Impact Your Credit Worthiness

If you currently have an above average or excellent credit rating, it's important to maintain it. Far too many people do things such as making mortgage payments late or skipping credit card payments, and the negative impact on their credit scores is disastrous.

If your credit scores are already below average as a result of unforeseen misfortune or poor financial decisions in your past, it's important to immediately begin rectifying the situation by taking steps to begin rebuilding your credit rating. This process can take months or even several years of diligence and responsible financial planning.

Strategies for Improving Your Credit Rating

Out of all the information that's packed into this book, the strategies offered within this chapter are the most important for rebuilding or protecting your credit rating. Some of these strategies may seem like common sense; however, they represent solutions to the most common reasons why the typical person develops a less than perfect credit rating.

Unfortunately, successfully completing just one or two of these tasks alone probably won't result in a fast and dramatic jump in your credit scores. However, utilizing most or all of these strategies simultaneously and over time will definitely give your credit scores upward momentum, the results of which you should start seeing within three to 12 months (possibly sooner), depending on your unique situation.

When it comes to repairing or rebuilding your credit rating, this is definitely something you can do yourself. There are, however, legitimate credit counselors, financial planners, and accountants who can assist you in better managing your finances and in learning to be more responsible when it comes to managing your credit. See Chapter 12 for information about seeking out reputable and knowledgeable experts who can help you rebuild or maintain your credit rating.

Dirty Little Secrets

Strategy 1: Pay Your Bills on Time, Every Time

This strategy may seem extremely obvious. However, late payments are the most common piece of negative information that appears on people's credit reports and is often responsible for significant drops in their credit scores. When it comes to loans and credit cards, it's vital that you always make at least the minimum payments in a timely manner, each and every month, with no exceptions.

($) Credit Tip

If you can't make your monthly credit card payment(s), call the credit card issuers immediately (before the payments become late), explain why you can't make even the minimum payment, and negotiate a solution that will keep the creditor from reporting negative information to the credit reporting agencies. If you take a proactive stance when trying to work with your creditors and lenders, they're more apt to understand and work with you in order to help you salvage your credit rating.

The impact on your credit reports and credit scores will be considerable if you're late or skip one or more mortgage payments. However, making late payments on other types of loans, or defaulting on any loans, will also have a disastrous impact on your credit scores. The negative impact will last for up to seven years.

The benefit to having credit cards is that you can determine how much you spend using them, then decide how much you wish to pay back each month, as long as that amount is equal to or greater than the minimum monthly payment due. This allows you to budget your money and make intelligent decisions, based on your financial situation.

Simply paying the minimums on your credit cards will keep those accounts from being late, however, the costs associated with this action (in terms of fees and interest charges) will often be significant over time. Plus, the strategy of only making minimum payments will keep you from greatly reducing or paying off the outstanding debts.

One of the worst mistakes you can make, aside from making late mortgage payments, is having any account go to collections (i.e. be turned over to a collection agency). This means that you've neglected to pay your monthly minimums or have skipped payments for several months, and the account gets closed and turned over to a third-party company in an effort to recover the outstanding debt. Once this happens, regardless of whether or not you ultimately make the payments or settle the account, your credit score will be negatively impacted for up to seven years.

Contrary to popular belief, failing to pay any of your bills could result in those debts being turned over to a collection agency. Once this happens, the collection agencies will report negative information to the credit reporting agencies and your credit scores will take a significant negative hit. Thus, it's important to pay your medical bills, utility bills, telephone, internet and cellular phone bills, gym membership fees, and other bills on time, or negotiate with the companies you do business with if you're unable to meet your financial obligations.

Warning

While the telephone company or your doctor's office, for example, typically can't or won't report negative information to the credit reporting agencies, once an account gets turned over to a collection agency, the credit reporting agencies will be notified and the collection agency will take whatever legal actions are necessary to recoup the money that's owed. Be sure to read Chapter 6 for tips on how to best deal with your creditors, lenders, or collection agencies if you encounter difficult times from a financial standpoint.

Dirty Little Secrets

Warning

Paying off a collection account will not automatically remove that negative trade line from your credit reports, nor will it boost your credit score. Once an account is reported as having been turned over to a collection agency, your credit scores will suffer regardless of the actions you subsequently take.

A few bad decisions today could keep you from buying or leasing a new car, getting approved for a mortgage, or qualifying for credit cards, for example, several years down the road. Think about your future and know that your current actions will impact it.

People who get themselves into financial trouble often tend to ignore the problems until they become huge legal issues. Simply by taking a responsible approach, paying what you can, and working with your creditors and lenders, you can almost always keep your delinquent accounts out of collections, which in turn will protect your credit rating and ultimately save you a fortune (not to mention a lot of hassle and pestering from collection agents).

Credit Tip

If you have trouble paying your bills on time, consider asking your creditors/ lenders to change your monthly due date for payments. Schedule your due dates for later in the month, for example, to be immediately after you receive your paycheck. Thus, you'll know you will have the funds available to pay your bills. This can often help you improve your cash flow and avoid being late on payments.

It's true that your creditors want to be paid in a timely manner. However, most also understand that people sometimes run into financial problems, especially in a poor economy.

The easiest and most straightforward thing you can do to protect your credit rating and credit scores (or begin repairing them) is simply to pay your bills on time. It's that easy!

Strategy 2: Keep Your Credit Card Balances Low

The fact that you have credit cards impacts your credit scores in several ways. Likewise, your payment history related to those credit card accounts also impacts your scores.

Another factor that's considered in the calculation of your credit scores are your credit card balances. Having a balance that represents 35 percent or more of your overall available credit limit on each card will actually hurt you, even if you make all of your payments on time and consistently pay more than the minimum due. If you have a $1,000 credit limit on a credit card, ideally, you want to maintain a balance of less than $350, and make timely monthly payments on the balance that are above the required monthly minimums.

Keeping this in mind, if you have a credit card that allows you to earn frequent flier miles for every dollar you spend, for example, and

 Credit Tip

If you have an average or better credit rating, consider asking your credit card issuers to increase your credit limits. However, do not utilize this extra credit by making more purchases. By increasing the amount of credit that's available on your credit cards while working to reduce your debt, you will improve your credit utilization. Doing this will help to increase your credit scores.

during one month, you opt to pay for a new flat-screen TV with that credit card in order to earn extra frequent flier miles, even if you plan to pay the full balance of that credit card at the end of the billing cycle, for a short time, your utilization of your available credit will change for the worse (since you'll be using a higher percentage of your available credit), and as a result your credit scores could temporarily drop (for up to two or three billing cycles). Thus, if you need the highest possible credit scores to apply for a mortgage, avoid making large credit card purchases for several months prior to applying for that mortgage.

On an ongoing basis, demonstrate (through your credit history) that you're actively reducing your balances, while properly and responsibly utilizing your credit cards. Depending on your personal situation, it could make sense to spread your credit card debt over three, four, or five cards, while keeping your balance on each of them below that 35 percent of the total credit limit mark, as opposed to maxing out one credit card. If you do this, make timely payments on each card and keep them all in good standing. Managing your credit card debt appropriately will not only keep your score from dropping, it could give it a boost.

You Should Know . . .

Need help making financial calculations related to your credit cards? You can utilize a free, online credit card debt calculator at www.bankrate.com/calculators/index-of-credit-card-calculators.aspx.

Deciding to spread your credit card debt among several cards might help your credit score. However, before adopting this strategy, calculate the interest you'll be paying and compare interest rates between cards.

In some cases, you may save money by consolidating your credit card balances onto one low-interest card, as opposed to having that same balance spread over several higher interest-bearing cards. This debt consolidation strategy could save you money, but could also hurt your credit scores since on that one card, you'll be using more of your available credit than 35 percent of your total credit limit. Do the math to help you make the decision and take the action that's best for you.

Strategy 3: Having a Long History Counts, So Don't Close Unused Accounts

One of the factors considered when calculating your credit scores is the length of time you've had the credit established with each creditor. You are rewarded for having a positive, long-term history with each creditor, even if the account is inactive or not used. The longer your positive credit history is with each creditor, the better.

Knowing this, avoid closing older and unused accounts. If you have a handful of credit cards you never use, instead of closing the accounts, simply put those credit cards in a safe place and forget about them. Although you don't want to have too many open accounts, having five or six credit card accounts open, even though you only actually use two or three cards, can be beneficial. Likewise, if you have a five-year car loan, for example, showing three, four, or five years of positive payment history (with no late or skipped payments) will benefit you.

Warning

Closing an account does not remove the information from your credit reports. The trade line for that account will remain on your credit reports for seven years from the time it gets closed. The trade line will include details about the action you've taken to close the account and also state whether the account was paid in full, settled, or sent to collections.

Strategy 4: Only Apply for Credit When Needed, Then Shop for the Best Rates on Loans and Credit Cards

If you're shopping for a bunch of new appliances or other big-ticket items, it's common for consumers to walk into a retailer and be offered a discount and a good financing deal for a large purchase if they open a charge or credit card account with that retailer. Before applying for that store's credit card, read the fine print. Determine what your interest rate will be and what fees are associated with the card.

Next, only apply for new credit if you absolutely need it. Applying for a retail store card you're going to use once or twice, when you could just as easily use an existing credit card, might not be the best idea. Over the long term, if you maintain a balance on a store credit card, for example, the fees and interest charges are often much higher than a major credit card.

Unless you pay off the balance quickly, you'll wind up paying significantly more for that new appliance or whatever it is you opened the new credit card account to purchase. If the store credit card offer includes no interest for six months and 10 percent off of your purchase, do some number crunching before accepting the offer.

After that initial six-month period, what will the interest rate be? Chances are, the APR will be at least 20 percent. What additional recurring fees will you be responsible for? Will you be charged interest calculated on the initial date of your purchase or starting one day after the initial six-month period if you're still carrying a balance from that purchase?

Applying for and obtaining multiple new credit cards (including store credit cards) within a six-month period will also be detrimental to your credit scores. Unless you can save a significant amount of money on your purchase over time and can justify accepting a reduction in your credit score, don't apply for credit you don't actually need.

Chapter 8 offers more information on obtaining, utilizing, and managing your credit card debt. If you want or need to apply for a new credit card, shop around for one with the best offer in terms of rates and rewards. There are a handful of websites, like CreditCards.com, that can help you quickly find and then apply for a new credit card, assuming you meet the qualification requirements based on your credit scores.

According to Charles Tran, founder of CreditDonkey.com, a credit card comparison website, "Store credit cards were my favorite go-to recommendation for young adults looking to build credit. Now, with the CARD Act of 2009 restricting how those under 21 get credit, I would rarely recommend a store credit card over a traditional credit card. Sure, you'll get 5 or 10 percent off at that store, but usually only at that store. Traditional rewards credit cards usually give you cash back almost everywhere you shop. Plus, traditional rewards cards offer card holders access to online discount malls, such as www.bonuscashcenter.citicards.com."

Strategy 5: Separate Your Accounts After a Divorce

During a marriage, it's common for a couple to obtain joint credit card accounts and co-sign for various types of loans. Coming into the marriage, the information on each person's credit report and their credit scores will eventually impact their spouse, especially when new joint accounts are opened or a spouse's name is added to existing accounts.

Warning

Even if a judge orders one person in the marriage to take full responsibility for a specific debt, such as a mortgage, car loan, or credit card bills, as long as it remains a joint account with both names appearing on the account, both parties remain financially responsible for it as far as the creditors, lenders, and credit reporting agencies are concerned. Thus, if your ex-spouse pays a bill late or skips a payment, if that account is also in your name, it will be negatively reflected on your credit reports as well.

Credit Tip

Be sure to close or separate all joint accounts after a divorce is finalized. This can be done by calling each creditor directly. You should also follow up the request in writing and make sure you receive confirmation that the change to the account has been made. Until all accounts are closed or separated, be sure to make on-time payments to all joint accounts. Remember, even one missed or late payment will show up on both of your credit reports and remain there for seven years.

Consolidating all of your accounts once married makes record keeping easier. If a couple gets divorced, however, this can create a whole new set of credit-related challenges.

First, understand that just because you obtain a legal divorce, it does not release one or both people from their financial obligations when it comes to paying off a joint account. As long as both names appear on the account, both parties are responsible for it.

As your divorce proceedings move forward, be sure to pay off and close all joint accounts, or have one person's name removed from each account, meaning only one person will remain responsible for it.

It will probably become necessary for one or both parties in the marriage to re-establish their independent credit. When doing this, start off slowly and build up your independent credit over a few years. Immediately applying for a handful of new credit cards, a new car loan, and/or a new mortgage within a short period of time after your divorce won't help to improve your credit rating or credit scores. Try to spread out new credit card acquisitions and new loans by at least six months each.

In the event of a spouse's death, creditors cannot automatically remove the deceased person's name from a joint account and make the debt the sole responsibility of the living spouse.

Dirty Little Secrets

> ### $ Credit Tip
>
> Depending on your situation, in order to re-establish your credit, it may
> be necessary to find a co-signer, such as a family member or close friend.
> Remember, when someone cosigns a credit or loan application, they're
> taking on equal responsibility for the debt you incur. If you make late pay-
> ments, default on the loan, or skip payments, it will be reflected on your
> credit reports as well as your co-signer's credit reports and negatively impact
> both parties' credit scores. As you're establishing or rebuilding your credit, it
> becomes more important than ever to pay all of your bills on time.

It will be necessary to contact each creditor separately. In some cases, the widow or widower may need to reapply for the credit card or loan as an individual borrower. Keep in mind that the credit reporting agencies regularly update their records using information provided by the Social Security Administration. As a result, joint accounts that include someone who is deceased will be flagged when the creditors are notified.

Strategy 6: Correct Inaccuracies within Your Credit Reports and Make Sure Old Information Is Removed

One of the fastest and easiest ways to quickly give your credit scores a boost is to carefully review all three of your credit reports and correct any erroneous or outdated information that's listed. If you spot incorrect information, you can initiate a dispute and potentially have it corrected or removed within 30 days.

Remember, inaccurate information can be removed from credit reports. Information that is negative, but accurate, is much harder, if not impossible to get removed from your credit reports. If you want

Dirty Little Secrets

information from your creditors or lenders to be reported differently to the credit reporting agencies, that's something you'll need to negotiate directly with your creditors or lenders, not with the credit reporting agencies that simply collect and report data provided by creditors and lenders. Likewise, legal judgments against you, for example, can only be removed by a court.

Strategy 7: Avoid Too Many Hard Inquiries

Every time you apply for a credit card or any type of loan, a potential creditor/lender will make an inquiry with one or more of the credit reporting agencies (Experian, Equifax, or TransUnion). This inquiry information gets added to your credit report(s) and will typically remain listed for two years. For one year, however, the inquiry will slightly reduce your credit score. If you have multiple inquiries in a short period of time, whether or not you get approved for the loan or credit you apply for, this can dramatically reduce your credit scores.

In other words, if your application for a credit card gets rejected, do not immediately apply for additional credit cards from other banks or financial institutions that will most likely also reject your applications. First, find out why your initial application was not approved, rectify the situation, and then apply again for the credit card or loan in a few months.

(\$) *Credit Tip*

If you know you'll be applying for a mortgage or car loan within the next six months, do not apply for any other types of loans or credit cards in the interim. Excessive inquiries in a short period of time will lower your credit scores and decrease your chances of getting approved.

Keep in mind, when shopping for a mortgage or car loan, it's permissible to have multiple inquiries for the same purpose within a 30- to 45-day period, without those multiple inquiries hurting your credit scores. In this situation, the multiple inquiries will be counted as one single inquiry.

"Soft inquiries" are inquires made by creditors or lenders without your authorization in order to pre-qualify you for a credit card offer or some other special financing deal, for example. Often, if you have a credit card, car loan, or mortgage, those lenders will periodically and automatically check your credit reports. Soft inquiries have no impact on your credit scores or credit rating whatsoever, but they do get listed on your credit reports.

Strategy 8: Avoid Bankruptcy, If Possible

There are a lot of misconceptions about the pros and cons of filing for bankruptcy if you encounter serious financial problems. In terms of your credit reports, credit rating, and credit scores, filing for bankruptcy is one of the absolute worst things you can do.

If your credit scores have not already plummeted as a result of late payments, missed payments, charge-offs and defaults, when the bankruptcy is listed on your credit reports, you will notice a large and immediate drop in your credit scores. Furthermore, that bankruptcy

Just filing bankruptcy papers with the court is enough for it to negatively impact your credit reports, credit rating, and credit scores. Even if the court rejects your bankruptcy papers, the negative information will still appear on your credit reports within the "Public Records" section, and that will impact your credit scores.

Warning

Filing for bankruptcy does not wipe clean all of your debt. You will still be responsible for alimony, child support, student loans, and taxes, for example. Be sure to consult with a bankruptcy attorney or accountant before pursuing this option.

will continue to plague your credit reports for up to ten years and could keep you from getting approved for any type of loan or credit during that period.

For most people, bankruptcy does not offer an easy way out of their financial responsibilities or offer a quick fix. Instead, you're setting yourself up for long-term financial difficulties, because obtaining any type of credit or loans in the future will be significantly more difficult. Plus, bankruptcy does not always dissolve or remove all of your debts. Many mortgage brokers (and lenders) and car loan financing companies will automatically reject applicants with bankruptcies listed on their credit reports.

If you do file for bankruptcy, the best thing you can do is slowly rebuild your credit by paying all of your bills on time from that point forward, with no exceptions. Rebuilding your credit in this situation will most likely take years, with no quick fixes available. One way to start rebuilding your credit is to obtain a secured credit card, which is described in Chapter 8. (As you'll discover, secured credit cards typically come with very high fees and interest rates, plus offer very low credit limits.)

Strategy 9: Avoid Consolidating Balances onto One Credit Card

Unless you can save a fortune in interest charges and fees by consolidating balances onto one credit card, this strategy should be avoided. One reason to avoid this is that maxing out any of your credit cards will detract from your credit scores, even if you make on-time payments. Assuming the interest rate calculations make sense, you're better off distributing your debt over several low-interest credit cards. An alternative is to pay off high-interest credit card balances using another type of debt consolidation loan or by refinancing your mortgage with a cash-out option. See Chapter 8 for more information about credit card debt consolidation options.

Strategy 10: Negotiate with Your Creditors or Collection Agencies

Contrary to popular belief, your creditors and lenders aren't your enemies (at least they don't have to be). Your creditors are in business. The nature of business dictates that they strive to earn a profit. When you don't pay your bills, this impacts a creditor's ability to do business and impacts its bottom line. Many creditors are willing to be understanding of difficult financial situations and short-term financial problems, especially if you openly communicate with them in a timely manner.

In other words, instead of skipping a handful of payments or defaulting on a loan, contact your creditors and lenders as soon as a problem arises and negotiate some form of resolution that's acceptable and within your financial means.

Forcing a creditor to turn your debt over to a collection agency will simply cause you bigger problems in the future because many collection agencies are relentless when it comes to recovering money. (You can expect non-stop collection calls and even legal action to be taken against you by a collection agency in an effort to recoup the money that's owed.) Furthermore, the negative information that's placed on your credit report will have a long-term negative impact on your credit rating.

Depending on the level of your financial difficulties, your creditors may be willing to do one or more of the following things to assist you,

Dirty Little Secrets

You Should Know...

Although you can easily negotiate with creditors on your own behalf, to learn more about what's possible to rectify or improve your situation before it gets too far out of control, consider seeking help from a professional credit counselor. In the past, accepting help from a credit counselor was detrimental to your credit report and credit scores. This is no longer the case.

For information about credit counseling, contact the National Foundation for Credit Counseling (NFCC) at (800) 388-2227, or visit the organization's website (www.nfcc.org). From this nonprofit organization, which has more than 1,450 offices throughout the country, you can receive low-cost or free guidance that can help you work with your creditors and develop a realistic budget for you based on your personal situation.

NFCC member agencies provide a handful of free and/or affordable services to consumers, including:

- Budget counseling and education
- Counseling referral services
- Financial literacy courses
- Bankruptcy counseling and education
- Housing counseling

Be sure to read Chapter 6 to discover proven strategies for negotiating successfully with creditors, lenders, and collection agencies.

assuming you make the effort and show good faith in contacting them quickly (when a negative situation, such as the loss of a job, death of a spouse, or serious illness/injury arises) to discuss your situation:

- Reduce your interest rate
- Reduce your monthly minimum payment
- Waive extra finance charges and late fees
- Allow you to skip one or more monthly payments (and extend the length of the loan)
- Close the account and allow you to make affordable payments to slowly reduce the outstanding balance over time
- Close the account and accept a settlement for less than the amount you actually owe. (In some cases, you may be able to settle an overdue account for 50 cents on the dollar or less.)
- Allow you to refinance the loan at a lower interest rate and/or for a longer term to reduce your monthly payments

Warning

Simply ignoring a debt, closing an account (or allowing an account to be closed by a creditor for nonpayment), or moving without providing a creditor with your new address will not cause the outstanding debt to disappear. In many cases, the longer you hold off paying your debts, the more you'll spend in interest fees, late fees, legal fees, and other types of penalties.

Avoiding Credit Repair Scams

There's a big difference among "credit repair," "debt consolidation," and "credit or debt counseling." Credit repair services are typically a scam. Companies falsely advertise that for a fee, they will have accurate but negative information removed from your credit reports, which will quickly boost your credit scores.

These services don't work and in many cases are scams designed to prey on people suffering from financial difficulties. Only the credit reporting agencies or your actual creditors/lenders can remove information from your credit reports.

For example, the BankRate.com website (www.bankrate.com/brm/news/advice/19980720c.asp) features an article, "Credit Repair Scams," in which Jodie Bernstein, the director of the FTC's Bureau of Consumer Protection in Washington, DC, is quoted as saying, "While there are legitimate, not-for-profit credit counseling services, the FTC has never seen a legitimate credit repair company." If you see a "credit repair" service advertised, proceed with extreme caution before utilizing this type of service.

Debt consolidation involves taking out a new, larger loan at one predetermined interest rate so that you can pay off multiple overdue outstanding debts that are potentially charging much higher interest rates. Assuming you obtain a debt consolidation loan from a legitimate company, this can be an excellent way to begin rebuilding your credit and fixing financial problems.

There are, however, debt consolidation loan companies that aren't legitimate or that charge exorbitant fees or interest rates. Make sure you fully understand the type of loan you are applying for and what your responsibilities are before proceeding. Consulting with a reputable (and licensed) personal financial planner, accountant, credit counselor, or attorney before moving forward with a debt consolidation loan is an excellent strategy.

Credit counseling is a service that teaches you how to better manage your finances and often includes negotiation with creditors on your behalf to help you regain your financial stability and rebuild your credit. There are often fees associated with credit counseling services, even if the organization you work with is a nonprofit corporation.

Some companies advertised as "credit counseling services" are really debt consolidation loan companies offering high-interest (and/or high fee) debt consolidation loans. Consumer beware! Make sure the debt consolidation firm you choose to work with is reputable.

Dirty Little Secrets

The National Foundation for Credit Counseling (800-388-2227, www.nfcc.org) is an excellent place to start your search for a reputable and affordable credit counseling service.

According to the FTC, "Every day, companies target consumers who have poor credit histories with promises to clean up their credit report so they can get a car loan, a home mortgage, insurance, or even a job once they pay them a fee for the service. The truth is, these companies can't deliver an improved credit report for you using the tactics they promote. It's illegal: No one can remove accurate negative information from your credit report. So after you pay them hundreds or thousands of dollars in fees, you're left with the same credit report and someone else has your money."

If you see an advertisement for a "credit repair" company, here are some things to look for in order to determine if what's being offered is a scam:

- The company wants you to pay for credit repair services before they provide any services. Under the Credit Repair Organizations Act, credit repair companies cannot require you to pay until they have completed the services they have promised.
- The company doesn't tell you your rights and what you can do for yourself for free.
- The company recommends that you not contact any of the three major national credit reporting companies directly.
- The company tells you they can get rid of most or all of the negative credit information in your credit report, even if that information is accurate and current.
- The company suggests that you try to invent a "new" credit identity—and then, a new credit report—by applying for an Employer Identification Number to use instead of your Social Security number.
- The company advises you to dispute all the information in your credit report, regardless of its accuracy or timeliness.

Dirty Little Secrets

The FTC reports, "If you follow illegal advice and commit fraud, you may find yourself in legal hot water, too: It's a federal crime to lie on a loan or credit application, to misrepresent your Social Security number, and to obtain an Employer Identification Number from the Internal Revenue Service under false pretenses. You could be charged and prosecuted for mail or wire fraud if you use the mail, telephone, or internet to apply for credit and provide false information."

Learn How to Better Manage Your Finances and Expenses

If you're currently experiencing financial troubles which have led to problems with your credit rating, consider the reasons for this. Are your problems a result of poor financial management and decisions on your part? Sure, some people run into serious credit problems as a result of circumstances that are outside of their control (such as sudden loss of a job, illness, injury, or death of a spouse), but far too many people run into credit problems as a result of poor money management, out-of-control spending, and a lack of understanding when it comes to personal finance issues.

If you've made mistakes in your past and now must recover from the situation, make sure you learn from those mistakes and take steps to ensure you never repeat them. Adapting a more responsible personal finance management plan can almost always help. Consider using personal financial management software, such as Intuit's Quicken software (www.quicken.com), to help you better manage your finances, control your spending, and remind you to pay your bills on time. Later, in Chapter 14, you'll learn more about software, online services, and mobile phone (and tablet) apps that can help you better manage your finances and protect your credit rating.

While software packages such as Quicken are relatively easy to use, also consider either hiring an accountant or personal financial planner to help you develop and stick to a budget and take control of your spending. Likewise, sitting down with a career counselor can help you develop a strategy for advancing your career, finding a higher-paying job, and boosting your income over time.

Refer back to the financial goals you set when reading Chapter 1 and make sure you have a realistic plan in place to achieve those goals, keeping in mind that dedication on your part will be essential to achieving success.

Reading personal finance books, taking part in adult education classes related to money management, and participating in seminars sponsored by your bank or financial institution can also be useful for improving your financial situation and finance-related knowledge.

The following interview with a credit expert offers additional advice for finding and utilizing the help you'll need to recover from financial/credit problems. You'll also discover more tips for building and maintaining your credit rating.

Advice from a Credit and Debt Counseling Expert

Bradley M. Wood is the vice president of operations for Advantage Debt Management of America in Cincinnati, Ohio (877-245-5435, www. helpwithbills.org). His organization is a credit counseling agency that has been supplying financial assistance to the greater Cincinnati area for over 75 years.

According to Wood, "We are one of the oldest credit counseling agencies in the United States. We are a 501c3 nonprofit agency that provides free advice to consumers on the options that are available to them to resolve the financial problems they are facing, and free budgeting seminars to employers, communities, service groups, etc. We also offer bankruptcy counseling for consumers who are having to choose that option to resolve their overwhelming debt."

Wood is a graduate of Michigan State University. He has personally been providing financial counseling and education since 1988.

What is credit and debt counseling?

Bradley M. Wood: "Credit and debt counseling at our agency comes in two stages. First is the initial intake, where a counselor reviews with a consumer their income, living expenses, assets, and liabilities to assess the consumer's situation and to give them a plan of action for resolving the problems they're facing.

"If consumers can't resolve their problems on their own and need direct assistance, then they move into the second stage, which is a debt management plan. This program is where our agency acts on the consumer's behalf to set up repayment arrangements with their creditors that fit within the consumer's budget and are acceptable to the lenders. These plans usually include the reduction of payment amounts and the reduction of interest, as well as a snowball payment system that rolls payments from one creditor to another as debts are paid off."

What is the difference between a debt and credit counselor (if any)?

Bradley M. Wood: "It's all semantics: Some agencies call their counselors debt counselors and some call them credit counselors."

From a consumer's standpoint, how does the credit or debt counseling process work?

Bradley M. Wood: "The consumer goes through the intake process, and then takes that information to make a decision about which option(s) to follow. There are usually more than one, or multiple options that may have to be followed. Every consumer receives a printout of the counseling session with advice included.

"If the consumer's decision is to set up a debt management plan through our agency, they then come back for a follow-up appointment, sign the nonbinding agreement, and make their first deposit. At that point we begin contacting their creditors to negotiate the arrangements the consumer can afford. If their decision is to just make the changes to their budget we recommended, they can then contact us at anytime for follow-up advice, or attend one of our free budgeting seminars to get further assistance on creating and maintaining a budget. If their decision is to file [for] bankruptcy, the consumer will then come back to us for the certification needed to file."

On average, how long does it take to see positive results?

Bradley M. Wood: "It depends on which path they choose. If you are referring to the debt management plan, then positive results are seen within 90 days, as this is the most it will take for the collection calls to stop, and for the interest and payment amounts to be reduced. The average term of a repayment plan is a little over four years, but this differs with each individual based upon the amount of debt they have and how much they have available to put toward it."

How much does credit counseling cost the consumer?

Bradley M. Wood: "All counseling is free. But if a consumer opts to use a debt management plan, then there will be fees involved, which are voluntary, meaning that the consumer can ask for free help, or the counselor will remove the fee due to the client's inability to pay it.

"Almost every state now has a law on their books regulating how much a credit counseling agency can charge the consumers in their state. We offer debt management plan assistance mainly in Ohio, Indiana, and Kentucky. Ohio and Kentucky allow a fee of $30 or 8.5 percent of the money received to disburse per month, whichever is greater, while Indiana has no minimum, just the 8.5 percent. We voluntarily cap our fees at $50 a month, regardless of how much the state would allow. We are also allowed to charge a one-time startup fee of $50 in each state."

Who can best benefit from debt and debt counseling?

Bradley M. Wood: "Actually everyone can benefit from credit counseling. The main consumers who come to us are those who are behind on their bills, or who are about to be behind, or are over extended. However, since they are still not teaching money management in school, we are really the only 'in-person' assistance consumers have available to talk with a certified professional. Just as you would go to an attorney for legal advice, a credit counselor is there to answer questions regarding debt and credit."

What is a debt management plan and how does it work?

Bradley M. Wood: "A debt management plan is a structured repayment plan set up by the credit counseling agency with a consumer's creditors to assist in the reduction of payments and interest making the debt repayment more affordable so that it can fit within the consumer's existing budget. The consumer makes payments to the agency, which disburses those funds to their creditors, based upon the arrangements that were set.

"Once a consumer enrolls in the debt repayment plan, proposals are sent to their creditors requesting they agree to the terms the counselor has determined the consumer can afford. Once the consumer makes the first payment the agency disburses those funds based upon the arrangements set. If a proposal is rejected, the agency negotiates with the creditor for the client until a plan can be agreed upon.

"The consumer continues to make the monthly deposits to the agency until the debt is retired or until the consumer is comfortable in handling their finances on their own again. As the consumer pays off debts through the plan, their payment does not change, but instead the 'freed' money is moved to the next creditor to speed up the process of repayment."

At what point should someone seek out the services of a debt or credit counselor? When is it too soon or too late?

Bradley M. Wood: "It is never too late to ask for help, and there are always options open to the consumer. A consumer should seek assistance when they have questions about their financial situation or feel that it is getting out of their control."

What are the pitfalls to avoid when working with a debt counselor?

Bradley M. Wood: "Make sure that the counselor is not a salesman in disguise. If all he does is try to promote his plan, he is a salesman, even if he also offers budget advice. Consumers should also be wary of statements that sound too good to be true. It took years to get into their situation, so it will take years to pay off.

"Consumers should also understand the effect a debt management plan may have on their credit. Although over the long run using an agency generally improves a consumer's credit, it may come with an initial hit to the credit score as accounts may continue being or become delinquent until the proposals are agreed to.

"Consumers should also be wary of the fees the agency is going to be charging them, as they should be within the state's regulations and should not be exorbitant. Finally, a consumer needs to be aware that any account put on the plan will no longer be open for further borrowing. Creditors are not going to agree to reductions and then let the consumer keep using the credit card or credit line."

How does working with a credit and debt counselor impact someone's credit report, credit rating, and credit scores?

Bradley M. Wood: "Using a credit counseling agency does not directly impact a consumer's score. Creditors may report to the credit reporting agencies that the consumer is using third-party assistance, which is displayed on the report, but that does not affect the FICO Score. Consumers who are actively on a debt management plan are discouraged from obtaining any new credit until the plan is completed, and some lenders require a letter of approval from an agency if the consumer is trying to borrow while on or immediately after a debt management plan, since it is displayed on the report.

"That being said, there may be a reduction of the score when the client first starts the plan due to the accounts remaining delinquent until the proposals are accepted and the plans implemented. Generally, if a consumer successfully completes a debt repayment plan, he will find his credit score greatly improved. Although this is not the primary drive of the service—debt repayment is—we pull our clients' reports annually to keep an eye on the score and make sure that it is improving and that no new debt is accruing."

How can someone find the most reputable debt/credit counselors to work with? What credentials should someone look for?

Bradley M. Wood: "I would recommend that any consumer look for a local brick and mortar agency within their community. There is at least one in every major city in the U.S. If that is not an option, use the internet or Yellow Pages. Any agency a consumer uses should be a 501c3 nonprofit that is licensed in their state, if the state requires it.

"All counseling should be free, and the monthly fees for a debt management plan should be within state guidelines and reasonable. I would also recommend the consumer use the Better Business Bureau and their state's attorney general's website to check for complaints."

What scams should consumers look out for when seeking out a debt and credit counselor?

Bradley M. Wood: "Consumers need to make sure they understand the services they are signing up for, how those services will work, what the benefits and drawbacks are, and exactly how much the fees will be if they sign up for a debt management plan.

"There are services out there we refer to as "debt settlement" agencies that pass themselves off as credit counselors, when in fact the services are not the same. These are those companies that state they can get you out of debt for pennies on the dollar. They charge large fees upfront, and are usually unable to provide the services they promise during enrollment.

"There have been plenty of stories about these agencies in the national press, and many states have written laws to regulate their practices; limiting what they can promise, and how much they can charge, and when they can charge their fees.

"Even if a consumer contacts a debt settlement agency that is licensed and insured, they need to be fully aware of how the services work and the impact they are going to have on their finances and credit. Lenders certainly will agree to settlements, but not before the account is severely delinquent, which means the consumers' credit rating/score will be trashed in the process of waiting for the lender to agree to a settlement.

"Keep in mind, a credit report with a bunch of charge-offs on it is going to have a huge impact on that overall credit scores. In my professional opinion it would be better for the consumer to file bankruptcy when their credit score is still high than it would be to take this route, as you would be able to rebuild that score much quicker.

"Second, the debt settlement agency usually takes all of their fee upfront, which means typically the first six monthly payments the consumer pays into the plan are going just to cover that fee, with nothing being saved toward the proposed settlements.

"Third, the debt settlement company has no authority to keep the lender from taking further action against the consumer, even if that settlement agency is run by an attorney. Credit cards typically charge off at six months, at which point legal action is considered. So, if the consumer has no money to start the plan, and has to pay the fee in installments, by the time they start saving money for the settlements the lenders are already moving forward with getting a judgment that will allow them to garnish wages, seize assets, etc."

"We are finding with the bankruptcy counseling we do that a lot of the customers who have worked with debt settlement agencies are having to file for bankruptcy anyway, in order to stop legal action. This leaves them with even worse credit scores, and they will have a much harder time rebuilding their credit.

Dirty Little Secrets

"Fourth, the consumer needs to understand that just because the agency quotes certain settlement amounts when enrolled, those settlement amounts may not still be valid when the money is finally saved. Most accounts accrue interest and charges, which means that as the consumer is saving to do the settlement, the balance is still growing, which also means the amount the creditors will be willing to accept is still growing.

"The final thing to be wary of with debt settlement services, which again are very different from debt counseling services, is that if the settled amount is greater than $600, it will be reported to the IRS, which will view the waived amount as income. Thus, the consumer will be required to pay taxes on it. Yes, they will still be saving, but most people are not aware of this fact and find themselves unable to pay the extra fees come tax time."

If someone decides to work with a credit and debt counselor, can this be done online or over the phone, or does it need to be done in person?

Bradley M. Wood: "My advice is to find a local agency to work with, but even then most agencies nowadays offer multiple forms of access: face-to-face, telephone, and internet. Generally, the larger the agency, the easier it is to access, and the more contact options you have."

What types of information will a consumer need to provide to the credit and debit counselor?

Bradley M. Wood: "A consumer is going to need four types of information ready when contacting a credit counselor in order to complete a counseling session. This includes details relating to their income, including their monthly net pay. They'll also need to provide details about their living expenses. These are the averages they spend on rent, utilities, food, gas, insurance, etc. Information about their liabilities will also be needed. This includes the names, account numbers, monthly payments, and balances of their debts. Finally, the consumer will need to provide details about their assets, which is the value of the things they own."

Do credit and debt counselors help someone declare bankruptcy, or can a company like yours help people avoid this?

Bradley M. Wood: "The main drive of our business is to increase financial literacy and help consumers avoid bankruptcy, but it is definitely an option that needs to be disclosed to consumers so that they can make an educated decision with regard to which path they are going to follow.

"We do not help consumers file for bankruptcy. An attorney can do that, although consumers can easily file on their own. However, with the Bankruptcy Reform Act, consumers must now complete two certifications if they are filing bankruptcy. The first certification is needed within six months of the filing. This certification attests that the consumer has reviewed his finances with a U.S. Trustee approved agency and has been made aware of all his options. This certificate is submitted with the bankruptcy filing paperwork. The second certification is done after the filing, but prior to the discharge. This certification attests that the consumer has completed a two-hour financial education course concentrating on budgeting, money management, and the laws that cover finance."

By working with a debt or credit counselor, will someone get out of paying some or all of their debt? Does a credit counselor negotiate with creditors/lenders on the consumer's behalf? What is the impact of this on someone's credit report and their credit scores?

Bradley M. Wood: "The only reduction a consumer might negotiate when using a credit counselor is a reduction in the interest being charged and a cessation of late charges and over-the-limit fees. None of the principal is reduced in this kind of arrangement. Because we are trying to salvage the client's credit while repaying the debts, lenders can't offer principal reduction due to federal regulations."

What can someone expect to get out of working with a credit and debt counselor?

Bradley M. Wood: "Consumers who use a credit counseling agency will find their financial knowledge has increased, with better comprehension of financial terms. Consumers will also have a better understanding of what a budget is and how to establish and maintain one, allowing them much greater control over their financial future. Consumers will also, hopefully, have better financial habits, reducing their risk of falling back into unmanageable debt in the future."

What tips can you offer for someone who wants to negotiate with their creditors/ lenders on their own? What pitfalls should they avoid?

Bradley M. Wood: "Understand that the first person they get when calling for assistance is the employee with the least amount of authority to alter the contractual obligations, depending upon how delinquent they are. Customer service representatives usually only follow a script from which they cannot deviate, so the consumer needs to expect to have to talk to multiple people before they reach a representative with enough authority to agree to and implement changes. Because of the CARD Act, most credit card companies are going to automatically refer consumers to a credit counseling agency if a consumer calls asking for help in the form of reductions. The more delinquent they are, the easier it will be to negotiate, but before paying anything the consumer needs to get the agreement in writing, as this is a deviation from the original contract. Many collectors have been known to make promises that they later do not honor, just to get payment, and if nothing was in writing the original contract can continue to be in force and the consumer is stuck."

What tips can you provide for someone to work successfully with a debt or credit counselor?

Bradley M. Wood: "Stay involved, watch the statements from the agency as well as the ones they still get from their creditors, and make sure they match up. Be sure that the payments being sent by the agency are showing up on the statements from the creditors, and that the balances match up. Also, meet with your counselor at least once every 12 months to review your account and to go over your credit report. Many consumers just want to enroll and forget, but those are the ones who can blame no one but themselves if something does not turn out the way they were hoping it would."

Is there anything else you'd like to share about yourself, your company, or your service with the book's readers?

Bradley M. Wood: "Most consumers are not aware that there really are only five ways to repay debt, whether you are delinquent or not. There is no easy tip or magic remedy to debt resolution, whether you are delinquent or not. The five options are: Contractual repayment (paying your debts as agreed); budget revision (increasing your income and/ or decreasing your living expenses); asset reallocation (selling off or borrowing against existing assets to pay down the debt and reduce the money needed to make payments); credit counseling (third party intervention to make repayment affordable); and bankruptcy (using the courts to intervene on the consumer's behalf to relieve them of dischargeable debts or create a structured repayment, usually for a percentage of the outstanding principal)."

What's Next?

One of the biggest causes of overspending and credit problems in America is the poor judgment many consumers utilize when taking advantage of their credit cards to make purchases. The next chapter offers advice on how to properly obtain, use, and manage credit cards and related credit card debt.

Credit Card Management
Strategies

What's in This Chapter

- Discover how credit cards work

- Find the best credit card deals

- Learn to better manage your credit card debt

- Tips for consolidating credit card balances

Credit Cards Can Be Your Best Friend or Biggest Credit Foe

For the responsible consumer, utilizing credit cards can be a tool for making life easier and used as a way to maintain and build a positive credit rating. For the irresponsible consumer, however, credit cards can be the biggest cause of problems due to excessive spending and irresponsible debt management.

Using a credit card is a privilege, not a right. So, before you apply for and begin using one or more credit cards, it's essential that you develop a thorough understanding of how they work and how to properly utilize them.

Statistics released by the Federal Reserve indicate that more than 40 percent of all American families are spending more than they earn. The most popular way of doing this is through the misuse or abuse of credit cards. While a credit card can periodically be used to compensate for a short-term cash shortage, as well as to provide convenience when making almost any type of purchases, improper use of credit cards winds up costing consumers a lot of money in fees and interest charges, plus leads to growing debt.

If you pay only the monthly minimum payment due on an outstanding $8,000 credit card debt that has an 18 percent interest rate, it will take you more than 25 years to completely pay off that debt, at a total cost of more than $24,000 (assuming that once you rack up that $8,000 debt, you stop putting new charges on the card and just work toward paying it off). Talk about wasting money!

 Credit Tip

Based on your own credit card balances, to see how long it'll take to pay them off if you only make minimum payments, use the free online calculator found at CardTrak.com (www.cardtrak.com/tools).

If you use credit cards to cover your regular living expenses because you're spending more than you earn, eventually all of your credit cards will get maxed out (you will have reached their credit limits). At this point, not only won't you be able to pay your monthly living expenses, you also will not be able to pay the monthly payments associated with those high credit card balances. This will ultimately put you in greater debt, damage your credit rating, and could quickly lead to financial disaster.

Contrary to popular belief, even though a credit card is considered an unsecured loan, if you stop paying your monthly minimums, the creditor charges off your account (after closing it) and you wind up owing money to a credit card issuer, they'll come after you legally for the money you owe.

At first, you'll receive an obscene number of collection calls and letters from your creditor. If you still don't pay, your account will eventually be turned over to a collection agency. At this point, your credit scores will take a huge dip, even worse negative information will be placed on your credit reports (and stay there for seven years), and the collection agency will most likely take legal action to collect what's owed.

This will often result in a legal judgment against you, and potentially a lien being placed on your home (if you're a homeowner). The creditor or collection agency could also get a judge to garnish your future wages. In other words, it's not possible to simply walk away from credit card debt unless you declare bankruptcy, and even that has become extremely difficult.

The potentially good news for people in serious debt is that it's often possible to negotiate a payoff settlement with your credit card issuers and wind up paying up to 50 percent less than the overdue balance, plus have late charges and some interest charges waived. However, your credit card accounts will be closed, you must be willing to make a lump-sum payment (or divide that total payment into two payments), and be prepared for your credit rating to be damaged for up to seven years. Chapter 6 offers more information about negotiating settlements and payment plans with credit card companies.

In addition to finding yourself in legal trouble for defaulting on credit card debt obligations, these actions will destroy your credit rating and credit scores, which will prevent you from obtaining any type of additional loans or credit for at least seven years. This includes your ability to get a mortgage, finance a car, or obtain a student loan for yourself or your kid(s).

The credit card companies are making billions of dollars each year thanks to consumers badly managing their credit cards and ultimately not applying basic smart money management principles to their credit card usage. There's no reason whatsoever why you can't use credit cards, but at the same time, you always want to implement management strategies to save yourself money and protect your credit rating over the short and long term.

What Are Credit Cards?

Credit cards, like MasterCard, Visa, Discover, and many of the products offered by American Express, for example, are a form of revolving credit. Retail store chains, department stores, gas stations, and other companies that cater to consumers often offer their own store credit cards.

Credit cards provide the cardholder with a pre-set credit limit, but unlike a mortgage, for example, there are not a fixed number of payments associated with the amount borrowed. Purchases can be paid off over time. The amount available to the cardholder will decrease or increase as funds are borrowed and then repaid. Cardholders make payments based only on the amount they've actually borrowed, plus interest and fees.

Each month, the cardholder is responsible for making at least a minimum payment, which is typically between two and two-and-a-half percent of the total balance owed. While payments toward the outstanding balance are often made over time, the entire balance can be paid off at any time with no penalty.

Buying anything using a credit card is just like taking out a loan that must be paid back. Credit cards are *not* free money or a license to spend money on random things until you reach your credit limit and max out the card! They're only cost-effective and worthwhile if they're used responsibly.

Every credit card issuer offers a unique set of terms that the cardholder (you, the borrower) must adhere to in order to keep the account active and in good standing. These terms are described in the cardholder agreement that's provided when the account is opened.

Read this document carefully (even the tiny fine print)! Also, be sure to read any supplements or revisions to the cardholder agreement that are mailed to you by the credit card issuer (they're often disguised as junk mail, but contain information about rate hikes, increased fees, or other new rules associated with the use of the card).

In addition to all of the rules and regulations the cardholder must adhere to, the card's annual percentage rate (APR) will also be listed in the cardholder agreement. The APR is the cost of credit that's expressed as a yearly rate. This number, along with the "periodic rate," will help you calculate how much maintaining a balance on the credit card will cost you over time.

The terms *credit card* and *charge card* are often used interchangeably. However, they are not the same. While purchases made using a "credit card" can be paid off over time, a "charge card" requires the cardholder to pay off their balance, in full, each month when their statement arrives. Some products offered by American Express, for example, are "charge cards," not credit cards.

The Potential Benefits of Credit Cards

The following is a list of potential benefits of using a major credit card to make purchases:

Dirty Little Secrets

■ You can buy and afford items you need right away, without having to save up for them. You can use your credit cards as a "buy-now, pay-later" tool. They provide you with the opportunity to utilize an unsecured loan from a financial institution (the credit card issuer). On the other hand, using cash, a check, or a debit card to make the same purchase involves using a "buy-now, pay-now" tool. A debit card, however, does not typically have an interest rate, finance charges, or fees associated with it.

■ There's no need to carry around a lot of cash in your wallet.

■ As you make purchases, your monthly statement offers a detailed record of your purchases.

■ Using a credit card to make purchases is faster and much more convenient than writing checks.

■ If managed properly, you can consolidate multiple bills into one payment.

■ Using a credit card to make a purchase is typically more secure than using cash or checks.

■ You can benefit from the perks associated with certain credit cards, such as cash-back rewards, the ability to earn airline frequent flier miles, or other benefits.

■ If you shop around for the best credit card deals and manage your accounts wisely, you can benefit from low-interest credit cards, special introductory offers, balance transfer offers, and other cost-saving benefits.

The Potential Drawbacks of Credit Cards

Just as credit cards offer convenience and benefits, they also have some potential drawbacks, especially for people who don't manage them wisely. Some of these potentially costly drawbacks include:

■ Thanks to interest, fees, and finance charges, you'll pay extra for the items and services you purchase using the credit card, especially if you pay back the balance of your credit card(s) over time.

- Thanks to the ease-of-use and convenience of credit cards, it's extremely easy to spend beyond your means, which will result in financial difficulties and large amounts of debt.
- If you don't pay your credit card bills on time every month, you will negatively impact your credit rating and credit scores. This will ultimately make it more difficult and much more expensive to get a car loan, a mortgage, or even acquire insurance in the future.
- There are often many different fees associated with credit card usage, beyond just the interest rate, that many consumers aren't aware of until they wind up having to pay them. Some of these fees include: an annual fee, over-the-limit fees, late-payment fees, online payment fees, telephone payment fees, balance transfer fees, cash advance fees, and currency exchange fees (when you make purchases abroad).
- If you make one or more late payments, skip credit card payments, or don't adhere to the terms of the cardholder agreement, your regular interest rate could automatically switch to the much higher "default rate," which will make it considerably more costly to maintain a balance on that credit card. The default rate can be upwards of 30 percent, while the regular APR might only be 5 percent, depending on your credit rating and the terms offered by your credit card issuer.

What to Consider *Before* Using a Credit Card

If you're going to successfully possess one or more credit cards and use them, you'll need to consider your actions from three unique perspectives.

First, consider the financial consequences of using those credit cards and what the long-term cost will be. This means finding the best credit card deals, shopping around for the best rates, focusing on the card's APR and fees, and then being wise with how the credit cards are used.

Dirty Little Secrets

Second, focus on the impact your credit card usage will have on your credit scores and on your credit reports. The number of active credit card accounts you possess, the balances you maintain, and whether or not you make your monthly payments in a timely manner all get reported to the credit reporting agencies, who then incorporate this information into your credit reports. This information also directly impacts your credit scores.

Finally, only acquire the credit you need, when you need it. Maintain manageable balances, shop around for the best deals, and have a plan to pay off the debt in a relatively short period of time in order to avoid paying ongoing interest and fees on insignificant purchases.

As you'll discover from this chapter, charging insignificant purchases on your credit cards, such as dining out, movie tickets, dry cleaning, or a pack of gum, for example, and then taking months or years to pay off that debt is simply throwing away money. It's a classic example of poor credit card usage and irresponsible debt management.

If you're going to use a credit card to make insignificant purchases for convenience or to utilize the credit card's reward system, that's fine, as long as you have a plan to pay off the balance at the end of the month, especially if it's a high-interest credit card. There are situations, however, when it might make sense to carry a balance on a credit card, especially if you're offered an introductory or promotional zero percent interest rate for a few months, for example. Taking advantage of these special offers often makes sense, as long as you read all of the fine print and adhere to the terms of the offer.

Types of Credit Cards

Not all credit cards are alike. In addition to offering different interest rates and fees, some are offered by banks or financial institutions (creditors) that target people with less than perfect credit, while others offer rebates, bonuses, or other incentives for using the card. The following is a summary of the different types of credit cards available.

■ *Affinity Credit Cards.* This is a traditional credit card with a twist. In addition to working as a Visa or MasterCard, because it's offered by two separate organizations—a lending institution and a non-financial group—it entitles cardholders to special discounts or deals from the non-financial group. Major retailers, like Barnes & Noble Booksellers, Sony, Walmart, Starbucks, Jet Blue Airlines, American Airlines, The Walt Disney Company, and thousands of other companies, plus hundreds of charitable organizations, offer affinity credit cards with special perks, bonuses, or money-saving incentives to cardholders. Most affinity credit cards have an annual fee and a slightly higher interest rate connected to them, but the incentives or perks can make the added costs of having the card worthwhile. Chase (https://creditcards.chase.com), for example, offers more than 180 different affinity MasterCard and Visa credit cards to choose from.

■ *Debit Cards.* This is a payment card that is linked directly to a customer's bank account. Some cards require a personal identification number. Others require a customer's signature. A PIN-based or direct debit card removes the purchase price from a customer's checking account almost immediately. A signature-based or deferred debit card has a Visa or MasterCard logo and removes the purchase price from a customer's bank account in two or three days. A debit card is very different from a "credit card" or "charge card." While a debit card may display the Visa or MasterCard logo, meaning that it can be used to make purchases from companies that accept Visa or MasterCard, when you make a purchase using a debit card, the amount of that purchase is automatically withdrawn from your checking or savings account within a few days. A debit card is a more convenient alternative to writing a check or paying for something with cash, however, no credit is actually being extended to you. Using a debit card also does not impact your credit rating or credit scores at all, as long as it's used appropriately and responsibly.

Dirty Little Secrets

- *Premium Credit Cards.* These are credit cards that offer incentives, such as cash-back rebates on purchases made, airline frequent flier miles, insurance, etc. They tend to be made available to people with excellent credit and offer high credit limits. An affinity card can also be a premium credit card.

- *Pre-Paid Cards.* A pre-paid credit card is different from a secured credit card. With a pre-paid card, you pay the card issuer, in advance, the pre-determined face value of the card (plus fees). You can then use that card to make purchases wherever Visa or MasterCard, for example, are accepted. Once you've used up the pre-paid balance on that card, you must obtain a new pre-paid card or give the card issuer additional funds to replenish a positive balance. Pre-paid credit card issuers do not report to the credit reporting agencies, so your usage of these cards has no impact on your credit rating, credit reports, or credit scores. They're simply a convenience for people who don't have a traditional credit card.

- *Secured Credit Cards.* A secured credit card is often available to people with very bad credit. This type of card requires the cardholder to open and maintain a savings account with the financial institution that issues the credit card. The balance of your savings account is typically the credit limit of your credit card, although in some instances, a small credit line is granted by the card issuer to the cardholder. You're still required to pay your monthly credit card bill and all related interest and fees, but the savings account balance is used as collateral against you defaulting on your debt. Secured credit cards often come with extremely high interest rates and a wide range of high fees, but they're an option for helping rebuild credit after it's been badly damaged. Companies that issue secured credit cards report to the credit reporting agencies.

- *Traditional/General Use Credit Cards.* These are traditional, revolving credit cards, such as a Visa, MasterCard, Discover, or some

American Express cards. These credit cards are issued by banks, credit unions, and other financial institutions.

Remember, if you have one or more active credit card accounts, your credit limit, monthly balance, and how responsible you are at making your payments on time are regularly reported to all three credit bureaus: Equifax, Experian, and TransUnion. This impacts your credit rating and credit scores on an ongoing basis.

Using Credit Cards Intelligently

Out of all the ways consumers can borrow money and acquire debt, credit cards tend to be the most troublesome. Most consumers don't fully understand how credit cards work and the financial implications of using them. Even fewer take the time to shop around for the best credit card deals, properly manage their credit card accounts, and take steps to implement intelligent usage strategies in order to save themselves money and preserve their credit rating and credit scores.

Because most credit card purchases are paid for over time, which means interest and fees need to be paid, the average purchase made on

 **Warning**

Even credit cards issued by the same bank or financial institution and that look identical can have vastly different terms, credit limits, and fees associated with them. If you have two credit cards from Capital One, for example, don't assume that the terms outlined in the cardholder agreements are identical. Always read the initial credit card offer carefully before applying, and then make sure you understand the terms and fees associated with using each individual card, which are outlined in their respective cardholder agreements.

Dirty Little Secrets

a credit card winds up costing the consumer considerably more than if they were to use cash for that same purchase. According to CardWeb. com, "On average, the typical credit card purchase is 112 percent higher than if using cash."

Since most consumers don't bother to shop around for the best credit card deals, they wind up paying extremely high interest rates and fees. In fact, Americans pay an average of 18.9 percent interest on each of their credit cards. Simply by shopping around for better credit card deals, you can save a fortune every year, especially if you have an average or better credit rating.

The following are some of the basic strategies you should apply to your credit card usage and management on an ongoing basis:

- Apply for credit cards that have the lowest interest rates and fees associated with them. Read the fine print of the initial credit card offer and the cardholder agreement carefully to make sure you understand all of the fees associated with that card. In addition to the annual fee (if applicable), the credit card may also have account maintenance charges, over-the-limit charges, late fees, cash advance fees, ATM fees and other charges associated with it that can add up quickly.
- Don't use credit cards for everyday purchases unless you have a plan and the funds to pay off the balance at the end of the month, before interest charges start to accumulate.
- To maintain the highest possible credit scores, always pay at least the minimum monthly payment on time for each credit card.
- To maintain the highest possible credit score, keep your credit card balances below 35 percent of your card's total credit limit. Instead of maintaining a high balance on one or two cards, try to maintain lower balances on several cards that offer competitive interest rates.
- Don't use your credit cards for cash advances, especially if the interest rate and fees for this "convenience" are high.

Dirty Little Secrets

- If you already have high balances on several high-interest-bearing credit cards, consider applying for lower interest credit cards that offer attractive balance transfer offers and take advantage of the no-interest or low-interest offers to save money. Credit card balance transfers are described later in this chapter. Ultimately, you want to maintain a zero balance on your high-interest credit cards.
- Never apply for multiple credit cards in a short period of time. The excessive hard inquiries will negatively impact your credit scores. Try to spread out your new credit card applications by at least six months.
- As a general rule, store-issued credit cards and charge cards typically have higher fees and interest rates associated with them than traditional credit cards. Even if the initial offer for the retailer's credit card seems attractive, read the fine print carefully. In most

 **Warning**

Before applying for a new credit card, read the entire credit card offer carefully. The headline is almost always a bit misleading, especially if you have less than perfect credit. For example, many credit cards associated with an airline's frequent flier program promote that a new cardholder will receive 25,000 to 50,000 bonus frequent flier miles just for signing up for the card and using it once. That's enough miles for one or two free round-trip tickets on most airlines. This statement, however, is always followed by an asterisk (*). If you read the fine print, this offer is only extended to people with excellent credit. People with less than excellent credit might get approved for an airline's credit card, but it might come with a higher annual fee, a higher APR, and a bonus of just 5,000 frequent flier miles, for example.

Dirty Little Secrets

cases, you're better off utilizing one of your regular, low-interest bearing credit cards to buy that new TV, appliance, or computer, for example. If you don't absolutely need an additional credit card or store credit card to make a purchase, don't apply for it, no matter how many times the salesperson tells you how much money you could save.

Credit Card Lingo You Should Understand

Responsibly managing your credit card accounts involves understanding the terms and conditions imposed by the credit card issuer. To help you better understand credit card offers, here are a handful of terms you'll need to understand when comparison shopping for the best deals:

- *Annual fee.* This is a fee that's charged to the consumer every year for the privilege of having a specific credit card. Depending on the card, the annual fee might range from free to $150 per year. Ideally, you want a credit card with no annual fee. If the card has some type of reward for usage (such as airline frequent flier miles) or a cash-back bonus tied to it, an annual fee will often apply.
- *Annual percentage rate (APR).* This is a measure of the cost of credit, expressed as a yearly interest rate. This is the amount of interest you'll pay per year on your balance from purchases with that card. The APR could be different if you use the card for cash advances or transfer a balance from another card. This APR will remain in effect as long as you adhere to the terms of the card-holder agreement (or unless the card issuer sends you an updated or revised cardholder agreement.) If you fail to adhere to the terms described in the cardholder agreement, your interest rate will automatically switch to the much higher "default" interest rate.
- *Average daily balance.* This is the method the credit card issuer uses to calculate your payment due. Your average daily balance is

determined by adding each day's balance and then dividing that total by the number of days in a billing cycle. Your average daily balance is then multiplied by a card's monthly periodic rate, which is calculated by dividing the APR by 12.

■ *Balance transfer and balance transfer rate.* A balance transfer involves moving an outstanding balance from one credit card presumably to a lower interest bearing credit card in order to save money. (The balance would remain the same, but you'd then be paying a lower interest rate.) In order to entice consumers to utilize them, many credit card issuers offer a special incentive or teaser rate on balance transfers. Keep in mind, however, there are always additional fees associated with balance transfers, so understand the terms and conditions on both credit cards. The balance transfer rate is the interest rate you'll receive on the amount of money you transfer to the new card. If you're being offered a special teaser rate, determine what the rate will be when that teaser rate expires. Again, read the cardholder agreement carefully.

■ *Cardholder agreement.* This is the "fine print" associated with each credit card. It lists all of the terms and conditions, fees, and other information a cardholder should know pertaining to the use of that card. All fees, for example, will be listed within the cardholder agreement. In the future, the card issuer might issue a revised cardholder agreement that lists new fees or terms of usage. This updated or revised agreement will be mailed to you, but will often be disguised as junk mail.

■ *Cash advance fee.* Many credit cards are assigned an ATM PIN (personal identification number). This allows you to obtain cash advances using that credit card. Depending on the credit card issuer, there might be a flat fee associated with each ATM transaction, or you could be charged a percentage of the amount withdrawn (and possibly a flat fee as well). Withdrawing money from an ATM using a credit card is referred to as a "cash advance." Often, the portion of your outstanding credit card balance that's a result of

Dirty Little Secrets

cash advances will be charged a higher interest rate. Read the card-holder agreement associated with the credit card carefully.

■ *Charge-off.* This term indicates that a creditor does not expect a credit card debt to be paid and is listing it as such on the cardholder's credit reports. When this happens, the account is automatically closed, but the debt still exists and attempts will be made to collect it. Charge-offs look very bad on credit reports and hurt credit scores.

■ *Grace period.* For someone who makes a credit card purchase during a given month, the grace period is the time between the day of the purchase and when finance charges (interest, etc.) will start being added to the new balance. A grace period is typically between 15 and 30 days. If no grace period is offered, finance charges will accrue starting the moment a purchase is made with the credit card.

■ *Minimum payment.* This is the lowest amount a cardholder must pay to keep their credit card account from going into default (and being reported negatively to the credit reporting agencies). The minimum payment is typically about 2 percent of the outstanding balance. Remember, simply paying the minimum payment due each month will do very little to help lower your balance. This strategy will ultimately cost you more in interest charges. For your specific credit cards, use the Minimum Payment Calculator offered at the BankRate.com website (www.bankrate.com/calculators/managing-debt/minimum-payment-calculator.aspx) to see how much maintaining a positive credit card balance is costing you over time. For example, if you currently have an outstanding balance of $1,000 on a credit card that charges 18 percent interest, if you pay just the minimum monthly payment of 2 percent ($20) each month, it will take you 232 months (over 19 years) to be rid of your debt. In that time, you will pay $1,931.33 in interest. This does not include annual fees and other charges.

- *Over-the-limit fee.* If your charges and fees combined go over your credit card's credit limit in any given billing cycle, you will be charged this additional fee. Many credit card issuers charge a $39 over-the-limit fee.
- *Transaction fees and other charges.* These are extra fees you'll need to pay to use your credit card for certain types of transactions, such as ATM (cash advance) withdrawals, making a late payment, or going over your credit limit.
- *Telephone or online payment fees.* These are fees that are applied if you attempt to make a monthly credit card payment over the telephone or using the card issuer's website. These fees can be anywhere from $2.95 to $15.95 per payment. Even if you make a telephone or online payment, read the fine print to determine how quickly that payment will be posted to your account. Some card issuers still take up to 48 hours to post these payments to an account, so if you're close to your payment due date, you don't want to get hit with a late payment fee or have negative information reported to the credit reporting agencies.

Shop Around for the Best Credit Card Deals

Choosing the best credit card offer(s) to apply for requires careful shopping and comparisons between offers, especially if you have average or below average credit. While many credit card issuers (such as Capital One, First Premier, and Orchard Bank) will approve a credit card application from someone with low credit scores, the APR and fees associated with those credit cards will often be astronomical, while your credit limit will be very low.

For someone who has a low credit score and a poor credit history, in order to reestablish credit and begin rebuilding their credit score, it is often necessary to take advantage of less than attractive credit card offers for a few years. When you pursue this option, however, make sure you're able to carefully manage your credit card usage to stay current and avoid any excess charges (late fees, etc.).

In addition to contacting your local bank, credit union, or financial institution, to do your own credit card or secured credit card comparison shopping, point your web browser to one or more of these sites:

- https://creditcards.chase.com
- www.bankrate.com
- www.cardratings.com
- www.cardweb.com
- www.creditcards.com
- www.creditdonkey.com
- www.e-wisdom.com/credit_cards/chart.html

Managing Your Existing Credit Card Accounts

Use the "Credit Card Management Worksheet" in Figure 8-1 on page 189 to help you manage the credit card accounts you currently have.

 Credit Tip

As you're reviewing each of your credit card accounts, determine which, if any, of your cards have a high interest rate and a high balance. Could you benefit from opening another credit card account (one with no annual fee, a low interest rate, and an attractive balance transfer offer) and transferring your balance to that card? See "Take Advantage of Special Balance Transfer Offers," below for details on how to do this effectively to save money.

Take Advantage of Special Balance Transfer Offers

One of the ways credit card companies entice consumers to apply for their card is to offer extremely attractive balance transfer offers. Suppose you currently have a credit card that has an 18-percent interest rate and a $6,000 balance. Your minimum payment would be $150,

FIGURE 8–1: **Credit Card Management Worksheet**

Use this worksheet to help you manage your credit card debt, decide whether or not to consolidate your balances, and understand the cost of maintaining the debt over time. Fill out the form for each of your credit card accounts.

Credit Card #1 Account Information

Credit Card Name	
Account Number	
Interest Rate (APR)	
Credit Card Issuer's Phone Number	
Credit Card Issuer's Website Address	
(Username & Password)	
Credit Limit	$
Target Balance (35% of the Credit Limit)	$
Current Balance as of __/__/__	$
Monthly Minimum Payment	$
Actual Monthly Payment Made	$
Monthly Interest Paid	$

Credit Card #2 Account Information

Credit Card Name	
Account Number	
Interest Rate (APR)	
Credit Card Issuer's Phone Number	
Credit Card Issuer's Website Address	
(Username & Password)	
Credit Limit	$
Target Balance (35% of the Credit Limit)	$
Current Balance as of __/__/__	$
Monthly Minimum Payment	$
Actual Monthly Payment Made	$
Monthly Interest Paid	$

Dirty Little Secrets

FIGURE 8–1: **Credit Card Management Worksheet,** cont.

Credit Card #3 Account Information

Credit Card Name	
Account Number	
Interest Rate (APR)	
Credit Card Issuer's Phone Number	
Credit Card Issuer's Website Address	
(Username & Password)	
Credit Limit	$
Target Balance (35% of the Credit Limit)	$
Current Balance as of __/__/__	$
Monthly Minimum Payment	$
Actual Monthly Payment Made	$
Monthly Interest Paid	$

Credit Card #4 Account Information

Credit Card Name	
Account Number	
Interest Rate (APR)	
Credit Card Issuer's Phone Number	
Credit Card Issuer's Website Address	
(Username & Password)	
Credit Limit	$
Target Balance (35% of the Credit Limit)	$
Current Balance as of __/__/__	$
Monthly Minimum Payment	$
Actual Monthly Payment Made	$
Monthly Interest Paid	$

FIGURE 8–1: **Credit Card Management Worksheet,** cont.

Credit Card #5 Account Information	
Credit Card Name	
Account Number	
Interest Rate (APR)	
Credit Card Issuer's Phone Number	
Credit Card Issuer's Website Address	
(Username & Password)	
Credit Limit	$
Target Balance (35% of the Credit Limit)	$
Current Balance as of __/__/__	$
Monthly Minimum Payment	$
Actual Monthly Payment Made	$
Monthly Interest Paid	$

Credit Card Debt Summary Worksheet

Total Credit Card Debt	$
Total Monthly Minimum Payment (All Credit Card Accounts)	$
Total Actual Monthly Payment (All Credit Card Accounts)	$
Total Monthly Interest Paid	$
Percentage of Total Credit Actually Being Used (Example: 100 percent would mean all of your credit cards are maxed out.)	

of which $90 would go toward interest charges. If you don't add any new charges to the account but only pay the minimum payment each month, it would take 331 months to pay off the debt. Ultimately, you'd pay $8,615.25 extra in interest (plus a wide range of fees).

To reduce the amount of interest you'd pay and save money in the short and long term, you could seek out and apply for a

Dirty Little Secrets

new, low-interest-bearing credit card that offers an attractive balance transfer rate. This means that your current $6,000 balance could be moved to the new credit card and you'd take on the terms associated with the new credit card while immediately paying off the balance of the old card.

Taking advantage of special balance transfer offers is a "quick fix" to stop paying high interest rates on a small number of high-interest-bearing credit card accounts. However, if you're already in serious debt and have many high-interest credit cards that are maxed out (or close to it), you should consider a debt consolidation loan as a more viable long-term fix to your situation.

If you shop around and your credit scores are average or better, you can often find very attractive new credit card offers that allow for a no-cost or low-cost balance transfer with zero percent interest for the first six months to one year, for example. After that, normal interest charges apply. The benefit to transferring your high-interest balance to a zero-interest credit card, even if it's only for six months to one year, can be significant. On that existing $6,000 balance, used in the earlier example, you could save up to $90 per month in interest charges, even if you only make the minimum monthly payments.

When the zero-percent interest offer runs out, you could do another balance transfer to another credit card offering an attractive balance transfer offer, or you could make your regular monthly payments as you

 Credit Tip

To pay off your credit card debt even faster, one strategy is to transfer your existing balance to a zero-interest card (taking advantage of the introductory rate being offered), but keep paying the same minimum payments you were before on the old card (at least 2 percent of the balance). Instead of spending your newly found savings, apply it to paying off your existing debt faster.

have been. Hopefully, the new credit card you transferred your balance to will have a lower interest rate (after the special offer expires) than what you were paying before.

To initiate a balance transfer between credit cards, the first step is to analyze which of your current credit card accounts would make sense to transfer to lower interest bearing accounts. Take a look at the "Credit Card Management Worksheet" earlier in this chapter. Select the accounts that currently have the highest balances and the highest interest rates.

Next, start shopping around for new credit card offers that feature a zero-percent or extremely low interest rate for balance transfers. Carefully read the cardholder agreement from the new credit card company to ensure you understand all of the terms, how long the introductory offer lasts, and what happens when the introductory period expires.

You Should Know . . .

Depending on the credit card issuer, the special offer for an introductory balance transfer rate and the fees associated with making a balance transfer may be very different from the "Introductory APR" offered for new purchases made with the card. Make sure you know the APR, fees, and expiration dates associated with the balance transfer on the new credit card and that you have this information in writing.

When you've found a new credit card to apply for, fill out the application. Be sure to make it clear that you intend to take advantage of the balance transfer offer. You will need to provide details about your current credit card (and the balance you wish to transfer). Because this process could take several weeks, continue to make the minimum monthly payments on your existing credit card account. Keep paying

Dirty Little Secrets

the monthly minimums until you receive written notice that the balance transfer has been made and that your old card now has a zero balance. You may want to call the old credit card company to confirm the balance transfer has been made.

You Should Know . . .

In many cases, an attractive balance transfer offer only applies to new accounts. The balance transfer must be initiated at the time the credit card application is completed. Otherwise, the introductory balance transfer rate will not apply once the new account is opened and the card is issued. Read the "Terms and Conditions" of the credit card offer in addition to the cardholder agreement.

Keep detailed records of the date when the balance transfer took place and calculate when the special introductory offer will end. You may want to take additional action as you get closer to the expiration date before interest charges start accumulating on the outstanding balance.

The CreditCards.com website (www.creditcards.com), along with similar online services, allows you to quickly shop around for credit cards offering attractive balance transfer rates to new cardholders. As you search for the best offers, look for statements like "0% interest for up to 12 months on all purchases and balance transfers," "0% APR on balance transfers for 12 months," "This credit card features a low 0% introductory APR on balance transfers for up to 6 months" or "0.00% intro rate for 6 months on purchases and balance transfers."

Should You Consider Debt Consolidation?

A debt consolidation loan could allow you to take several high-interest-bearing credit card accounts and combine them into one lower interest bearing loan. If you have three, four, or more credit cards with high balances and a 10-percent, 15-percent, or even 20-percent interest rate associated with them, you could combine all of those balances into one loan that has an interest rate of less than 8 percent, for example, assuming you have a decent credit rating.

Not only will you immediately begin saving money each month in interest charges, you'll also zero out your credit card balances and now only have one payment to make each month. The trick is to either close your existing credit card accounts once they're paid off or have the discipline to stop using them altogether.

Debt consolidation loans are typically offered to homeowners. You can refinance your existing mortgage, apply for a second mortgage, or utilize a home equity loan or home equity line of credit to pay off your existing credit card debt and consolidate the balances. The potential drawback to this is that you're transferring your debt from an unsecured loan to a secured loan, where your home is being used as collateral. Thus, if you default on your loan, you could ultimately lose your house.

If, however, you're able to make the monthly payments on the refinanced mortgage or other debt consolidation loan, you will save significant money, plus be able to protect your credit rating. It's important to take this step early on—before you get so far behind with your credit card payments that your credit score takes a huge hit.

Keep in mind, a debt consolidation loan doesn't eliminate the debt altogether. It simply allows you to take multiple high-interest credit card balances, combine them into one lower interest loan, and then pay off that new lower interest loan over time while saving money each month on interest charges.

Make sure the fees, closing costs, and interest charges associated with the new loan allow you to achieve the financial objectives you're striving for and that you're not simply trading in one high-interest loan for another of a different kind.

An accountant, financial planner, or credit counselor will be able to help you determine if a debt consolidation loan is worthwhile based on your current financial situation, amount of debt, and credit rating.

What to Do if Your Credit Card(s) Get Lost or Stolen

Let's face it, people sometimes lose their wallet, misplace a credit card, or become the unwitting victim of a theft. Having your credit card, debit card, or ATM card information fall into the wrong hands is one of the biggest causes of identity theft, which can ultimately cost you a fortune. If one or more of your credit cards gets lost or stolen, or you believe your confidential account information is in any way compromised, it's vital that you call the credit card issuers immediately to report the problem, have the account suspended, and have a new credit card (with a new account number) issued to you.

At the same time, if the card or your confidential account information is stolen, contact the police department and fill out a crime report and contact all three of the credit reporting agencies. Then, for the next six to 12 months, watch your credit card statements and your credit reports carefully. Look for any unauthorized charges or new accounts being opened in your name that you didn't authorize.

If your credit card is lost or stolen, time is of the essence in terms of reporting the situation to the credit card issuer. The phone number to call is on the back of the credit card and should appear on your monthly statement. It's a good idea to keep all of the information from the Credit Card Management Worksheet (found earlier in this chapter) in a secure place at home so you will have it handy if you need to contact the credit card issuer.

In addition to calling the bank or financial institution that issued the credit card, you can also report a lost or stolen card to Visa, MasterCard, Discover, or American Express directly using the following phone numbers that are available 24 hours a day, seven days a week:

■ Visa Global Customer Assistance Center—(800) 847-2911

Dirty Little Secrets

- MasterCard Assistance Center—(800) 622-7747
- Discover—(800) 347-2683
- American Express Emergency Card Replacement—(800) 528-2122

While having to deal with a lost or stolen credit card can be a hassle, the good news is that you're only liable for unauthorized charges up to $50 per card, assuming you report the loss or theft in a timely manner. Some homeowners insurance policies cover lost or stolen credit cards.

One strategy for limiting your liability is to only carry one or two credit cards with you at any given time. Keep the rest of your cards in a safe or secure location within your home. Most people have no need to carry more than their ATM card, one credit card, and some cash with them in their wallet. Keep a detailed inventory of your wallet at home, which includes information about all of your credit cards, ATM cards, debit cards, membership cards, driver's license, insurance cards, etc. This way, if your wallet does get lost or stolen, you know exactly who to call and have all of your account or membership numbers handy.

Remember, someone doesn't need to possess the physical credit card in order to make unauthorized charges. It's important to keep your credit card number, expiration date, PIN, and the three-digit security number on the back of the credit card as private as possible. If you throw away old credit cards or statements, be sure to shred them so the numbers and confidential information is no longer legible. Also, never carry the PIN associated with your debit or credit card in your wallet. This is a number you should memorize.

Advice from Experts Representing Three Credit Card Comparison Websites

The following interviews offer advice about applying for and managing your credit cards, directly from three financial experts who have founded or represent popular, online-based credit card comparison websites.

Dirty Little Secrets

Meet Curtis Arnold, Founder of CardRatings.com

When shopping around for the very best credit card deals or for help understanding the terms of a particular credit card offer, the CardRatings.com website is an information-packed resource that was founded by Curtis Arnold.

While this is an advertiser-supported service (and some of the credit card issuers are sponsors of the website), Arnold explains that the editorial content and card reviews published throughout CardRatings.com are totally unbiased, allowing customers to learn about the best deals available to them based on their credit rating.

In this interview, Arnold offers advice to consumers about finding the best credit card deals available, as well as tips for properly managing your credit cards and keeping your debt under control.

What exactly is CardRatings.com?

Chris Arnold: "I founded CardRatings.com over a dozen years ago. At the time, I pioneered the concept of reviewing and rating cards for consumers. Our niche is helping consumers to level the playing field and make intelligent choices when shopping for credit cards. There is no one single credit card that is right for all consumers. We are a comprehensive source for comparing credit card offers. We also offer an open forum for consumers to discuss credit cards amongst themselves through free messaging boards. Plus, consumers can rate and review their own credit cards."

How do you rate the credit cards?

Chris Arnold: "We use a five-star rating system to review each credit card that's offered to consumers. All of the editorial on our site is unbiased, but we are advertiser supported and a for-profit company. Just because a particular credit card issuer advertises with us, they receive no preferential treatment in terms of our reviews or editorial coverage. There are and have been card offers that advertise with us that on the editorial side receive the lowest possible rating based on our review system. The only advantage these advertisers receive is that their offers are given featured placement on our site, but that's disclosed to consumers. They are, however, rated just like any other card.

"If you go to some of our competitors, they only list and review credit card offers from card issuers that advertise with them. Our database of reviews includes all credit card offers from all credit cards issuers, regardless of whether they advertise with us."

What type of information is in your credit card reviews that consumers can use?

Chris Arnold: "We break everything down into categories to make finding and understanding information easy for consumers. Most consumers have an inkling about the type of credit card they're looking for. We categorize our reviews based on card type. For example, you can easily compare all credit cards that allow you to earn frequent flier miles or cash-back rewards.

"Each card review is based on our five-star rating system. Each review lists the highlights of the card and its related terms and conditions, which are broken down into 35 to 40 different data points that can be compared between offers. In addition to comparing APRs, annual fees, and introductory rates, we also look at more obscure things, like the default rate and what actions actually trigger the default rate. This varies greatly from one card issuer to the next and can make a huge financial difference for the consumer.

"People assume that all cards and card offers are fairly similar, but this is very untrue. For example, we recommend secured credit cards for people looking to rebuild their credit, but the various secured credit card offers out there vary greatly. Between high interest rates, strict policies, and high fees, some of these cards don't represent good deals at all. We looked at one card that had competitive rates, slightly higher than normal fees, but that had a grace period of zero days. This was something that most consumers would overlook, until they made a payment just one day late and got hit with high fees. Most cards offer a 15- to 30-day grace period."

Dirty Little Secrets

What are some of the things people should look for when evaluating a credit card offer?

Chris Arnold: "In addition to the APR and annual fee, look at the default rate, the grace period, and at all of the fees that go along with using the card. Also, determine if the APR is a fixed rate or variable rate, because this, too, will impact how much interest you pay. In a declining rate economic environment, consumers will benefit from a variable rate offer. However, the opposite is true if interest rates in general are on the rise.

"Other things to look at are the balance transfer rates and the fees associated with the card offer. If an introductory rate is being offered, make sure you understand what this rate applies to, because it, too, varies greatly. In many cases, the advertised introductory rate does not apply to balance transfers or cash advances, for example.

"Credit card fees are definitely on the rise, and I see this as a trend that will continue. If you're looking at the fees associated with balance transfers, look for a card that caps its fee below $100. More and more card issuers are eliminating the cap on balance transfer offers. Get out your calculator and do some basic number crunching to determine if the balance transfer is worthwhile, even if you're going from a higher interest rate to a lower one. The savings might get lost once you pay the fees."

What are some of the other fees associated with credit cards that consumers should watch out for?

Chris Arnold: "Most people know about late fees and over-the-limit fees, but they don't realize how much these fees have recently gone up. Right now, they average about $39 each. What's equally important to know, however, is what triggers these fees. Some card issuers are more trigger happy than others. Some credit card issuers are strict about payment cutoff times, not just cutoff dates. For example, if your payment is due on a Friday at 2:00 P.M. (EST), but you make the payment that Friday at 2:05 P.M. (EST), you will get stuck with a late payment fee.

"Typically, if you get hit with just one late fee or over-the-limit fee, you can call up the credit card issuer and get that fee reversed. But they'll typically do this only once per year.

"The easiest way to avoid a late fee is to make your monthly payments online and to sign up for an automatic payment service from the credit card issuer, so you know that your monthly minimum will automatically be deducted from your checking or savings account to pay a card's minimum payment due. It's then your responsibility to make any additional payment you desire to lower your balance, but this will ensure you never accidentally skip a payment or are late. If you sign up for this type of automatic payment service, make sure you have ample funds in your checking or savings account, or your bank will charge you overdraft fees.

"If you'll be making your credit card payments online or over the telephone, determine if the credit card issuer will charge you for this privilege. I have seen card issuers charge up to $15.95 for making a single telephone payment, for example."

What are some of the biggest misconceptions people have about credit card offers?

Chris Arnold: "People pay too much attention to the marketing messaging associated with a credit card offer. These headlines are often captivating, but very misleading. If the offer says, 'Up to 5 percent cash back,' for example, the words 'up to' in the headline should tip you off that it's necessary to carefully read the fine print. Also look for phrases like, 'As low as zero percent.' In this case, it's the words 'as low as' that could be misleading.

"Pay attention to headlines in credit card ads or offers that are followed by an asterisk. This too is an indication that the offer does not apply to everyone. These offers are always based on someone's credit worthiness and are given only to people with an excellent credit rating.

"The biggest mistake consumers make is not properly reading and understanding the entire credit card offer. They simply apply for a credit card offer based on the ad's attractive headline. People should take the time to comparison shop. Don't fall for phrases like, 'You're pre-approved' that come in the mail. You can often find better deals and offers by searching them out online, for example.

"Even if you think you're being inundated with credit card offers in the mail, in reality, you're only seeing a small number of the actual credit card offers that are out there and available to consumers. Instead of adopting a reactive strategy by responding to credit card offers you receive in the mail, take a proactive strategy and seek out the very best credit card deals you can find, regardless of whether or not you're pre-approved for them. Often, the 'pre-approval' is simply a marketing ploy."

What should people understand about reward credit cards?

Chris Arnold: "Often, the actual cash value of the reward is significantly less than what you pay in annual fees, additional charges, and higher interest rates associated with carrying a balance on the card. Crunch the numbers before utilizing one of these rewards cards that allow you to earn frequent flier miles or cash back, for example. This applies especially if you'll be carrying a high balance on the card and paying a high interest rate plus fees on that balance.

"It's often cheaper to utilize a regular credit card that has no annual fee, low ongoing fees, and a very competitive interest rate to make your purchases. With the money you save on fees and interest charges, you can pay for your own airline ticket and still save money."

If someone encounters financial problems, what are the key things they should do in terms of communicating with their credit card companies?

Chris Arnold: "The first thing I recommend is picking up the phone and calling the card company. Be open and honest about your situation, but make it clear you'd also like to honor your debt. You'll typically discover the credit card company will work with you and be understanding of your predicament. Before you look at credit counseling, consolidation loans, bankruptcy, or your other options, try talking to the credit card company directly, as soon as you begin experiencing a problem. Don't wait or force the credit card company, or its collection agency, to chase after you to collect the debt.

"Because of the state of the economy, the credit card default rate amongst consumers is very high, which means the credit card issuers are losing money. If you demonstrate good faith when working with the credit card companies so they don't have to come after you, it's always in your best interest. They'll often offer you a payment plan or the option to settle for much less than the amount owed. To protect your credit rating, you always need to be proactive."

CreditDonkey.com also Allows Consumers to Compare Credit Card Offers

In this interview, Charles Tran, the founder of CreditDonkey.com, talks about the online credit card comparison service his company offers, and provides some additional tips related to shopping for and managing credit cards successfully.

Tran's professional background is in finance and technology. Instead of building platforms to help only institutional Wall Street traders, his goal is to help "Main Street" consumers better understand credit.

What does CreditDonkey.com offer to consumers?

Charles Tran: "CreditDonkey.com provides easy-to-understand financial tips to help consumers understand and take advantage of the best credit card deals available."

How is the CreditDonkey.com website supported?

Charles Tran: "CreditDonkey.com receives compensation from advertisers, such as credit card issuers (i.e., if a visitor is approved for a credit card)."

Dirty Little Secrets

In our current economy, has it become more difficult for a consumer to get approved for a credit card? How has this changed in recent years?

Charles Tran: "The credit landscape is improving. It's always darkest before the dawn. The U.S. suffered a major credit freeze in 2008, but the market has thawed over the last couple of years. Issuers are mailing more credit offers, especially to those with high credit scores."

What should people look for when choosing a credit card to apply for?

Charles Tran: "People who tend to carry a balance should look to minimize interest with a low-interest rate credit card. For those who pay off their balance in full each month, look for rewards that you'll actually redeem. There's no point accumulating buckets of airline miles if you don't plan to fly anywhere."

What FICO credit score does someone need to get approved for a good credit card offer?

Charles Tran: "Most good credit card offers require excellent credit. While 720 used to be a good rough estimate, now to get a leg up and the best deals, I would strive for 760 or even 770.

"For some credit offers, the spread between the low range of the APR and the high range can be as much as 10 percent."

What tips can you share for saving money on credit card fees?

Charles Tran: "The squeaky wheel gets the grease. It doesn't hurt to pick up the phone and call your credit card company. Ask about the interest rate. Or if you're having difficulties making payments, tell them so. It's in their interest to work with you."

What hidden fees/charges should someone look out for?

Charles Tran: "Balance transfer fees. Before the CARD Act of 2009, issuers had more flexibility in raising your rates on existing balance. Now, most issuers charge a fee, around 3 percent, to do a balance transfer."

Dirty Little Secrets

What are some of the pitfalls people encounter when applying for new credit cards?

Charles Tran: "It's best to make sure you're realistic about your credit worthiness and spending profile. If you have bad credit and the offer says it's only good for excellent credit, you'll most likely not get the card, plus you'll get an inquiry hit on your record.

"Another pitfall is the high thresholds with some of the bonus deals. If you don't usually hit the credit card's spending threshold, such as $3,000 in three months, it's best not to imagine you'll suddenly be able to rack up the charges just to qualify for the deal. The last thing you want to do is to incur unnecessary credit card debt."

Are there any really good deals when it comes to credit card rewards or cash-back cards? What should people look for or avoid?

Charles Tran: "Airline credit card deals are usually lucrative for travelers. Just before the holiday shopping season, some issuers ramp up the incentives on cash-back credit card sign-up bonuses. The gas station branded credit cards offering five cents off per gallon are not as hot of a deal now that gas is well over $3 per gallon."

If someone is trying to increase their credit score, what tips can you offer in terms of how they use their credit cards?

Charles Tran: "Avoid late payments. If you have difficulties making payments, contact your credit card company so they can work with you. Don't forget to check your credit report for mistakes."

What tips can you offer about balance transfers or consolidation?

Charles Tran: "Pay attention to all the different fees: balance transfer fees, annual fees, and minimum finance charges. While the CARD act offers you new safeguards, if you don't pay your bills on time, you might trigger a penalty that can skyrocket your interest rate. Read the fine print. Most issuers won't look kindly on a balance transfer from another credit card from the same issuer."

For zero-percent APR credit cards, what does that really mean? What happens after the intro period? What should consumers look out for?

Charles Tran: "Don't take teaser rates at face value. Make sure you know what the zero-percent introductory APR applies to. It could just be for balance transfers or for new purchases. You don't want to buy a new TV thinking your credit card offers zero percent interest, when the promo rate only applies to balance transfers."

How much over the minimum payment should someone pay each month to maintain or improve their credit rating?

Charles Tran: "It's important to make sure you pay at least the minimum payment on all your credit cards. Beyond that, you'll want to target any extra money to reduce the amount of overall debt you owe, first targeting the higher interest credit cards."

If someone has poor credit, what are the problems they run into when applying for subprime credit cards targeted to them?

Charles Tran: "With subprime credit cards, you'll have to watch out for high annual fees, 'account setup' fees, and counterproductive interest rates."

If someone winds up with a credit card's default rate, what recourse do they have?

Charles Tran: "Get back in the saddle and make it a habit to pay on time. Once you've triggered the default rate because you've been 60 days delinquent, you need to make sure you pay on time for six months consecutively. Then, the credit card companies will re-evaluate. If you've once again proven your reliability, your interest rate will be returned to its original rate within an additional 45 days."

Additional Advice From Ben Woolsey, the Founder of CreditCards.com

Ben Woolsey is the director of research for CreditCards.com, yet another extremely successful and reputable credit card comparison website that helps consumers find the best credit card deals and compare credit card offers from a wide selection of banks and financial institutions.

Woolsey's professional background is in banking, risk management, financial analysis, and credit card marketing. With more than two decades of experience, he founded CreditCards.com in 2004.

What does CreditCards.com offer to consumers?

Ben Woolsey: "CreditCards.com is a marketplace that connects consumers and credit card issuers in one place. Our service allows consumers to compare credit card offers and choose what's best for them. Consumers can compare bank offers and rates, and then apply securely online for the credit card they choose through our website, although they are not obligated to do this. Visitors to our website can simply use CreditCards.com as a learning tool. We offer a wide range of educational articles.

"The site is free to consumers. We do not collect any personal information from our visitors. If someone wants to apply for a credit card, we offer direct links to the websites of banks and financial institutions that accept online credit card applications.

"At CreditCard.com, we generate revenue when a consumer uses our website to apply for a credit card online from a bank or financial institution that we direct them to, and that consumer gets approved for the credit card they've applied for. At that point, we receive a referral fee from that bank or financial institution. The information on our website, however, is objective and unbiased. We never push any one credit card offer over another."

How does CreditCard.com evaluate credit card offers?

Ben Woolsey: "We use a fairly complex algorithm that evaluates a credit card offer based on a variety of criteria. We also track how consumers respond to different card offers and take into account the popularity of specific credit cards from that perspective. Thus, we try to showcase the more popular credit card offers that also offer the best deals to consumers."

Dirty Little Secrets

Based on the current economy, how difficult is it for consumers to get approved for a new credit card?

Ben Woolsey: "I would say that since 2011, after the recession, the credit card issuers have loosened up a bit and are approving applications these days at a fairly robust clip. The banks do not share with us their underwriting criteria. What we receive from them are their broad qualification guidelines, such as people with fair credit or excellent credit, and we categorize credit card offers based on those guidelines that are provided. We try to encourage consumers to avoid applying for credit cards they won't qualify for.

"We definitely see banks favoring consumers with higher credit scores in terms of their approvals. Fewer banks are offering subprime credit cards targeted to people with poor or below-average credit."

What should a consumer look for when evaluating a credit card offer?

Ben Woolsey: "The main thing is to understand how you'll be using the credit card, and then choose a credit card that caters to your needs. For example, if you'll be using a card for your everyday purchases and plan to pay off your balance quickly, a credit card with rewards or cash back associated with it will benefit you. Your requirements for a credit card will be very different if you're planning to carry a high balance over an extended period, for example. In this case, the low interest rate the card offers is important.

"There are also credit card offers specifically designed for consumers looking to transfer balances from another card. Thus, you want to choose the best card offer based on how the card will be used, and what your habits are as a consumer in terms of paying off your debt."

What should someone look for when choosing a credit card that offers rewards?

Ben Woolsey: "As long as you pay off the credit card debt quickly, credit cards that offer rewards can be lucrative for consumers. However, these cards in particular have to be used properly to generate the best results.

Dirty Little Secrets

Otherwise, the extra interest and additional fees you wind up paying will be far greater than the value of the reward you receive, whether it's cash back on purchases or frequent flier miles from an airline, for example.

"Not all rewards offered by credit cards have the same value. Cash back is easier to measure than the value of airline frequent flier points or merchandise you receive by collecting reward points, for example. Part of your decision about the type of reward credit card to apply for should be based on your spending level. If you don't spend a lot using a credit card and don't pay off that debt quickly, you may not benefit at all from the reward being offered.

"When comparing rewards, think of frequent flier miles or reward points as being worth one cent each. Figure out what you could receive in a typical year based on your credit card spending, and then determine if that reward is better than receiving cash back, or if paying a lower

---

You May Be Better Off Paying For Your Own Airline Ticket, Not Earning Miles

Instead of paying higher interest charges and an annual fee for a credit card that earns frequent flier miles for a particular airline, you may be better off obtaining a credit card that offers lower fees and interest charges, but no rewards. You can then use an online-based travel website, such as Hotwire. com, Priceline.com, Kayak.com, or Orbits.com to find low-priced airfares that you pay for outright. Keep in mind, most airlines require that you redeem at least 25,000 frequent flier miles to receive a free round-trip ticket within the United States, assuming seats are available and no blackout dates apply. Frequent flier miles also expire after a pre-determined period. So if you don't collect enough miles and they go unused for too long, you could wind up losing them altogether.

Dirty Little Secrets

interest rate and no annual fee for a credit card that does not offer rewards will work out better for you. If after you analyze the reward, if it's worth less than one penny per point, for example, you should probably seek out a better card offer."

What tips can you offer to consumers when it comes to keeping credit card fees low?

Ben Woolsey: "Apply for credit cards that have no annual fee and a competitive interest rate. If a credit card does have an annual fee associated with it, in most cases, the first year's fee is waived. The vast majority of credit cards being issued these days have no annual fee.

"If you're applying for a subprime credit card, because you have a below average credit rating, the initial fees you pay to obtain that credit card cannot be more than 25 percent of the initial credit line you're offered. However, in this situation, don't expect to receive a credit limit higher than $300 to $500. Instead of or in addition to charging account setup fees and other initial fees, the banks that offer subprime credit cards to consumers with poor credit typically have very high interest rates associated with their credit cards.

"Someone with poor credit might consider applying for a secured credit card to help them build up their credit rating. A secured credit card is different from a pre-paid credit card. The issuer of a secured credit card reports to the credit reporting agencies. Thus, if you manage your use of the secured credit card properly, you will be able to build up your credit rating over time."

How can someone utilize their credit cards to help boost their credit scores?

Ben Woolsey: "As a consumer, you always want to work toward building and maintaining a strong credit rating. The best thing you can do is manage your credit cards properly and responsibly. For example, don't just make the minimum payment on your credit cards each month. Instead, always strive to pay more than that minimum payment. Also, pay attention to your credit utilization in terms of how much of your overall credit you're using at any given time."

Dirty Little Secrets

Do you have tips for negotiating with a credit card issuer to get them to lower your interest rate when the account is in good standing?

Ben Woolsey: "This is always possible. However, whether or not they'll be open to doing it will depend on a variety of factors. First, keep in mind the credit card issuer probably does not want to lose your business. Your request for a lower interest rate will be taken more seriously if you maintain some type of balance on the card over time, so the credit card issuer is making money on you, but at the same time, you pay your bills on time and have proven to be a responsible consumer. Having a high credit score will also improve your chances.

"If you have good credit, but pay off your credit card bill every month and maintain a zero balance, that credit card issuer is not making money on you. In fact, they could just be breaking even or be losing money on you. In this situation, they're not apt to lower your interest rate upon request. However, if you have a pre-qualification offer for another credit card in hand that offers a better overall deal than what you have now, this gives you more leverage when trying to negotiate a better rate with the credit card issuer you're currently doing business with.

"Consumers should understand that for every new credit card a bank or financial institution approves, it costs them several hundred dollars for that lead. So, instead of losing you to another bank or financial institution, they may take steps upon your request to keep your business. Thus, the banks have a built-in motivation not to allow customers to walk out the door if the customer allows them to break even or is profitable for them. If as a consumer you're not profitable, however, they're more willing to see you go."

What's Next?

Your ability to obtain a car loan to purchase a new vehicle (or your ability to lease a car) will be strongly impacted by your credit rating. Because this is a high-ticket item, lenders will pay careful attention to

Dirty Little Secrets

information in all three of your credit reports, as well as utilize your credit scores to help make their approval or loan rejection decision. The next chapter offers tips and strategies for finding and obtaining the best rate on an auto loan.

CHAPTER 9

Finding and Obtaining
the Best Rate on
an Auto Loan

What's in This Chapter

- The importance of your credit rating and credit score when shopping for a car

- Determine the interest rate and financing terms you qualify for

- Vehicle financing options for people with bad credit

If you plan to purchase a new car, unless you'll be paying for your vehicle entirely using cash, you'll probably need to finance at least a portion of the purchase. This means applying for and obtaining approval for a car loan from the dealership's financing department, a bank or credit union, or from another lending source.

For people with a strong credit rating and above-average credit scores, obtaining approval for a car loan will be a fast and relatively effortless process, even in a tough economy. You will, however, want to shop around for the very best deal you can qualify for in order to save money over the life of the loan.

You Should Know . . .

If you're planning to finance your new or used vehicle, in most situations you'll need to make a down payment of between 10 and 20 percent, based on the negotiated price of the vehicle, so plan your finances accordingly. Dealerships often look to obtain higher down payments from people with below-average credit.

If your credit rating is shaky and your credit scores are below average, you will probably find it much more difficult to get approved for an auto loan, especially if you're trying to finance a new car through a dealership. While almost anyone with a steady job can get approved for some type of auto loan (since there are some lenders out there willing to approve auto loans for people who are high credit risks), someone with below-average credit will always pay significantly higher fees and interest for a loan they're ultimately approved for. Over time, this dramatically increases how much you'll pay for the vehicle.

Paying too much in interest and fees over the life of a loan is one way you could wind up being upside down on a loan if you attempt to sell your vehicle before it's totally paid off.

Being upside down on the loan means you owe more on the car (in terms of the outstanding loan amount) than the car is actually worth should you try to resell it. Thus, to sell the now-used vehicle, you'd need to pay the difference between how much you sell the car for and what you still owe.

Dirty Little Secrets

For example, suppose you owe $10,000 on your vehicle and still have three years left of monthly payments to pay off the loan, yet for whatever reason, you want or need to sell the vehicle immediately. Upon doing research, you determine that in its current condition, your car is only worth $6,000 if you sell it privately (as opposed to trading it in when purchasing a new car at a dealership).

Thus, you still owe $4,000 on your loan, above and beyond the $6,000 you could potentially sell it for. When you sell your vehicle, you'll still need to come up with $4,000 in cash. This means you're upside down on the loan, which is a very bad position to be in. Also, by having to pay a high interest rate and high fees on your loan, less of your money goes toward the loan's principal each month and more goes toward interest charges and fees.

What Happens If You Don't Pay?

If you fail to make your monthly car payments in a timely manner, the finance company will eventually repossess your vehicle. This means the car will be taken away from you and sold (often at auction for below market value). The amount the vehicle is sold for will go toward what you still owe on your loan.

Even after a vehicle gets repossessed, you will still owe the money on the loan, as well as repossession and legal fees. Plus, the repossession will appear negatively on your credit reports for seven years and reduce your credit scores significantly. You will also find it considerably more difficult to be approved for another auto loan (or other forms of loans or credit) if a repossession appears on your credit report.

Understanding Your Credit History

When you apply for auto financing, after completing your written application—which will request information about you, including your full name, address, and phone number; employer; income; and Social Security number—one of the first things the dealership, bank, financial institution, or potential lender will do is obtain copies of your credit reports, typically from all three credit reporting agencies (Equifax, Experian, and TransUnion). They'll also obtain your corresponding credit scores for each credit report or, depending on the financing company, may calculate its own scores using a proprietary formula.

Information displayed within your credit reports and your credit scores will play tremendous roles in the potential lender's approval process. Your credit reports list information about you and your credit history, including your relationship with your current and past lenders and creditors. By looking at your credit reports, a potential lender can determine if you have a history of paying your bills on time. They'll look carefully at how timely you were paying off past car loans (or your auto lease payments, if you've leased a car in the past).

Between 60 and 90 days before you start shopping for a new or used car, obtain copies of your credit reports and credit scores. Reviewing your credit reports and credit scores in advance will help you determine how much of a loan and what loan terms you'd potentially qualify for. Thus, you can further narrow down your options in terms of vehicle makes and models, based on what you can afford.

Each time you apply for a loan, credit card, or some type of financing, the potential lender will obtain copies of your credit report and credit scores (which is referred to as "pulling your credit reports") from one or more of the credit bureaus. When this is done, it's considered a "hard inquiry."

The number of hard inquiries made on an ongoing basis is tracked by the credit reporting agencies and will be held against you. In fact, each time a hard inquiry is made and a potential creditor/lender accesses your credit report, your credit score will temporarily decrease slightly.

When you're shopping for a car loan, however, the credit reporting agencies allow you to have your credit reports pulled as many times as needed, by as many different potential lenders as you wish, during a 30- to 45-day period (depending on the credit reporting agency).

Dirty Little Secrets

Thus, whether you have one inquiry or 10 relating to potential vehicle financing during that period, it will only count as one inquiry in terms of the impact on your credit scores. While this will vary, one hard inquiry will typically reduce your credit scores slightly for six months.

All of the inquiries made by car dealerships or lenders will appear on your credit reports immediately. So, if you've shopped at six different dealerships, and you're currently visiting your seventh dealership, that dealership will be able to tell where you've already shopped and whether or not you were approved for financing if you completed loan applications at the places you've already visited. The dealership's financing department (or financial institution) can hold this information against you when making their approval decision.

 **Warning**

Unless you're serious about purchasing a vehicle from a specific dealership, don't allow them to pull your credit reports and don't fill out a loan application, even if you're pressured to do so by the salesperson or finance manager.

When you apply for a more substantial loan, such as a car loan, the financing company will typically access all three of your credit reports, then use the corresponding middle credit score as a tool to help make an approval decision. If only two credit scores are available, which is not unusual, then the finance company will rely on the lower of the two credit scores.

Because your credit scores are considered an extremely reliable indication of your credit worthiness, they can be used to make auto loan decisions extremely fast. A creditor or lender can obtain or calculate your credit scores in a matter of seconds, then often make a loan or credit approval decision in just minutes.

Dirty Little Secrets

($) *Credit Tip*

When you apply for an auto loan at a dealership, ask for a copy of your three-in-one credit report that they acquire. This is a free way for you to obtain a copy of this report (because it's paid for by the dealership or auto finance company).

If you discover you need to improve your credit score before applying for an auto loan, or you apply for a loan that doesn't get approved, see Chapter 7 for tips and strategies you can implement that will help you boost your credit scores within three to 12 months, depending on how badly damaged your credit score is and what caused that damage.

Your Credit Reports and Credit Score Directly Impact Vehicle Financing

Because the information on your credit reports and your credit scores directly impact your ability to obtain financing and get competitive financing deals from the car dealership's financing department, your bank, a credit union, or another lender, it's important that you make every effort to ensure your credit scores are as high as possible *before* applying for the auto loan.

Keep in mind, changes or corrections to your credit reports can take up to 30 to 45 days to show up, so plan accordingly. For example, if you pay off one or more credit cards prior to applying for an auto loan, those credit card payments will take time to register on your credit reports, since the credit card companies typically report new data to the credit reporting agencies only once each month.

Once you know what your credit scores are, you can do some research online to figure out what the best loan rates are that you can qualify for. You'll find that the interest rates and loan fees charged by different lenders will vary dramatically, so knowing what you can potentially qualify for and then shopping around for the best deals can save you money.

The BankRate.com (www.bankrate.com) website is one online service that takes a national survey of auto loan lenders each week and reports its findings as to the best new and used car financing deals available.

Using this site, you can select your state, city, and loan term (36, 48, 60, or 72 months) and then choose new or used car financing in order to find current rates for someone with an average or excellent credit score. You'll probably discover that if between five and ten banks or finance companies are listed, there will be a discrepancy of up to two full percentage points in terms of the rates being offered. This is why shopping around for the best rates pays off.

The Bankrate.com website also offers an online auto loan calculator that can be used to calculate the monthly payment on a loan if you provide the loan amount, term (number of months), and interest rate.

 **Warning**

Never just accept whatever loan offer a car dealership makes. Try negotiating the rate and terms. You might be able to get a more competitive rate or better loan terms working with a local bank, credit union, or another lender, for example. Credit unions tend to offer very competitive rates, especially to people with an above average or excellent credit rating.

Credit unions also offer car loan refinancing options, so if you wind up with a car loan that has a high interest rate now, but you work toward improving your credit rating over the next six months, during the life of the loan, you can refinance in order to get better terms and save money.

($) *Credit Tip*

To ensure you'll qualify for the best rates and experience the least amount of hassle getting approval for an auto loan without needing a co-signer, work on getting your credit score to an "above average" classification. Your chances of having an auto loan approved will increase if you can make a 20 percent (or more) down payment on the vehicle (thus financing 80 percent or less of the purchase price).

Shop Around for the Best Vehicle Financing Options

When it comes to shopping around for the best deals—after you've selected the make and model vehicle you're interested in purchasing and you've selected a dealership you'd like to work with—you can shop around for the best rates by completing a loan application with the dealership. Most dealers have relationships with many lenders and can quickly shop around to get your loan approved.

However, when you finance through a dealership, you are *not* automatically guaranteed to be offered the lowest interest rate and loan fees you'd qualify for. You'll probably want to negotiate a bit with the dealership, and then contact one or more banks, credit unions, or other lenders for a second or third opinion.

If you already know your credit scores, most lenders will be able to offer you a ballpark figure in terms of the loan interest rates they offer over the telephone, without you having to complete a full application. However, no financing company will guarantee a rate until they actually process your application and can offer you an approval.

You can (and should) also shop around for auto financing via the internet. There are many services, including Bankrate.com, that allow you to find the best rates from local banks and lenders, then complete an online application.

To begin shopping for competitive auto financing on the internet using any search engine (such as Google or Yahoo!), enter the search phrase "Auto Loan." If you have low credit scores, you can use the search phrase "Bad Credit Auto Financing."

Some of the car and auto financing websites worth checking out include:

- American Automobile Association—www.aaa.com
- Autobytel—www.autobytel.com
- AutoLoan123—www.autoloan123.net
- Capital One Auto Finance—www.capitaloneautofinance.com/Application/apply.html
- Cars Direct—www.carsdirect.com/auto-loans
- Cars.com—www.cars.com/finance
- E-Loan—www.eloan.com
- Kelley Blue Book—www.kbb.com
- Lending Tree—www.lendingtree.com/auto-loans
- Smart Car Loan—www.smart-car-loan.com
- Wells Fargo Auto Loans—www.wellsfargo.com/autoloans
- Yahoo! Autos—http://autos.yahoo.com/car-finance

Vehicle Financing Options for People with Bad Credit

If you know you have poor credit, you have four main options when it comes to obtaining auto financing. These include:

1. Taking steps to improve your credit scores *before* applying for a loan. How long it'll take to see a dramatic increase in your credit scores will depend on what type of negative information currently appears on your credit reports and what steps you take to improve negative information. This option might result in your having to wait for six months or more to purchase or lease a vehicle.

2. Accepting the fact that you'll be paying a significantly higher interest rate (plus higher fees) if you can find a lender who will

Dirty Little Secrets

approve your loan immediately based on your credit scores. You'll also most likely need to make at least a 20-percent down payment on the vehicle. The greater a down payment you're willing and able to make, especially if you have below average credit, the better your chances of getting a loan approved.

3. Finding someone with good credit to co-sign your loan. This means the co-signer will take responsibility for the loan if you default on the payments. Down the road (no pun intended) making late payments or defaulting on the loan will damage your credit scores as well as your co-signer's.

4. Saving up and purchasing a new or used car using cash for the entire purchase (so no financing is needed.) You may find that based on your current financial situation, it makes more sense to purchase an inexpensive used car right now. You can then work toward improving your credit scores and purchase a new vehicle (using financing) in six to 24 months.

Now that you're aware of your current credit situation and can determine whether or not you'll qualify for a loan, you can focus on deciding if purchasing a new or used car is in your future, or if it makes more sense to lease a new vehicle.

What's Next?

While getting approved for an auto loan becomes more difficult in a poor economy, the recent and very serious problems within the mortgage industry has made it extremely difficult for people with average or even above average credit to get approved for a mortgage (or to get refinancing of their mortgage approved). The next chapter deals with qualifying for a mortgage in a tough economy.

CHAPTER 10

Finding and Obtaining
a Mortgage

What's in This Chapter

- Challenges you might face getting approved for a mortgage in today's economy

- Finding a reputable mortgage broker or lender

- Pre-qualification versus pre-approval

- The pre-qualification process

Pre-Qualifying for a Mortgage Makes Sense

There are many reasons to pre-qualify and obtain pre-approval for a mortgage prior to finding and choosing your new home and then making an offer. The most important reason is that this process will help you determine exactly how much you can afford. Plus, it will allow you to narrow your home search based on financial scenarios that make sense for you.

When you begin searching for a home and potentially working with a Realtor® or real estate agent to find the ideal home (or condominium), some of the very first questions you'll need to answer about the potential home itself are:

- Where would you like to live?
- What type of home are you looking to purchase, in terms of size and features?
- How much can you afford?

From a financial standpoint, you'll also need to determine:

- How much of a down payment you can afford (plan on at least 20 percent of the home's purchase price; more if your credit rating is not above average)
- What your current credit rating and credit scores are
- Whether you'll be approved for a mortgage based on your own credit rating as it is right now, or whether you'll need to improve it before you'll get a mortgage approval
- How much of a mortgage you can qualify for
- In addition to being able to make the mortgage payments, will you be able to afford all of the costs associated with home ownership, such as utilities, insurance, real estate taxes, home maintenance, etc., as well as your ongoing living expenses?

Based on your own personal or family budget and by pre-qualifying for a mortgage, you'll be able to calculate a price range for the home that you know you can afford before you start your real estate search.

Dirty Little Secrets

There Are Many Reasons to Pre-Qualify for a Mortgage

Several important factors go into determining how much you can afford when looking for a new home, including the size of the mortgage you're qualified to obtain based on your credit rating, income, savings, current debt, and employment situation. By pre-qualifying for a mortgage, you begin the process of searching for a home and potentially working with a mortgage broker or lender knowing how much you can afford, based on the size of the mortgage you qualify for. Knowing this also allows you to easily calculate how much of a down payment you'll need to make in order to help pay for the home you ultimately choose, based on the type of mortgage you'll be applying for.

Pre-qualifying for a mortgage will help determine where you can live and the size of your home, for example, plus save you time because you won't look at properties you simply can't afford.

You might want to move into a $375,000 home with a large front lawn and state-of-the-art appliances. In reality, however, you might only qualify for a $200,000 mortgage. If you only have a down payment of $25,000, the maximum price of the home you should be searching for is $225,000, not $375,000. Knowing this from the beginning of your search will help you pinpoint what you can afford, what neighborhoods

---

You Should Know . . .

The size of the mortgage you pre-qualify for (plus any money from savings, for example, you plan to use as a down payment) is the maximum you can spend on the home. It is not, however, the price you should agree to pay. Always negotiate with the seller for the lowest purchase price possible. Just because you qualify for a certain size mortgage doesn't mean you need to spend that entire amount.

Dirty Little Secrets

you can afford to live in, and allow you to find the most suitable home within those parameters.

Pre-qualifying for a mortgage also gives you greater negotiation leverage with potential sellers, especially if you're bidding against other potential buyers who aren't pre-qualified.

By becoming a pre-qualified buyer, sellers know you potentially have the necessary funds available to purchase the home. The chances of your financing falling through are greatly reduced. This is important if the seller is looking to sell their home quickly and can't afford to waste time with potential buyers who don't have the finances available to purchase the home.

Once you pre-qualify for a mortgage, you can still shop around for the best financing deals and continue to explore your mortgage

Warning

Even if you pre-qualify for a specific loan amount, it's important to develop a realistic budget for yourself and determine, in advance, that you can actually afford to take on that mortgage and the expenses associated with it. Remember, becoming a homeowner requires more than just making your monthly mortgage payments on time. There are also real estate taxes, homeowner's insurance, and ongoing home repair/maintenance fees to consider. There may also be monthly homeowners association fees if you're moving into a housing community or condominium complex, for example.

Make sure you'll be able to afford these ongoing expenses, plus have available funds needed for furniture, landscaping, new appliances or any other home improvements you might want or need to make. Oh, and there are still day-to-day living expenses, car payments and many other costs to consider.

options. Plus, before you actually begin searching for a home, you'll be able to determine if you need to take steps to improve the information on your credit reports (such as correcting inaccuracies or paying off credit card bills) in an effort to boost your credit scores and qualify for better mortgage rates.

Finding a Mortgage Broker or Lender

In three words, the trick to obtaining the best mortgage is to *shop, compare,* and *negotiate* with the lender or broker you ultimately decide to work with. That lender could be a local bank, a credit union, a mortgage company, or some other type of financial institution. As you'll discover, various organizations (such as mortgage brokers) specialize in different types of mortgage products that are suitable for different types of borrowers.

People with below-average credit will have an extremely difficult time getting approved for a mortgage these days, even if you have a steady, good paying job. The banks and lending institutions have become very strict in terms of their approval guidelines, especially when it comes to subprime loans (loans for people with poor credit). An experienced mortgage broker or lender will be able to help you quickly determine if you'll be able to qualify for any type of mortgage before you invest too much time and effort into the process.

These days, it's essential to boost your credit scores as high as possible before you start shopping for a mortgage and going through the approval process. With less than "above average" credit, you may need to find a co-signer with excellent credit, be able to make an extra-high down payment, and/or look into other options.

Dirty Little Secrets

Virtually all lenders are happy to work with people with excellent credit and a steady, good paying job. If, however, you don't fall into this category (and plenty of people don't), you may need to spend some extra time shopping around for the best lender or mortgage broker to work with—one that specializes in subprime loans—in order to obtain an approval and receive the best possible rates and overall deal.

What Is a Mortgage Broker?

Instead of actually loaning money, a mortgage broker serves as the middleman between the borrower (that's you) and the lender (a bank or financial institution). Most mortgage brokers represent multiple lenders and will work to find a lender for you that's most apt to approve your application, based on your unique financial and credit situation.

Mortgage brokers can typically offer a broader range of mortgage products than a traditional bank. It's important to understand, however, that while a mortgage broker will work to land your business, they are not obligated to give you the best rates. Thus, it's your responsibility to shop around, determine what you should be able to qualify for in terms of mortgage rates and terms, and then negotiate with the broker.

Mortgage brokers earn a fee for the services they provide. These fees may be separate from the fees the actual lender charges. Be sure to ask how the mortgage broker you choose gets compensated, and consider those fees when shopping around. Negotiating with a mortgage broker to obtain the lowest possible fees and interest rate is expected.

Over 80 percent of the home buyers in the U.S. work through a mortgage broker. Back in 2005, there were over 20,000 mortgage brokerage companies in America. However, due to recent troubles in the mortgage industry and extremely high foreclosure rates nationwide, a significant percentage of mortgage brokers have gone out of business or have altered the focus of their business.

Due to the recent upheaval in the mortgage industry and the recession that took place in the United States, obtaining an approval for a new mortgage has become more difficult than ever, especially if you don't have an excellent credit rating, a significant down payment, and a steady job.

A typical mortgage broker will handle these tasks:

- Assess the borrower's current circumstances and finances and evaluate their credit rating and employment situation (as appropriate).
- Help the borrower find the best mortgage product to fit their needs, based on current rates and offerings by various lenders. This includes educating the borrower about the various financing options available to them.
- Assist the borrower in getting pre-approved for a mortgage with one of their lenders.
- Gather all documentation (bank statements, pay stubs, tax returns, etc.) on behalf of the lender.
- Work with the borrower to complete the application form(s) for the mortgage.
- Submit the application and materials to the lender
- Work as the liaison between the borrower and lender throughout the application processing and closing process.

Choosing Your Lender or Broker

Finding a mortgage broker or lender to work with is relatively easy. They advertise everywhere! The trick, however, is finding someone who is reputable, extremely knowledgeable, and who is willing to work with you and invest the necessary time to help you get the best deal possible based on your personal situation.

To accomplish this, utilizing a referral from a friend, neighbor, co-worker, or relative is always a good option. Otherwise, you can find lenders and mortgage brokers online; advertising in newspapers, on radio, or on TV; in the Yellow Pages; or through a referral from your real estate agent.

Dirty Little Secrets

If you're a first-time homebuyer, seriously consider participating in a free workshop offered by the U.S. Department of Housing and Urban Development (HUD). These workshops are offered throughout the country on an ongoing basis. To learn more, call (800) 569-4287, or visit this website: www.hud.gov/buying/localbuying.cfm.

The Mortgage Bankers Association (MBA) (www.mortgagebankers. org) is a professional trade association comprised of lenders and mortgage brokers. The organization publishes guidelines and requirements for how members should do business with their clients (borrowers).

The "MBA Best Practices" guidelines can be found on the organization's website. It's a good idea to review them to ensure your mortgage broker is adhering to them if he or she is a member of this organization. These guidelines relate to compliance with state and federal laws, training, equitable treatment of clients, pricing, advertising and marketing guidelines, and other factors that can impact a borrower.

Before committing to work with a lender or broker, check them out with your local chamber of commerce and/or the Better Business Bureau (www.bbb.org). It's important to understand that just because a lender or broker advertises the best rates or makes appealing statements in their ads, those statements might not be true, or what's offered might not be best suited to meet your own needs.

You'll often find that the brokers and lenders that advertise the most and have the catchiest radio and TV jingles also charge the highest

Warning

Avoid the bait-and-switch tactics used by some mortgage brokers. They advertise a very low interest rate or a very appealing financing deal, but when you apply, you're told that you don't qualify, but that an alternative, less attractive mortgage option is available.

fees and don't necessarily offer the personalized service you'll want and need as a homebuyer.

There are many free online mortgage comparison-shopping sites. When you utilize one of these services, you'll be required to enter all of your pertinent personal and financial information on the site's forms. Those details will then be forwarded to a handful of potential brokers or lenders who will pre-qualify you and compete for your business.

If you then choose to utilize one of these mortgage comparison websites, you can expect to be bombarded by telemarketing phone calls, emails, and direct mail from potential lenders and brokers who will solicit your business. While this can make shopping for the best deal easier, it can also get frustrating and annoying, since some brokers and lenders will be relentless in trying to contact and do business with you.

Several popular online-based mortgage comparison shopping sites include:

- Bankrate.com—www.bankrate.com
- Free Rate Update—www.freerateupdate.com
- LendingTree.com—www.lendingtree.com
- LowerMyBills.com—www.lowermybills.com
- Mortgage Marvel—www.mortgagemarvel.com

Important Considerations When Choosing a Lender or Broker

As you choose your lender or broker, your four primary concerns should be:

1. Ensuring that the broker can actually get your loan on time and has a good working relationship with their lenders. You don't want your deal to fall through because the broker misrepresented their ability to get the loan approved and closed within a pre-determined period of time.
2. The lender or broker has competitive rates.

Dirty Little Secrets

3. The lender or broker is willing to offer you the best possible deal you qualify for, regardless of how much they earn in commissions and fees off of the transaction.

4. The lender or broker you choose is knowledgeable and trustworthy.

Work Closely with Your Loan Officer

A loan officer is the person who works for the mortgage broker and is your primary contact person throughout the application, approval, and closing process. Their job is to work with you, the borrower, and help you choose a mortgage product, complete the mortgage application, get approved by the lender, and prepare you for the closing. The loan officer will often work on a commission basis, based on the mortgage product he or she sells.

The mortgage broker you work with should never encourage you to provide false information or inaccurate financial documents to the lender, nor should you be encouraged to leave signature lines blank on any application or loan forms. The mortgage broker should be open and honest when explaining all of the fees associated with the loan, including what they charge for their services, and everything should be put in writing. Never simply trust what a mortgage broker tells you.

Fewer Mortgage Options Are Available These Days

Even for people with excellent credit, an available down payment, and a steady job, the types of mortgages available these days have diminished. While dozens, perhaps hundreds, of different mortgage products were available just a few years ago, many of these mortgage types are no longer available because lenders are no longer funding them.

Banks, credit unions, savings & loans, and other types of financial institutions offer only their own mortgage products. As a result, their offerings and ability to negotiate rates may be limited due to these limitations and strict guidelines.

Because a mortgage broker represents multiple lenders, there's a bit more flexibility in terms of what they offer and charge. When you start shopping around for a mortgage, you'll quickly discover that different lenders and mortgage brokers will quote you different prices and rates for what appear to be the same type of loan. When comparing offers from lenders or brokers, make sure you know the loan amount, loan term, and the type of loan, so you can easily compare the quoted fees and rates.

Other things you'll need to determine when evaluating an offer from a lender or broker is whether or not the rate is fixed or adjustable. If you're taking on an adjustable-rate mortgage and interest rates go up, so will your monthly payment. Meanwhile, depending on the terms of your loan, your monthly payment might not drop, even if interest rates fall.

Be sure to determine the loan's annual percentage rate (APR). The APR takes into account the interest rate and points, brokers' fees, and other fees associated with the loan. Points are fees you may pay to the lender or broker. Typically, the more points you pay, the lower your interest rate on the mortgage will be. When a mortgage lender or broker is describing a product to you, ask that the points be quoted to you as a dollar amount, so you can easily determine what you're responsible to pay.

Fees are another component of a mortgage you need to be concerned about. As you'll discover, when you take on a mortgage, a wide range of fees are involved. When you begin working with a broker or lender, be sure to ask for a summary of all fees you'll be responsible for. Otherwise, at the closing, you could be surprised at how much you're actually paying and realize you could have negotiated those fees down if you had learned about them sooner. Some of the fees you're responsible for must be paid when you actually apply for the mortgage. Other fees will be due at your closing or built into the loan.

Another question to ask the lender or broker early on is what size down payment will be required to get the mortgage application

Dirty Little Secrets

You Should Know . . .

Interest rates for mortgages change daily. The deal you discuss on a Monday, for example, most likely will not still be available on the following Thursday or Friday, unless you take steps to lock in the rate with the lender or broker. Likewise, the same loan could be offered at different rates to different people, based on their credit rating and credit scores.

---

approved. Depending on the type of mortgage, the down payment required will typically be 20 percent (or more) of the purchase price. Of course, the more money you offer as a down payment, the lower the amount of your mortgage will be. Thus, your monthly payment will be lower. Until recently, mortgages were available that required zero down payment or a small down payment, but many of these mortgage products are no longer available, even to people with excellent credit.

Money-Saving Strategies for Mortgage Shoppers

When shopping for a mortgage and evaluating offers, consider the overage. This is the difference between the lowest available rate for a mortgage and the rate you're actually quoted and agree to. When an overage occurs, the broker or lender will keep this amount as "bonus" compensation, so it's not in their best interest to bring it to your attention. An overage can be the result of how the points, fees, and/or interest rate are quoted and calculated.

It's important to review the fees charged by the lender or broker early on and negotiate to have as many of them waived or reduced as possible in order to save money. Not all fees can be waived or reduced, but many of them can. It's these fees that often determine the profit the lender or broker will receive. Once you negotiate all of the fees, make sure that no additional fees are added and that your interest rate or the points you're required to pay don't increase.

After you've reached an agreement with the lender or broker, it's in your best interest to obtain a written lock-in to ensure what you've agreed to will be binding. The lock-in should list the rate you've agreed to, a summary of fees, and the period the lock-in will last. At this point, you may be charged a fee to lock in your rate. If rates rise before your closing, you will be protected. However, unless you negotiate this in advance, if rates fall, you could wind up paying a higher rate.

If your credit is average or below average, you may be forced to work with a high-cost lender who will charge you extra fees and offer you a higher interest rate, because you represent more of a risk based upon your credit rating. If you have unusual circumstances relating to your personal finances and credit rating, it's important that your lender or mortgage broker understand your situation before recommending specific mortgage products to you.

Realistically, if your credit rating is below average (or even just average, for that matter), getting approved for a mortgage will be extremely difficult, so you might have to contact several mortgage brokers and complete several pre-approval or full applications before actually getting approved. If you do get rejected for a mortgage, determine why before re-applying, or you could be wasting your time.

One way to potentially improve your chances of getting the best rates is to review your credit reports early in your decision-making process and take steps to correct any inaccuracies or outdated information that could be negatively impacting your credit scores. If you have negative information on your credit reports that you know is hurting your credit scores, consider paying off your creditors and/or negotiating with them to have the negative information modified or removed.

While your choices may be more limited than they were one or two years ago, there are still several different types of mortgage products available, such as fixed-rate loans, adjustable-rate loans, and non-traditional loans. Sitting down with a mortgage broker who will explain the differences between these mortgage products will help you choose which one best meets your individual needs. Once you determine this, you can shop around to find the best possible rates by speaking with several lenders or brokers.

Pre-Qualification vs. Pre-Approval

When initially approaching a potential lender, it's important to understand the difference between being pre-qualified for a mortgage and pre-approved. The pre-qualification process is a fast, informal process that involves you providing the potential lender with basic financial information (without documenting it). Based on the information you provide, the lender will give you a ballpark figure in terms of the amount of money you'd be eligible for if you were to formally apply for a mortgage.

The borrower can use the pre-qualification process to determine what price range they can potentially afford when looking for a home. The pre-qualification process can be done over the phone, in person, or online. It takes just a few minutes, but it's not binding.

A pre-approval requires the potential lender to gather financial information from you, evaluate your credit reports (and credit scores), and review a variety of financial documents (such as tax returns, pay stubs, bank statements, and W-2 forms). If you meet the qualification requirements for the mortgage you're interested in, the lender will offer you a commitment to grant you the loan, provided that when you actually complete the full application, you continue to meet the same qualification requirements. Some lenders will put an expiration date on a pre-approval. This process takes a bit longer to complete and will require you to fill out forms and provide financial documentation, such as tax returns and pay stubs.

Keep in mind, if you take on additional debt, such as a car loan, or lose your job after the pre-approval (but before your full mortgage application was completed, processed, and approved), there's a good chance your mortgage application will not be approved.

Dirty Little Secrets

Make sure that when you begin working with a potential lender, you understand what you're being offered in terms of a pre-qualification or pre-approval, how long it will remain in effect, and what limitations there are. Remember, everything you agree to should be put in writing.

The Pre-Qualification Process

The pre-qualification process for a mortgage begins with a bunch of questions that will be basically the same no matter what type of lender or broker you go to. Once you begin the process, based on the information you provide and your credit worthiness, the lender will be able to offer you different types of mortgage options and help you choose one that's affordable and will meet your needs.

Remember, by pre-qualifying for a mortgage, you are not actually completing the full mortgage application. This process is simply to give you an idea of how much of a mortgage and the type(s) of mortgage products you'd qualify for.

Once you find a lender, some of the pre-qualification questions you'll be asked include:

- Your full name, current address and phone number(s)
- Will you have a co-borrower? If so, you'll need to provide the co-borrower's full name, current address, and phone number(s)
- What state are you looking to buy a home in?
- What type of property are you buying (single-family home, condo, etc.)?
- How will you be using your new property (as a primary residence, vacation home, etc.)?
- Are you a first-time buyer?
- What is your gross monthly income (before income taxes) for yourself and your co-borrower (your spouse, if applicable)? Your income should include your base pay, bonuses, commissions, tips, overtime, child support (received), retirement income (if applicable), annuity income (if applicable), alimony

Dirty Little Secrets

(if applicable), and any other money you receive or earn on a regular basis.

■ Will you be documenting your income for the lender by providing tax returns, pay stubs, etc., or will you state your income but not provide documentation?

■ How much cash (from all sources, including savings, investments, gifts, and assets that can be converted into cash) do you have for your down payment and to cover closing costs? Approximately what percentage of the purchase price does this down payment represent? (For most types of mortgages these days, being able to make at least a 20-percent down payment based on the purchase price is one of the qualifications you'll need to meet to obtain the loan.) Your down payment must come from savings, earned income, an inheritance, or be a gift. You *cannot* borrow the down payment as a loan that needs to be paid back.

■ How would you define your credit history (excellent, good, average, below average, or poor)?

■ What is your approximate credit score? (If you don't know this, the lender/broker will obtain your credit reports and corresponding credit scores.)

■ Your current debt, including auto loans, student loans, credit cards, child support, alimony payments, other mortgages, etc.

■ Your current employment situation (including length of employment, job title, etc.)

Based on the information you provide during the pre-qualification process, your debt ratio will be calculated. This is the amount of debt you have compared to your income. Many lenders require borrowers to have a debt ratio within a pre-determined range in order to qualify for their mortgage products. Again, they've become much stricter about approval requirements since 2008.

Based upon your current income, an analysis of your current debt, and your estimated down payment, your lender/broker will be able to provide you with the maximum mortgage amount you could qualify for.

Once you provide the necessary information, including answers to the previous questions, the pre-qualification process will often take just minutes. This process is often referred to as a "pre-qualification analysis." It is meant to provide you with a ballpark figure that you could qualify for in terms of a mortgage. As you provide this initial information to the potential lender, don't exaggerate the numbers. This will result in you being given a false indication of what you can afford and ultimately hamper your ability to actually get approved for the mortgage once you apply.

The pre-qualification analysis will often remain valid for between 30 and 90 days, depending on the lender. Until you provide detailed information to the lender and actually complete a full application, however, it is not guaranteed that you'll actually be approved for the mortgage or that you will receive the interest rate being discussed.

Actually completing a full mortgage application will require at least one to two hours of your time, plus involve you providing the lender with a variety of financial documents, including tax returns, W-2's, pay stubs, and bank statements.

You Should Know . . .

There should be no cost or commitment required when you begin working with a lender to participate in a pre-qualification analysis. Based on the results of this analysis, the potential lender should be able to offer you a variety of mortgage products that you'd qualify for. There will, however, be a mortgage application fee of several hundred dollars if you choose to initiate the mortgage application process.

Dirty Little Secrets

If you choose to pursue a pre-approval (as opposed to a pre-qualification), you'll need to provide your Social Security number, along with your co-borrower's Social Security number, to begin the pre-approval process, and also agree to allow the potential lender/broker to obtain your credit reports from the three credit reporting agencies.

It's important to understand that a variety of different mortgage products are out there, beyond a traditional 15-, 20-, or 30-year fixed-rate mortgage offered by a bank. Each type of loan and each individual lender have different sets of qualifications and approval guidelines. Even if you don't qualify for one type of mortgage, you may qualify for another. The trick is to work with one or more potential lenders/brokers to learn about all of the potential options available to you.

Remember, a loan officer working for a mortgage broker is a middle person between you and the lender(s) he or she represents. The mortgage broker is typically not the actual lender nor does the mortgage broker make the final approval decision for the loan.

You're Pre-Qualified or Pre-Approved, Now What?

Now that you've found a mortgage broker, bank, financial institution, or lender to work with and you have a general idea of a mortgage you'd actually qualify for, you can begin searching for the perfect home.

For first-time homebuyers, it's easy to get confused or overwhelmed by the different types of mortgage products out there. You'll also need to figure out how to obtain the best financing deal possible, find the perfect home, and negotiate the best purchase price with the seller.

Knowing you're not a real estate expert, learn as much as you can yourself, but be sure to surround yourself with a lender/broker, real estate agent, and real estate attorney whom you trust and who can offer their guidance as you work your way through this entire process. It's always okay to ask lots of questions and to check and re-check all of the information that's provided to you.

Never allow yourself to be tied to a mortgage or pushed into purchasing a home that you simply can't afford, regardless of whether or not you find a lender willing to approve you for the mortgage needed to purchase the home. It's your responsibility to calculate your own budget and perform some of your own financial calculations to ensure you're not taking on too much debt or overextending yourself financially in the short or long term. A mortgage is typically a 15-, 20-, or 30-year commitment. Failure to meet that commitment down the road could result in a foreclosure and/or put you in serious debt.

What If Your Application Gets Rejected?

Unfortunately, with so much turmoil in the mortgage industry, applications that would have easily been approved a few years ago are now being rejected. People with less than perfect credit are finding it harder and harder to get approved for a mortgage.

If your mortgage application does get rejected, sit down with your mortgage broker and determine exactly why the rejection decision was made. Next, study your credit reports carefully and look for ways you can improve them and boost your credit scores. It may be necessary to put off the home-buying process for 6 to 12 months while you work to pay off outstanding debts, lower your credit card balances, and boost your credit scores before reapplying for a mortgage.

Find out if increasing your down payment would increase your likelihood of getting approved. If you determine this would help, start increasing your savings so you can make a larger down payment in 3, 6, or 12 months when you reapply.

Another option may be to get someone with excellent credit to become a co-signer, such as a parent or your in-laws. You may discover, however, that to move into the neighborhood you're looking at, you'll first need to improve your income and pursue a pay raise, or it may be necessary to investigate less expensive neighborhoods or less costly houses.

Dirty Little Secrets

Chances are, the economy will improve over time. Yet, if you can't wait for the entire U.S. economy to repair itself, work closely with a mortgage broker and personal financial planner who can help you position yourself as a viable candidate to get a mortgage application approved.

During this process, understand that the approval (or rejection) process is not at all personal. Many thousands of potential homeowners are having their mortgage applications rejected every month for a variety of reasons that stem from current economic conditions and the mortgage industry's own problems.

As a potential homebuyer, the best thing you can do as you get involved with this process is to begin with the highest credit scores and best credit rating possible, have at least a 20-percent down payment ready, and be able to show you have steady employment (with a salary that will allow you to meet all of your financial obligations if you were to take on a mortgage). In today's economy, this is realistically what's required.

What's Next?

Just as applying for and getting approved for a new mortgage is a challenging process, especially in today's tough economy, many current homeowners with mortgages are experiencing huge difficulties getting their existing mortgages refinanced—especially if they're stuck in an adjustable-rate mortgage and their monthly payments are on the rise. The next chapter focuses on offering strategies for refinancing an existing mortgage.

CHAPTER 11

All About Refinancing
in a Tough Economy

What's in This Chapter

- How recent economic changes will impact you

- What's refinancing?

- Reasons to refinance a mortgage

- When to refinance

- Additional mortgage products for refinancing

How Recent Changes in the Mortgage Industry Will Impact You

As a homeowner, chances are you've already gone through the process of applying for a mortgage, getting approved, and participating in a closing; three of the major steps that lead to home ownership.

The rate and terms of the mortgage you got approved for when you purchased your home were based on your financial situation, what information was on your credit reports, your credit scores, your employment situation, your income, the interest rates being offered at the time, and the type of mortgage you got approved for.

In the early to mid-2000s, there were literally hundreds (maybe thousands) of unique mortgage products available. Some were offered to people with very poor credit or who didn't really have the financial stability and wherewithal to make their monthly mortgage payments over the long term.

For a variety of reasons, many people who got approved for a mortgage should not have been, and all of these bad loan decisions finally caught up with the mortgage industry and the U.S. economy. During much of 2008, the number of foreclosures was record breaking, and many major lenders wound up losing billions of dollars, while smaller lenders and many mortgage brokers simply folded.

As a result, lenders have become much stricter when it comes to approving mortgage applications and refinancing existing mortgages. Unfortunately, this has caused tremendous hardship for many American families that got locked into an adjustable-rate mortgage thinking they'd be able to refinance before the adjustable rate rose.

Today, with the newer and stricter approval guidelines, these people no longer qualify for refinancing and are potentially stuck with the mortgage they already have. As the initial fixed-rate period of their mortgages (if applicable) comes to an end, homeowners in this situation now face a variable rate and are experiencing huge increases in their required monthly payments. In too many cases, adjustable-rate mortgage holders can no longer afford their monthly payments and are at risk of foreclosure.

The U.S. government has gotten involved in an attempt to curtail the extremely high foreclosure rate. So, if you're in a situation where you can no longer afford your monthly mortgage payments, there is still hope even if your credit is below average.

Instead of trying to refinance your mortgage the traditional way, since this now typically requires having above average or excellent credit, contact your existing lender and explain your financial hardship. In many cases, the lender will voluntarily (upon your request) rework your existing mortgage, transform a variable-rate mortgage into a fixed-rate mortgage, or take steps to make your existing mortgage more financially manageable. This is referred to as a loan modification, not a refinancing. Typically, less paperwork is involved with this process.

If you opt to pursue a mortgage loan modification, the process will take several months. During this time, make sure the bank or the financial institution that services your current mortgage does not report negative information to the credit reporting agencies. This is something you may need to request and then confirm.

Getting your existing mortgage company to work with you, however, is something you'll need to initiate and potentially qualify for. You'll probably be asked to supply updated financial information, recent bank account statements, paystubs, and other records to demonstrate you're experiencing financial hardship. If you know your existing mortgage is about to transform into a variable-rate mortgage, or your monthly payments for an existing variable-rate mortgage have gotten out of control, contact your lender before you actually begin to experience serious financial problems. In the meantime, do absolutely everything within your power to avoid making any late mortgage payments.

One of the requirements for refinancing almost any mortgage these days, regardless of your credit rating, is not having any late mortgage payments within the previous 12-month period. You also need to have at least above-average credit and a steady income to get approved for a traditional mortgage refinance, whether you're working with a mortgage broker, bank, credit union, or a lender.

Unless you have excellent credit, a steady job, no late mortgage payments within the past 12 months, and often at least some equity in your home, refinancing in current economic conditions is going to be a challenge. (That is, unless you qualify for a specific government program or you're able to negotiate changes to your existing mortgage terms directly with your existing lender.)

Whether you obtained that original mortgage six months ago, several years ago, or more than one or two decades ago, chances are, things have changed in terms of your own financial and credit situation, as have interest rates and the selection of mortgage products

Warning

Don't get caught up in the hype for refinancing deals that sound good in the ads, but that in reality don't make financial sense for the borrower! Before refinancing, make sure you understand exactly how you will be benefiting from the process, what your savings will be over the life of the loan, how long it will take you to recoup the expenses associated with refinancing, and how much the costs and fees associated with refinancing will be. You also want to know what your out-of-pocket expenses will be prior to and at the closing.

now available from lenders and brokers. For any number of reasons, many of which will be described in this chapter, it might make sense for you to consider refinancing your existing mortgage.

Refinancing 101

The process of applying for and getting approved for a new mortgage with different terms to replace your existing mortgage on the same property is called refinancing. Despite the time and effort it takes to find a lender or broker, shop around for the best deal, choose a mortgage product to apply for, complete the mortgage application process, provide the necessary paperwork and forms to the lender, and participate in the closing, there are many reasons why you might want to refinance now or sometime during the term of your existing mortgage. In fact, between the time you buy your home and either sell it or pay off the mortgage debt, you might opt to refinance multiple times as economic situations change.

In order to refinance, you'll need to qualify all over again and go through virtually the same mortgage application process you did originally. Since you already have a mortgage, you can improve your chances of being approved for a lower interest rate and better terms on your new (refinanced) mortgage if:

- Your credit scores have increased since you obtained your original mortgage
- You can show that you've made all of your monthly mortgage payments on time (and have no late payments within the past 12 months)
- Your income has improved since you obtained your original mortgage
- You've built up equity in your home
- You plan to refinance a lower principal amount
- You can keep the costs associated with refinancing under control (this is easier to do if you have excellent credit)

Dirty Little Secrets

There are many ways to potentially save money when you refinance, as long as you take the time to crunch the numbers, fully understand the terms of the new loan, consider the costs associated with refinancing, and then shop around for the very best deal you qualify for. No matter what type of mortgage you currently possess, the monthly payment you now pay is determined by a variety of factors, including:

- The principal amount of the loan
- The interest rate of the loan
- The length of the loan
- The terms of the loan
- Additional fees you paid in conjunction with the loan, including closing costs

Often when you refinance, the closing costs and the majority of other fees associated with refinancing can be built into the new loan to avoid out-of-pocket expenses at the closing. You will often, however, need to pay for your home's updated appraisal in advance. For a typical single-family home, the price of an appraisal will be between $250 and $350, depending on your geographic area.

When you consider refinancing, if you can change one or more of the above elements in your favor, such as lowering your interest rate, you could potentially lower your monthly payment and/or save

Warning

Calculate all of the additional fees and closing costs associated with refinancing, and then do the financial calculations necessary to determine how long it will take you to break even and then start saving money. If your plan is to refinance again or move in just a few months or years, refinancing might not save you money.

a fortune on interest over the life of the loan. Whether you lower your principal, interest rate, or change your loan duration, the smallest reductions result in significant savings over the life of the loan.

As you consider your refinancing options, think carefully about your goals. Are you trying to lower your monthly payment? Are you looking to shorten the term of the loan? Are you looking to cash out on the equity in your home?

If, however, times are tough financially, you could potentially refinance in order to obtain much needed cash. When crunching the numbers to see if refinancing makes sense, knowing how long you intend to stay in the property (or retain ownership of it) can also become a factor, especially if you'll be dealing with an adjustable-rate mortgage.

 Credit Tip

If you're refinancing the mortgage for your primary residence, there's a mandatory three-day grace or cooling off period after the closing that allows you to change your mind and pull out of the deal with no strings attached.

For this reason, if you expect to receive cash as part of your refinancing, you'll have to wait three business days before you receive it from the lender, so plan accordingly. Likewise, the new lender will not fund the new loan (pay off your existing loan) until after that third day. Sundays and holidays do not count toward the three-day period.

During this three-day period, review all of the paperwork once again and make sure it's accurate, acceptable, and that you're comfortable with the terms of the new mortgage. If you choose to pull out before the rescission period expires, you need to fill out the appropriate paperwork (supplied at your closing) and follow the correct procedure, which will be explained at the closing.

Dirty Little Secrets

Depending on what you're trying to accomplish and your ability to meet a lender's qualifications for approval, the refinancing options available to you will vary greatly. Knowing what your goals are will help you and your lender or mortgage broker determine your best options.

As you shop for the best deals for refinancing your mortgage, consider some of the different mortgage products available and determine if any of them could potentially save you more money. For example, you could go from one fixed-rate loan to another, or you could go from a fixed-rate loan to an adjustable-rate loan, or switch to some other type of mortgage product altogether.

Watch Out for Pre-Payment Penalties

Some lenders build pre-payment penalties into their mortgages in order to deter the borrower from refinancing or paying off their debt faster than the loan's term dictates. By paying off the loan early, the borrower saves money (in interest fees). But the lender loses money because the interest you would have paid becomes lost income.

If your existing mortgage has a pre-payment penalty and you choose to refinance, you could be charged extra fees (penalties). Ideally, when shopping for a mortgage, look for products that contain absolutely no pre-payment penalty. Some loans have a pre-payment penalty only for the first few years of the loan. If possible, this too should be avoided by the borrower.

You never know when your financial situation, the country's economic situation, or interest rates in general will change dramatically, allowing you to refinance and potentially qualify for a mortgage with a better rate and more attractive terms. Having no pre-payment penalty attached to your loan provides you, the borrower, with additional options.

Popular Reasons Why People Choose to Refinance

There are many reasons why a homeowner might opt to refinance their existing mortgage. The reason(s) you choose to refinance will help determine what mortgage products you qualify for and are most suitable for your needs.

Once again, it's important to sit down with several lenders or mortgage brokers in order to review your current situation and determine what options are available to you when it comes to refinancing or cashing out on the equity in your home. If any additional expenses are added to the loan (such as closing costs or a cash-out), the "refi" is referred to as an equity take-out or cash-out refinance.

The following section describes the most popular reasons why a homeowner with a mortgage might choose to refinance.

Obtain a Lower Interest Rate

Interest rates offered by lenders change daily. The rate you qualified for when you were approved for your current mortgage was based on a variety of factors. If interest rates have gone down in general, even by a fraction of a point, it might make sense to refinance in order to reduce your monthly payment and cut the amount of money you'll be paying in interest over the life of the loan.

For example, if you originally had a $200,000, 30-year, fixed-rate mortgage at 7.25 percent interest, your monthly payment for the life of the loan would be $1,364.35. Thus, upon paying off the entire principal after 30 years, you would have paid $291,166 in interest. By refinancing if interest rates have dropped to 6.75 percent, using the same exact terms of the original loan (including the same principal), your monthly payment would be $1,297.20 and the total interest you'd pay over the life of the loan would be $266,992. Not only would your monthly payment drop by $67.15 per month, you'd save $24,174 in interest.

But wait, there's more! If you've already been paying off your original mortgage on time for five years, for example, your outstanding principal would be lower. You could now refinance that lower amount for either a full 30-year period (which would lower your payment even more), or you could cut the duration of the loan down to 25 years (or less). Potentially, you could save a fortune, plus cut the term of your mortgage.

Use an amortization calculator, like the one found online at www.realtor.com/home-finance/financial-calculators/mortgage-payment-calculator.aspx, to help you calculate the financial benefits of refinancing a fixed-rate mortgage. You can also find online calculators that'll help you determine if, based on your situation, refinancing with another type of loan makes more financial sense.

Even if interest rates in general have not dropped, you can still refinance and benefit from a lower interest rate in one of several ways. First, if your credit scores have improved since you were originally approved for your mortgage, you may now qualify for a better interest rate, especially if you've also built up more equity in your home and you've made all of your monthly payments on your existing mortgage on time.

When you refinance, you can pay points during the refinance to lower your interest rate. Or, you could potentially switch from a fixed-rate mortgage to some type of adjustable-rate mortgage product that offers lower rates and better terms. If there's a way to decrease your interest rate, even by a fraction of a point, the benefits of refinancing could be dramatic.

Get Better Terms on the Mortgage

When refinancing, you can adjust the terms of your mortgage or potentially save money by switching mortgage products altogether. You could go from a fixed-rate mortgage to some type of adjustable-rate mortgage (or vice versa, which is more common these days), or switch to another type of loan.

By switching to an adjustable-rate mortgage (with an initial fixed-rate period), the lender will typically offer you a more attractive interest rate that will save you money. The risk you run, however, is that after the fixed-rate period of the new ARM (adjustable rate mortgage) ends, your interest rate could increase significantly. This has become a huge problem for people who took on this type of mortgage sometime in the past few years.

Before choosing this type of refinancing option, consider how long you'll be in your home. If you know you'll be moving in four years, you can refinance now with an ARM that has a five-year fixed-rate period and benefit from the savings with no risk of a higher rate after the five-year period, because you'll be moving or selling the home. Of course, consult with your lender or broker to see if this scenario works for you.

Keep in mind, when comparing totally different mortgage products, you must evaluate more than just the interest rate, duration, terms, and fees to determine which deal offers you the best option based on what you're trying to accomplish. Use a financial calculator to calculate how your situation will benefit from each scenario.

Unfortunately, if you're evaluating different loan types, comparing the APRs (annual percentage rates) on the loans won't do you much good. The APR represents your cost to borrow money, but to objectively compare mortgage products among different lenders using the offered APRs, the loan products themselves must be similar.

Cut or Reset the Time It'll Take to Pay Off the Mortgage

Whether or not you can qualify for a better interest rate, you can still benefit financially if you can refinance and obtain better terms on your new mortgage. One way to do this is to refinance for a shorter period. If you go from a 30-year fixed-rate loan to a 25-year or 20-year fixed-rate loan, your savings in interest payments over the life of the loan will be dramatic. If you can combine an interest rate drop with a duration reduction, your monthly payment could potentially decrease as well.

One way to decrease your mortgage payment is to refinance your mortgage and reset its duration. For example, if you started off with a 20-year fixed rate but have been paying it off for 10 years, you could

Dirty Little Secrets

now refinance at the same or even a higher interest rate but set the length of the new loan back to 20 or more years. This would *not* save you money in the long term (in fact, it'll ultimately cost you more), but your monthly payment from the time you refinance forward would decrease, which might help you address current financial shortfalls or problems.

Cash Out on the Equity in Your Home

If you initially made a down payment on your home when purchasing it, that amount contributed to the equity you now have in your home. Since then, if you've been paying off a small portion of your mortgage's principal with each monthly payment, this too has slowly allowed you to build up equity.

Finally, if the appraised value of your home has increased since your purchase, the difference between its current value and your purchase price also represents equity in your home. Unfortunately, if you've lost significant equity in your home as a result of dropping real estate prices, this could make it more difficult to refinance or represent a financial loss for you if you sell the property.

Regardless of what mortgage product you use to refinance, the lender will almost always require you to maintain at least some equity in your home (at least 10 to 25 percent). The equity you have in your home is the current appraised value of your home, minus the amount you still owe on your mortgage (and/or other loans where your home was used as collateral). Thus, if your home is appraised at $200,000, but you currently have a balance on your mortgage of $150,000, your equity is $50,000.

As long as you have equity in your home and meet the loan qualification guidelines of the lenders, you can borrow against or cash out on the equity in your home in order to obtain cash. Doing this would increase the amount you owe on your mortgage (or other types of loans, such as a home equity line of credit), but you can gain access to cash quickly.

Some of the most popular reasons why people opt to cash out some or all of their equity are to:

- Pay for home improvements
- Pay for school or college tuition
- Debt consolidation (pay off other high-interest-bearing debt, such as credit cards)
- Pay off a divorce settlement
- Pay medical expenses not covered by health insurance
- Make a purchase of a big-ticket item, such as an expensive car or boat
- Invest in another property, such as a vacation home or investment property

Typically, tapping the equity in your home for a significant amount of money is ultimately cheaper than utilizing a high-interest credit card or taking out some other type of loan. Plus, there are certain tax advantages, since the interest you pay on your home loan is tax deductible, for example, while the interest you pay on other types of unsecured loans is not.

When you decide to refinance in order to cash out on your equity, you'll have a variety of options based on your credit rating and your ability to meet the eligibility and approval requirements of the various lenders and brokers. Aside from refinancing, second mortgages, home equity loans, and home equity lines of credit (HELOC) are other options potentially available to you if you wish to tap into your home's equity.

The Paperwork You'll Need to Refinance

Once you decide to refinance your existing mortgage, you'll want to gather pertinent information about your current mortgage and financial situation. This includes reacquainting yourself with the terms of your existing mortgage. In addition to all of the information you'd need if you were buying a home and shopping for a mortgage, as you start talking to lenders and brokers about refinancing, some of the additional information you'll need to provide early on in the application process includes:

- The current value of your home (an appraisal will be ordered by the lender or broker)
- The current amount owed on your mortgage
- The interest rate and terms of the current mortgage
- Your credit history and credit score (the broker or lender will order copies of your credit reports and obtain your credit scores)

During the refinancing application process, be prepared to provide the lender or broker with your pay stubs from the past 30 days, copies of W-2 forms for the past two years (or two years' worth of tax returns, depending on your employment situation), two months' worth of bank statements, two months' worth of statements for your investment and IRA accounts, plus information about your employment and housing history for the past two years.

You'll also need to provide copies of your current mortgage documents (provided to you at the closing of your original mortgage). To save time and avoid unnecessary delays, start gathering these documents early in the refinancing process.

Meet Greg McBride, Bankrate.com's Senior Financial Analyst

One of the internet's best resources for mortgage information and current rates is Bankrate.com, a free service offered by Bankrate Inc., which is the internet's leading aggregator of financial rate information.

The rate data offered by Bankrate.com is obtained by continually surveying approximately 4,800 financial institutions in all 50 of the United States. This allows the service to provide their site visitors with clear, objective, and unbiased rate information. As a homebuyer or homeowner looking to refinance, what you'll find on Bankrate.com is free rate information on hundreds of financial products, including mortgages and home equity loans.

In addition to providing the raw financial data someone needs to make intelligent home financing or refinancing decisions, the Bankrate. com website publishes original and objective personal finance articles, plus offers referrals to connect borrowers with lenders and mortgage brokers nationwide. While Bankrate.com is advertiser supported, the editorial content and rates offered by the website is unbiased.

Greg McBride is a senior financial analyst at Bankrate.com. In this interview, he offers advice on how a homebuyer or homeowner looking to refinance can use the free services offered by Bankrate.com to find the best deals.

What exactly is Bankrate.com?

Greg McBride: "Bankrate.com is a personal finance website. We offer award-winning editorial content, online calculators, and a search engine, which can be used to find the best rates on a wide range of consumer banking products, including mortgages and home equity loans. We conduct unbiased editorial surveys, which is how we compile our rate data. We are an advertiser-supported service. The information we offer is provided free to the consumer."

If someone is shopping for the best rates on a mortgage, what type of information will they need to provide when visiting the Bankrate.com website?

Greg McBride: "If we're talking about mortgages, you'll need to select your geographic area, the desired loan amount, and details about the type of mortgage product you're looking for rates on. Everything we present in terms of mortgage data is targeted to consumers with above-average or greater credit scores. We do, however, cater to consumers with lower credit scores who are searching for home equity loans, for example. By providing a small amount of basic information, Bankrate.com will

Dirty Little Secrets

provide an overview of available rates for various mortgage products. We can also provide referrals to lenders or brokers offering those rates in your area. It's then up to you to contact those referrals to gather more information or embark on the application process."

At what point should someone first access Bankrate.com to begin their research?

Greg McBride: "I recommend someone use Bankrate.com throughout the process of obtaining a mortgage or refinancing. Borrowers can also use our online calculators to determine their financial situation, what they can afford, and then learn about various mortgage products available. When they're ready, they can shop for the best rates or get help finding a broker or lender to work with."

If someone uses your search engine to find a broker or lender referral, what should they do next?

Greg McBride: "I recommend comparison shopping between at least three different lenders. When you first contact a lender, ask questions, compare the mortgage products each offers, and then focus on rates. Make sure you ask plenty of questions about the mortgage products themselves and the associated rates, costs, and fees."

How should someone who is looking to refinance use Bankrate.com?

Greg McBride: "Start off by using our online refinancing calculator [www.bankrate.com/calculators/mortgages/refinance-calculator.aspx] to see if refinancing makes sense based on your situation. This calculator can help you determine, for example, how quickly you'll break even based on the costs associated with refinancing.

"One strategy I always recommend is that someone interested in refinancing should always contact their current lender first. Not only does this lender already have all of your financial information, which can streamline the application and approval process, many lenders will work hard to retain your business. After contacting your existing lender, definitely compare rates with a few other brokers or lenders."

What should someone watch out for when shopping around for the best home financing deal?

Greg McBride: "When working with lenders or brokers, don't just focus on the interest rate or what the monthly payment will be. You also need to calculate in the fees involved. When comparing lenders offering similar mortgage products, instead of just focusing on the interest rate, focus on the loan's APR [annual percentage rate], which reflects the total cost of the loan."

Does it matter if someone uses a local lender or broker and is able to meet their loan officer in person (as opposed to working primarily over the telephone and via email)?

Greg McBride: "That boils down to personal preference. But it's always important to comparison shop. If you plan to visit your local bank, for example, also shop around with some of the larger brokers or lenders. It's your job to become an educated consumer so you know if you're being offered the best deal you qualify for. The mortgage business is highly commoditized."

What's Next?

Personal finance, managing your credit, and staying afloat in a tough economy can be an extremely confusing and difficult process, especially if you don't consider yourself to be too savvy when it comes to managing money or crunching numbers. If you find yourself experiencing financial or credit challenges that seem too great to overcome yourself, seek out the help of a personal finance or credit expert.

Obtaining the right help, at the right time, from someone who is knowledgeable, reliable, and competent could save you a fortune, plus help to ensure you maintain your financial stability and protect your credit rating, no matter what obstacles or challenges you face. If you have questions, get them answered! If you need help, seek it out before it's too late!

The next chapter offers advice on how and where to find the help you need when it comes to obtaining financial or credit-related guidance.

Getting the Help You Need to Fix Your Credit Problems

What's in This Chapter

■ Whom to call when you need help with credit problems

■ What credit counseling is and how it works

■ Working with a financial planner or accountant on an ongoing basis

■ Beware of credit repair scams

■ Debt consolidation loan options

Being too Proud to Ask for Help Can Lead to Worse Problems

Many people can avoid getting themselves into serious financial and credit problems simply by asking for help as soon as they realize they might have a problem. Whether it's a matter of pride, shyness, or lack of knowledge, people often ignore their impending financial or credit disaster and avoid seeking out help until it's too late.

Your credit rating can get destroyed for any number of reasons, some of which are outside of your control (such as a sudden job loss, injury, or illness). Many people, however, wind up experiencing serious credit problems as a result of situations that could easily be avoided (such as careless spending, or being irresponsible and simply forgetting to pay bills on time).

Whether your credit problems are a result of naïveté or carelessness, as soon as you determine you have a problem (or could be headed for one), seek out the advice and guidance you need from a qualified, reputable, and understanding financial or credit expert.

Not only can soliciting expert help keep you from utterly destroying your credit rating (if you haven't already done so), the advice you receive could save you thousands of dollars in late charges, interest fees, and even legal bills.

If, however, your credit rating has already been trashed, collection agencies are calling you incessantly, multiple lenders or creditors are threatening lawsuits, and you don't have the funds to dig yourself out of your current predicament, finding a financial and/or credit expert to work with could help you resolve your problems faster, save you money, and help you avoid much of the stress that's associated with being in this predicament.

The experts who are available to help you will not pass judgment, ridicule you, belittle you, or embarrass you in any way. In fact, some will work with you on a confidential basis, while all will offer you the guidance you need to help you avoid or overcome the situation you find yourself facing. The first step, however, is to find someone who is qualified, reputable, and reliable to help you.

For most people, the most difficult part of this process is overcoming their personal pride and simply asking for the support and guidance they need. If you're already in over your head, it may be too late to remedy the situation yourself. Or, even worse, you just ignore the situation and hope it'll go away. Not only will it not go away, with each passing day, week, or month, your situation will get worse, your debts will increase, and your credit rating and personal financial situation will further deteriorate.

If you've made mistakes that have led to financial and/or credit problems, take personal responsibility for having made those mistakes and then seek out the help you need to remedy your situation. Or, if you've experienced a situation that's outside of your control (such as loss of a job, illness, injury, or being a victim of identity theft), instead of panicking, seek out the guidance you need to retake control of your financial life and credit rating.

Nobody but you can make that first all-important call to obtain a free consultation with a financial or credit expert. At the same time, it's your responsibility to avoid putting your financial future into the hands of someone who isn't qualified to handle your particular situation. Be prepared to do some research in order to find an expert in your geographic area who is capable, qualified, and, if necessary, licensed by the state where you live, to help you.

Depending on the type of expert advice or services you need, you may have to pay to receive help. However, whatever fees you pay will be offset (and are often much less) by the legal fees, late charges, and high interest you're currently responsible for paying your creditors and lenders as a result of making bad decisions or mishandling your financial or credit situation yourself.

As you'll discover from this chapter, however, there are also free (nonprofit) services out there designed to help people in financial need, so regardless of your current situation, you're not beyond help or without recourse when it comes to finding the assistance you need.

Solutions for People with Credit and Financial Problems

There are countless reasons people get themselves into serious debt, max out their credit cards, and simply run out of money. Some of these reasons include:

- Bad investment decisions or serious financial losses as a result of poor stock market performance
- Becoming a victim of theft or fraud
- Carelessness with money and irresponsible spending habits
- Death of a loved one
- Getting laid off from a job
- Not developing a well-thought-out personal or family budget and then sticking to it
- Sudden illness or a medical emergency

Whatever the reason, people who are experiencing serious financial problems often don't realize or acknowledge it until it's too late. Then, because the problem has gotten so big and out of control, these people don't know where to begin in terms of fixing their situation, so they simply ignore it or develop a sense of denial, which only causes the problem to get increasingly worse. Does this pattern sound familiar to you? If so, you're not alone!

Whether it's the result of financial problems or the cause of them, what goes hand-in-hand with having personal financial problems is developing debt and poor credit. As you fall behind on monthly payments for loans and credit cards, negative information begins popping up on your credit reports. This leads to a steady reduction in your credit scores, which potentially causes the interest rates you're paying on your credit cards and loans to increase. Plus, when you attempt to apply for additional credit or loans, at first, you'll just pay more due to your lower credit scores, but after some time passes, you'll discover you're unable to qualify for new loans and additional credit at all.

This is the point when many people discover they're in serious financial trouble and don't know where to turn or what to do. When you discover yourself experiencing any type of short- or long-term financial problems, it's important to begin dealing with them immediately to avoid much larger problems down the road.

For example, if you can't make your car loan payment in a given month, call the lender and explain your situation and the reason. If the reason is valid, the lender will often work with you by extending the loan and allowing you to skip one or two payments, restructure or refinance the loan with a lower interest rate, waive interest fees or late charges, or work with you to develop a solution that will help keep you from experiencing further financial hardship. By being proactive in dealing with your creditors and lenders, you can often avoid negative information showing up on your credit reports, or at least minimize the damage to your credit rating.

Especially if you've recently and unexpectedly lost your job, experienced a medical emergency, or have some other extenuating circumstance surrounding your personal and financial life, the trick to avoiding long-term credit and financial problems is to immediately contact your creditors and lenders and work with them. Don't allow bills to pile up as you skip payments and ponder what you're going to do, or worse yet, ignore the situation.

In the United States alone, there are countless people every month who begin experiencing serious financial and credit difficulties, yet don't know where to turn. If you're fortunate to have worked with an accountant, CPA (certified public account), financial planner, or certified financial planner (CFP) in the past and who is familiar with your financial situation, this is definitely the type of financial expert to turn to now.

Even if you've never worked with any type of accountant or financial planner in the past, if you can afford to hire one, even for a few hours to review your current situation and recommend some solutions, this is the fastest and easiest way to begin seeking solutions to your financial and credit problems.

When seeking an accountant or financial planner, find someone with experience and expertise working with people in your situation, but beware of people advertising themselves as "credit repair experts." Find someone with some type of legitimate certification. For example, find a CPA instead of just an accountant. If you're seeking a financial planner, find someone who has earned their CFP certification. This will help guarantee that the person you ultimately hire is qualified, experienced, and reputable.

If you're experiencing credit problems, you could also seek guidance from a reputable credit counseling service. A financial planner can help you with all aspects of money management and budgeting. However, a skilled and experienced credit counselor can:

- Advise you about managing your money and your use (and utilization) of credit
- Provide solutions and strategies for dealing with your current financial problems

Credit Tip

The best way to find an accountant or financial planner is through a referral from someone you know. Otherwise, consider contacting a professional association, such as the Certified Financial Planner Board of Standards (www.cfp.net/find). Another resource for finding a CFP in your area can be found online at www.letsmakeaplan.org/choose-a-cfp-professional/choosing -a-financial-planner.aspx.

- Assist you in creating a personalized plan to help you prevent future difficulties
- Help you negotiate with your existing creditors and lenders
- Develop and help you implement a debt management plan (DMP) to bail yourself out of your financial predicament

When you begin working with a financial expert, whether an accountant, financial planner, or credit counselor, the personal and financial information you provide is typically kept confidential, unless you authorize the person you're working with to contact and negotiate with your creditors and lenders on your behalf.

Strategies for Finding a Qualified Financial Planner

In the United States, there are more than 50,000 CFPs. On its website (www.cfp.net), the Certified Financial Planner Board of Standards offers the following advice for finding a qualified financial planner to assist you in overcoming your financial and credit problems:

- *Know what you want.* Determine your general financial goals and/ or specific needs (insurance policy analysis, estate planning, investment advice, college tuition financing, etc.) to better focus your search for a suitable financial planner.
- *Be prepared.* Read personal finance magazines to maximize your familiarity with financial planning strategies and terminology.

Credit Tip

When hiring an accountant, CPA, or credit counselor, know what you want; be prepared; talk to others; look for competence; interview more than one planner; check the planner's background; know what to expect; get everything in writing; and reassess the relationship regularly.

- *Talk to others.* Get referrals from advisors you trust, business associates, and friends. Or, contact a financial planning membership organization to obtain a referral to a financial planner in your area.

- *Look for competence.* A number of specialty designations exist in the financial planning and services arenas. Choose a financial planning professional with the certification that indicates that he or she is ethical and has met standards of financial planning competency.

- *Interview more than one planner.* Ask each planner to describe their educational background, experience and specialties, the size and duration of their practice, how often they communicate with clients, and whether an assistant handles client matters. Make sure you feel comfortable discussing your finances with the planner you select. It's essential that you communicate openly and honestly with the financial expert you opt to work with in order to ensure the best results.

- *Check the planner's background.* Depending on the financial planner's area of expertise, call the securities or insurance departments in your state regarding each planner's complaint record. Call CFP Board's toll-free number (888) CFP-MARK or visit www.CFP.net to determine if a planner is currently authorized to use the CFP certification marks or has ever been publicly disciplined by the CFP Board.

- *Know what to expect.* Ask for a registration or disclosure statement (such as a Form ADV) detailing the planner's compensation methods, conflicts of interest, business affiliations, and personal qualifications.

- *Get everything in writing.* Request a written advisory contract or engagement letter to document the nature and scope of services the planner will provide. You should also understand whether compensation will be fee or commission-based, or a combination of both.

▪ *Reassess the relationship regularly.* Financial planning relationships are often long term. Review your professional relationship on a regular basis and ensure that your financial planner understands your goals and needs as they develop and change over time.

Credit Counselors Are Available to Help You

Many companies advertise "credit counseling" and "credit repair" services on late-night TV, on the radio, and in newspapers or magazines. Assume that any company that promotes itself as a "credit repair" specialist is *not* legitimate! It is impossible to legally repair your credit rating overnight, or to make accurate information disappear from your credit reports, regardless of what these companies advertise or promise.

It's harder to determine, however, if a "credit counseling" service is reputable. Instead of responding to ads on late-night TV or on the radio, for example, one of the best ways to find a reliable and reputable credit counseling service is to contact the National Foundation for Credit Counseling by calling (800)-388-2227 or going to www.nfcc.org for a referral in your area.

A legitimate credit counselor can assist you in rebuilding your credit rating, help you negotiate with lenders, creditors, and collection agencies, work with you to avoid getting sued by companies you owe money to, and they typically know what strategies will help you preserve

---

You Should Know . . .

If you need the help of a credit counselor, your first call should be to the National Foundation for Credit Counseling (800) 388-2227 (www.nfcc. org). It provides you with free information and the opportunity to speak with a certified credit counselor who will charge you little or no money for the consultation.

Dirty Little Secrets

or rebuild your credit rating over time. These specialists can also work with you to create payment plans and a budget you can live with, based on your current circumstances.

The National Foundation for Credit Counseling (NFCC) was founded in 1951 and is the county's largest and longest-serving national nonprofit credit counseling organization. The organization's mission is to set the national standard for quality credit counseling, debt reduction services, and education for financial wellness through its member agencies.

The NFCC's agencies have trained, certified credit counselors who offer low-cost and free educational information, management advice, and debt reduction services. NFCC members help more than two million consumers annually through nearly 1,000 agency offices nationwide.

A Debt Management Plan (DMP) Could Help You

The NFCC offers consumers step-by-step counseling to become debt free. This is done by providing each consumer with an individualized plan to help them pay off their debt. If you've accumulated severe debt, the organization can help you establish a debt management plan (DMP).

According to the Debt Advice website, "A DMP is a systematic way to pay down your outstanding debt through monthly deposits to a third-party agency, which will then distribute these funds to your creditors. By participating in this program, you may benefit from reduced or waived finance charges and fewer collection calls. And, when you have completed your payments, we'll help you reestablish credit . . . . A DMP is a carefully formulated, monthly program that reduces your bills and consolidates them into one simple payment."

If you choose to participate in a DMP, the process of repaying your debt could take anywhere from 36 to 60 months. After negotiating with your creditors, a DMP can help you repay your debts in an organized and efficient way and lead you toward reestablishing your financial stability. However, it remains your responsibility to make timely payments once you're involved with a DMP, or your financial and credit situation will become even worse.

The NFCC will work with you one-on-one by providing free or extremely affordable counseling services. The organization also offers free educational seminars through its regional offices.

The Debt Advice website reports, "What sets the NFCC agencies apart from other nonprofit organizations is that it receives funding from sources besides its clients. As a result, while other credit counselors charge high startup fees and monthly service charges, the NFCC's rates are extremely low and there are no hidden costs to immediately begin benefiting from the services offered."

You Should Know . . .

The NFCC operates an informative website offering consumers tools and information to help them develop short- and long-term strategies for fixing their credit problems. To learn more, visit Debt Advice.org (www. debtadvice.org).

Because a significant number of companies and individuals fraudulently pass themselves off as "credit counselors" in order to capitalize on the misfortune of people in severe debt, the FTC has developed a list of eight questions to help you determine if a particular credit counseling agency is reputable. These questions include:

▪ What services are offered? A reputable credit counseling service will offer budget counseling and debt management classes, plus be able to provide you with the services of someone who is trained and certified in consumer credit, money, and debt management. A credit counseling service should begin by discussing your personal situation with you, help you develop a personalized plan to solve your immediate money and credit problems, and then teach you how to avoid the recurrence of these problems in the future. During your first meeting with a credit counselor, be prepared to spend between 60 and 90 minutes analyzing your personal situation.

■ Is the credit counselor licensed in your state to provide the services offered? Many states require counselors to obtain a license before they're allowed to offer credit counseling, debt management plans, or other related services to consumers.

■ Does the credit counseling service offer free information?

■ Will you be required to sign a formal contract or written agreement with the credit counseling company? Make sure you never agree to pay for any services over the telephone. You should receive a written contract or agreement before being charged for credit counseling services or participating in a DMP coordinated by the credit counseling company.

■ Does the credit counseling agency or service you're interested in working with have a good reputation with the Better Business Bureau and your state's Attorney General? Determine if there have been any formal complaints filed against the company. From the Better Business Bureau's website (www.bbb.org), you can search for complaints against a company and find contact information for your local BBB office. Keep in mind that even if you can't find any complaints against a specific company, this is not an absolute guarantee that the company is reputable.

■ How much does credit counseling services cost? Be sure to obtain a detailed price quote in writing. Make sure that all of the fees are listed within the quote. Determine if there are any upfront or startup costs, monthly fees, or any other charges for the various services offered. Also, determine when you'll be paying for the services rendered. If the company's fees are being built into your DMP, for example, it's still important for you

($) *Credit Tip*

The FTC publishes free informational booklets about managing credit, rebuilding credit, and understanding credit, which can be obtained online at www.ftc.gov/bcp/menus/consumer/credit.shtm or by calling (877) FTC-HELP. These booklets provide useful information if you're looking to hire a credit counselor, apply for a debt consolidation loan, or filing for bankruptcy.

to understand how much these fees are and know exactly what you're paying for.

■ How are the individual credit counselors paid? Are they given a commission based on services you sign up for? According to the FTC, "If the organization will not disclose what compensation it receives from creditors or how employees are compensated, go elsewhere for help."

■ Will the information you provide to the credit counselor be kept confidential? Who will have access to the personal and financial information you supply?

As you evaluate a potential credit counselor, determine if he or she will communicate and negotiate on your behalf with your creditors and lenders. If this is a service that will be provided, determine in advance what their negotiation strategy and goals will be. Then insist on receiving written copies of all correspondence, plus a summary of all telephone conversations held between your counselor and each creditor or lender. Never allow the credit counselor to agree to any payoff or settlement offers, for example, without your approval.

Beware of Scams

As a consumer, you'll see many ads offering "credit repair" and fast and easy relief of debt. Many of these ads, however, are for scams. The

FTC reports that some of the most common headlines to watch out for include: "Consolidate your bills into one monthly payment without borrowing," "STOP credit harassment, foreclosures, repossessions, tax levies and garnishments," "Keep Your Property," "Wipe out your debts! Consolidate your bills! How? By using the protection and assistance provided by federal law. For once, let the law work for you!" Avoid services that utilize advertisements, websites, or sales brochures that feature these or similar headlines.

To help you choose a credit counseling or debt negotiation service to work with, the FTC has published a list of promises often made by disreputable companies who could be perpetuating some type of scam. If one or more of the following promises or claims are made, *do not* work with the company that makes them.

- The company or individual guarantees your unsecured debt can be erased or removed from your credit reports and that the creditors you owe money to will simply go away.
- The company promises or guarantees that unsecured debts can be paid off with pennies on the dollar.
- The company requires substantial monthly service fees and/or a startup fee.
- The company demands a percentage of savings as payment.
- The company tells you to stop making payments to or communicating with your creditors and lenders.
- The company requires you to make monthly payments to them, rather than to your creditors and lenders, without you participating in a legitimate, documented, and recognized DMP.
- The company claims that creditors never sue consumers for nonpayment of unsecured debt.
- The company promises that using its system will have no negative impact on your credit reports.
- The company claims it can remove negative, but accurate, information from your credit reports and/or that your credit scores will improve dramatically overnight.

Debt Consolidation May Be a Viable Option

As you learned in Chapter 8, if you have multiple credit cards with high balances, and perhaps other types of high-interest loans, debt consolidation may be a way for you to reduce the fees and interest you're paying on your outstanding debts.

Debt consolidation involves taking out one (lower interest) loan and then using that money to pay off multiple other loans and credit cards. Not only will this allow you to pay just one monthly bill, it could save you a fortune in interest charges and help keep negative information from appearing on your credit report.

Debt consolidation is often used by people with multiple high-interest credit cards with high balances. However, it can also be used to help pay off student loans and other types of debt (that also have high interest rates and/or fees associated with them), because a debt consolidation loan will often carry with it a much lower interest rate than what you're currently paying.

There are several types of debt consolidation loans. Some people choose to refinance their mortgages and cash out some of the equity in their properties in order to pay off a handful of credit cards or other loans. You could also apply for a home equity loan or second mortgage, or apply for some other type of personal loan and use it for debt consolidation purposes. Another option is to apply for a low-interest credit card and transfer your other high-interest credit card balances to that new card. Chapter 8 offers more information on managing credit card debt.

If used properly, a debt consolidation loan can be a powerful tool for regaining control over your debt, paying off past-due accounts, and saving a lot of money in interest fees. Contact your financial institution, mortgage broker, bank, or financial planner for information about how a debt consolidation loan could potentially help you deal with your current financial or credit problems. Remember, this isn't a solution for everyone. Whether you can benefit from a debt consolidation loan will depend on your personal situation.

Some companies that offer debt consolidation loans or mortgage refinancing for debt consolidation purposes charge hidden fees, plus add extra charges for their services in the form of "points" and closing costs. Or, they charge high interest rates, especially to borrowers with below average credit.

Make sure you understand the type of loan you're being offered, what the rates and fees are, and determine that the loan you ultimately select will actually save you money after the consolidation process is complete.

Understand exactly how the debt consolidation loan will benefit you in both the short and long term, based on the situation you're currently in. Simply trading several high-interest (credit card) debts for one new high-interest debt isn't necessarily beneficial, unless it can improve your credit rating, bring you up-to-date with your creditors, allow you to pay off old debt, and help improve your credit score. Thus, in six months to one year, you'd qualify for a much lower interest loan and will have dramatically improved your credit situation.

Don't Be Afraid to Seek Help

There's no shame or need to be embarrassed about seeking out guidance from a certified, licensed, experienced, and reputable financial planner, accountant, or credit counselor. No matter how dire your situation is, however, don't become a victim of a scam by believing a company's lies that your financial or credit problems can be solved quickly and easily without actually paying off your debt. Make sure you find someone who is trustworthy and knowledgeable and offers services you need and can afford.

Remember, even if you're in serious debt, there are organizations and credit counseling services that are willing and able to help you, either for free or for a very small fee. Seeking professional help with your financial problems could be one of the best investments you ever make, especially if you're willing to follow the advice that's offered and are able to eventually solve your financial and credit problems.

In reality, there are few situations that are so bad that they can't eventually be fixed, even if it means filing for bankruptcy and rebuilding your financial stability and credit rating from scratch. Filing for bankruptcy, however, should only be considered as an absolute last resort and only after you've consulted with a credit counselor, attorney, or personal finance expert.

Contrary to popular belief, filing for bankruptcy does not get rid of all of your debt or allow you to forsake certain legal obligations. There are also fees associated with taking this action, and declaring bankruptcy will haunt you at least for the next 10 years. While you can immediately begin to rebuild your credit after declaring bankruptcy, the negative information related to this action will continue to appear on your credit reports (and negatively impact your credit scores) for a decade. Thus, it will become very difficult (especially in a tough economy) to obtain a mortgage, refinance a mortgage, get approved for a car loan, acquire new credit cards, or obtain any other type of loan or credit in the foreseeable future.

Before pursuing the bankruptcy route and erroneously thinking this is the solution to all of your financial and credit problems, work with a credit counselor or financial expert to determine if other solutions are available to you that could help salvage your credit rating and help you more easily rebuild a positive relationship with your creditors and lenders.

Advice from a Certified Financial Planner

Kimberly Foss is a certified financial planner (CFP) and personal finance expert. She has almost three decades of experience. Foss is based in Roseville, California, and is the founder of Empyrion Wealth Management (empyrionwealth.com). In this interview, she offers advice about working with a CFP, as well as offers strategies for rebuilding your credit rating and managing your personal finances.

If someone decides to work with a CFP, does this need to be done in person?

Kimberly Foss: "With today's technology, it does not. I often communicate with my clients through Skype, email, by telephone, and through webinars. As long as you're comfortable working with someone through non-one-on-one in-person interaction, the results can be the same."

Who is your typical client?

Kimberly Foss: "I work with a lot of people who have lost their job and are either about to declare bankruptcy or are facing foreclosure, or people who have recently gone through this and are trying to rebuild. Even if someone has declared bankruptcy and has had their home foreclosed on, over time, they can rebuild and eventually reestablish their credit rating and ultimately buy another home."

When is the best time to seek help from a CFP?

Kimberly Foss: "I think the first step is that you need to admit to yourself that you need help. I have worked with married couples who have gotten themselves into serious financial problems, but the husband, for example, would not admit to the situation and was initially unwilling to accept any help. This person ultimately needed to admit the problem existed, but for him, this didn't happen until his wife threatened to file for divorce. Three years later, both his marriage and his finances are on solid ground.

"In my experience, something very bad has to happen for certain people to admit a problem exists and then seek out help for it. More often than not, this happens when someone is about to lose their home. The earlier a financial expert gets involved in the situation, the easier it will be to help that person and get them back on their feet.

"People should understand that there are many banks and financial institutions out there that prefer to foreclose on homes rather than work with their borrowers to help them keep their homes. Working with a CFP can help you keep your home, or sell it on your terms in order to avoid foreclosure."

What are some of the warning signs that someone is in deep financial trouble?

Kimberly Foss: "If someone has gone through their savings, has begun to rely on credit cards to pay their living expenses, and has racked up a tremendous amount of credit card debt, these are strong indications of a serious problem. Likewise, if someone has cashed out their investments or cashed in their retirement plan early, these too are indicators of a serious financial problem."

At what point should someone consider bankruptcy as a potential solution to their financial problems?

Kimberly Foss: "Bankruptcy should be avoided whenever possible. The first step to avoid this is to become aware that you can no longer afford the house you're living in. Instead of waiting too long and hoping that the situation will get better on its own, seek out help, and if necessary, sell your home before it gets foreclosed upon and your financial problems spin out of control."

If someone has already gone through a foreclosure and/or bankruptcy, what is the process to begin rebuilding?

Kimberly Foss: "Your credit scores and overall credit rating are based heavily on your history of paying your debts on time. Part of the rebuilding process means starting again from day one and re-establishing that credit history, which will take time. The first step toward doing this is to begin paying all of your bills on time. Do not miss any payments, and pay careful attention to your credit utilization.

"What I recommend to my clients is that they get one credit card, even if it's a secured credit card, and re-learn how to manage it perfectly. With the single credit card, use it, but pay off the balance in full every month, and do this for at least six months in a row. Once you prove to the credit card issuer you are responsible and have developed a positive 6- to 12-month history with them, ask for a credit limit increase. However, do not utilize this extra credit. Allow the higher credit limit to help improve your credit utilization percentage."

Why do you recommend an American Express card for someone trying to reestablish their credit?

Kimberly Foss: "I like the basic American Express green card because you must pay off the balance at the end of each month."

For someone with average or above credit, what advice do you have for someone looking to apply for one or more new credit cards?

Kimberly Foss: "There are many credit cards out there. I recommend people find a MasterCard or Visa that will meet the majority of their needs and that offers a good interest rate. I believe in keeping things simple, and only having two or three credit cards at the most, including an American Express card and a Visa or MasterCard. What I recommend people avoid is applying for a bunch of credit cards that have different features. You probably don't need one card with a low interest rate, one that earns frequent flier miles, another that offers cash back, and one that allows you to earn points that can be redeemed for merchandise. Try to find one or two cards that meet the majority of your needs. This will make managing the cards simple."

What should someone look for in a credit card offer?

Kimberly Foss: "Read the fine print of the offer and the cardholder agreement carefully. If you're offered an introductory interest rate, make sure you know exactly when the interest rate will go up, and plan accordingly. I also recommend setting up a schedule where you pay your monthly credit card bills at least 15 days prior to their respective due dates."

If someone knows they have trouble paying their bills on time, due to being disorganized or lazy, what advice do you have?

Kimberly Foss: "If you're someone who has trouble keeping track of when bills are due and then paying your bills on time, even if you have the funds available, I recommend using a service like Mint.com (www. mint.com), which is a free service that's operated by Intuit. It makes managing your bills and personal finances very easy, and you can do it from your computer, a tablet, or even your cell phone, as long as you have access to the internet.

"Mint.com allows you to manage all of your bills, credit cards, bank accounts, and your personal budget all from one place. You can also pay your bills online. Properly managing your finances will help you avoid costly late fees that can be associated with credit cards and other bills."

What's Next?

One of the fastest growing crimes in America is identity theft. If you become a victim of identity theft, not only could this cost you a fortune, it could utterly destroy your credit rating. What's worse, one of the latest trends among identity thieves is to steal (assume) the identity of infants and children. So, if you're a parent, it's essential that you take steps to protect your children from this type of crime as well.

Most people who become victims of this type of crime find recovering from it will require hundreds of hours of work, plus cost thousands of dollars. When your identity is stolen, it might take months or years for the impact of the theft to become apparent. There are, however, strategies you can implement to protect yourself and your identity, as well as your credit rating. These strategies for protecting yourself and recovering from identity theft are covered in the next chapter.

CHAPTER 13

Identity Theft and Bankruptcy

Two Credit Rating Killers to Avoid

What's in This Chapter

- What identity theft is and how to avoid it

- How criminals obtain your personal information

- How to determine if you've already been a victim of identity theft

- Advice about bankruptcy from an attorney

How Many People Out There Are Posing As You?

Out of the many scenarios and triggers that will cause your credit scores to nosedive and your credit rating to be destroyed, identity theft and bankruptcy are potentially the most damaging. In this chapter, we'll take a closer look at both of these all-too-common problems and offer strategies for avoiding them.

Watch Out! Identity Theft Is the Fastest Growing Crime in America

Discovering you've become a victim of identity theft or some other type of credit fraud can be an extremely stressful and costly experience if not handled swiftly and correctly. It's estimated that more than 10 to 12 million Americans (3.6 percent of the U.S. population) become victims of identity theft every year. Although you may be protected financially if you're a fraud victim, correcting the problem will still often require a significant time commitment on your part.

Identity theft involves the unauthorized use of personal identification information to commit fraud or other crimes. This could include someone using your credit card(s) to make unauthorized purchases, or using your identity to take out loans or establish credit in your name. It can also involve someone stealing and using your Social Security number for a wide range of illegal activities, including securing employment or stealing your tax refund.

Before you think to yourself, "Oh, that could never happen to me," consider these disturbing statistics offered by the FTC:

- If you become a victim of identity theft, it could easily require a time investment of 175 to 600 hours (or more) to recover your good name and recover financially.
- There's a new identity theft victim in the United States every four seconds.

How Criminals Obtain Your Private Information

Criminals can be very clever when they want to take over your identity or obtain your confidential credit or financial information. Just some of the most common ways identity thieves operate in order to acquire private information about others that they can ultimately use to commit fraud and other crimes include:

■ *Attempting to change your address.* A criminal might try to divert your billing statements or credit card account information to another location by completing a change of address form that you don't authorize or even know about. (If this were done, the new or additional address would eventually show up on your credit report, indicating you have a problem with identity theft.)

■ *Dumpster diving.* Criminals rummage through your trash looking for bills, pre-qualified credit card offers, bank statements, credit card statements, and other financial papers that include your personal information within them.

■ *Phishing.* Criminals pretend to represent a well-known financial institution or company and send unauthorized but authentic-looking email to get you to reveal personal information about yourself via the internet. This could also include luring you to a fraudulent or imposter website.

■ *Pretexting.* People looking to commit identity fraud will sometimes impersonate you on the telephone and use false pretenses in an effort to obtain your personal information from financial institutions, telephone companies, credit card companies, and other sources.

■ *Skimming.* Criminals steal credit/debit card numbers using a special storage device when processing your card at restaurants, stores, or other retailers.

■ *Stealing.* Pickpockets and thieves will steal wallets, briefcases, purses, smartphones, tablets, and/or computers, while other

$ Credit Tip

The best way to prevent identity theft is to subscribe to a credit monitoring service so you will be notified within 24 hours every time any type of change is made to your credit reports. Thus, if someone uses your identity to apply for a credit card or some type of loan, for example, you will find out about it immediately and can stop it before it's too late. Another method you can use to protect yourself is to subscribe to an identity theft prevention service.

criminals will go after your mail to obtain your bank and credit card statements, pre-approved credit offers, new checks from your bank, and/or tax information, for example. Identity thieves also sometimes illegally acquire copies of their victims' credit reports. On a larger scale, identity thieves sometimes hack into computer databases maintained by large companies and steal customer records (including each customer's name, address, and credit card information, for example.)

Once an identity thief acquires your personal and financial information, such as your name, address, phone number, date of birth, Social Security number, credit or debit card number(s), and/or bank account information, it's relatively easy for them to use that information for a wide range of illegal activities, including:

- Spending sprees using your existing credit and/or debit card(s)
- Opening new credit card accounts in your name once they obtain your name, address, date of birth, and Social Security number
- Obtaining a car loan in your name
- Establishing cellular telephone service in your name
- Creating counterfeit checks or a fake debit card with your account information and draining your bank account(s)

Dirty Little Secrets

---

⑤ *Credit Tip*

Do not carry your Social Security card or any documents that contain your unique Social Security number in your wallet. If your wallet is lost or stolen, you don't want to make it easier for a thief to gather the personal information about you needed to steal your identity or more easily utilize your credit or debit cards, for example. It's also important to protect kids' Social Security numbers. According to the FTC, about 5 percent of all identity theft involves victims under the age of 18.

■ Filing a fake tax return with the IRS in order to steal your tax refund

You May Already Be a Victim of Identity Theft and Not Even Know It

How can you determine if you're a victim of identity theft? There are several warning signs to be on the lookout for, including:

■ Your credit reports will list new credit cards as having been issued in your name that you never applied for or received.

■ Your credit reports will list information about accounts that you did not open and know nothing about.

■ You'll notice charges on your monthly credit card statements and/or bank statements that you didn't authorize.

■ You stop receiving monthly credit card statements or important bills altogether.

■ You begin receiving bills from companies you've never done business with.

■ You begin receiving calls from creditors and/or collection agencies about accounts you know nothing about.

Dirty Little Secrets

What to Do if You Become an Identity Theft Victim

If you even suspect you've become a victim of identity theft or some type of credit-related fraud, follow these steps immediately:

- Contact your creditors and bank(s) immediately to discuss your suspicions. If you've had a credit or debit card lost or stolen (or you notice potentially fraudulent charges on your statement), report that immediately to the bank or credit card issuer. The appropriate phone number will be listed on your statement and on your actual credit and debit card(s).

- Contact your local police department immediately and file a report. Be sure to obtain a copy of this written report. Do this even if the crime was not committed locally.

- Collect all documents, such as your credit report, monthly statements, or other written information that relate to your suspicion. From the day you suspect fraudulent activity, keep detailed notes about with whom you speak and what notices you receive. Do not destroy or throw away any related paperwork or files.

- If you believe someone is fraudulently using your Social Security number, contact the Social Security Administration.

- Change your password(s) and PIN(s) on all ATM, debit, and credit cards. Have your checking account number (and related passwords and PINs) changed as well.

- Contact the fraud victim assistance department at each of the major credit reporting agencies. Ask that a "Fraud Alert" be placed in your credit report file. From this point forward, creditors will be instructed to take additional steps to verify your identity before granting you (or someone impersonating you) credit. Contact: Equifax (800-525-6285), Experian (888-397-3742), and TransUnion (800-860-7289). In situations relating to identity theft, the credit reporting agencies share data; however, to protect your own best interests, contact all three of the credit reporting agencies individually.

Dirty Little Secrets

> # *You Should Know . . .*
>
> The FTC can also be helpful if you're a victim of identity theft. Contact the Identity Theft Data Clearing House at (877) ID-THEFT, or visit www.ftc.gov/bcp/edu/microsites/idtheft2012 or www.ftc.gov/bcp/edu/pubs/consumer/general/gen09.pdf. Once you report your identity theft or fraud suspicions, you may be required to complete an "ID Theft Affidavit" and/or a "Fraudulent Account Statement." A group of credit grantors, consumer advocates, and the FTC developed these forms to help consumers report information to many companies using one standard form. The necessary forms can be obtained, free of charge, by calling the FTC's Identity Theft Data Clearing House or by visiting the organization's website.

Consider Using An Identity Theft Prevention Service

The number of identity theft-related crimes that happen every day in the United States is staggering. For a typical consumer, it's no longer a concern about whether or not you could be become a victim of identity fraud, but when you'll be a victim and how much damage the crime will inflict on your personal finances and credit rating.

In addition to using common sense to protect your personal information and keep it out of criminals' hands, there are services you can subscribe to that will not only help protect you from identity theft, but provide financial insurance and personalized support services if you do get victimized.

Keep in mind that identity theft prevention services such as LifeLock (www.lifelock.com) or Identity Guard (www.identityguard.com) are fee-based. You can save money by doing everything these services do to protect your identity on your own, but you have to have

Dirty Little Secrets

the time, patience, and persistence to initially take and then maintain the necessary precautionary measures. If that doesn't sound like you, it will be worthwhile paying a monthly fee to an identity theft prevention company to handle these services on your behalf.

Meet Todd David, CEO and Founder of LifeLock

Phone Number: (800) LIFE-LOCK
Website: www.lifelock.com
Fee: $10 or $25 per month

What is LifeLock and why did you establish this company?

Todd Davis: "LifeLock was the first service of its kind to come to market. Our goal is to prevent identity theft before it happens. We take advantage of the existing laws that are on the books to help consumers protect themselves. Before I launched this company, I kept hearing in the news about how identity theft is the fastest growing crime in America, but I never heard anything about how someone could keep this type of crime from happening to them.

"Consumers have the ability to add fraud alerts to their credit reports as a preventative measure, but few consumers know they can do this or they don't take advantage of it. A fraud alert can be added to your credit reports for free, but they only last 90 days. This means that if you were to add these alerts yourself, but you have not yet been a victim of identity theft, you'd have to keep adding new alerts with each of the three credit reporting agencies every 90 days. A fraud alert requires all creditors or lenders to contact you by phone and confirm your identity before opening a new account in your name.

"People are required to provide their Social Security number, along with their date of birth and other personal information needed by identity thieves, to a wide range of companies and service providers that they utilize every day, including utility companies, insurance agencies, doctors, schools, lawyers, accountants, and their employer. So, simply telling people to guard their Social Security number is not an adequate way to protect their identity."

What services does LifeLock offer for the monthly membership fee?

Todd Davis: "In addition to requesting and obtaining for you free copies of your credit reports to review from all three credit reporting agencies, a complete list of what's offered with our service can be found on our website.

"For example, we take steps to ensure that if your personal information falls into the wrong hands, it becomes harder for the criminals to use it to make money or commit fraud.

"A credit monitoring service will only notify you after a change has been made to your credit report. In other words, you find out after someone has opened a credit card account, for example, in your name. We are in the business of protecting your data. Our core business is to protect people from the fastest growing crime in America.

"Using our WalletLock service, which is free to members, if you lose your wallet or it gets stolen, we will contact all of your credit card companies and help you change your account numbers and obtain replacement cards. We'll also help you get a replacement driver's license."

Who is the ideal customer for LifeLock?

Todd Davis: "Anyone who has a good credit rating and wants to protect it is our ideal customer. The reality, however, is that every American needs to take active steps to protect their identity whether they use our service or take the necessary precautionary steps on their own. Identity thieves can victimize anyone with a Social Security number, including infants, children, teens, adults, and senior citizens.

"When someone steals a valid Social Security number from an infant or child, for example, and the identity thief attempts to establish credit using that stolen Social Security number that's in your child's name, all that's reported by the credit reporting agency is that the Social

Security number and the person's name is valid, but that the person [your child] has no credit history.

"The credit reporting agencies and lenders/creditors don't compare data from a loan application against the accurate data related to the Social Security number. So, someone with your child's name and Social Security number can make up their age, address, and other information, and that false data never gets checked before a fraudulent credit card account, for example, is opened.

"The identity thief can take their time, over many years, and build up a credit rating using your child's name and Social Security number, and the fraud often won't get noticed for years. For a variety of reasons that benefit the credit reporting agencies, there are no checks and balances in place."

If someone has already become a victim of identity theft, can signing up for LifeLock now still benefit them, or is the damage already done?

Todd Davis: "LifeLock only takes responsibility for identity theft that happens after someone becomes a member of our service. However, if you believe your data has been compromised, but no fraudulent activity has yet occurred, we can still help you. It could take months or years for an identity thief to begin utilizing your personal data after they steal it."

What is the biggest misconception people have about identity theft?

Todd Davis: "It's that you only need to worry about it if you already have great wealth and an excellent credit rating. This simply isn't true. People with bad credit think there's nothing an identity thief could possibly do to hurt their credit rating any more or impact them financially. Even people with really bad credit ratings can become victims of identity theft and have money stolen from them. It can also become very difficult to ever fix your credit rating if you become an identity theft victim and don't do anything about it. The damage can be devastating."

Dirty Little Secrets

What are some of the things people can do for themselves, without LifeLock, to protect their identity?

Todd Davis: "Anyone can place fraud alerts on their credit reports for free, every 90 days. Anyone can also request free copies of their credit reports at least once per year to look for signs of fraud or credit theft. If necessary, it's possible for consumers to add a credit freeze to their credit reports, which means that nobody can access their credit report, for any reason whatsoever, without you knowing about it first. However, if you place a freeze on your credit reports, you have to lift the freeze anytime you apply for a loan or credit. In some states, a credit freeze costs money.

"Another thing anyone can do to help protect their identity is to opt out of receiving pre-approved credit card offers in the mail. To do this, call (888) 5OPT-OUT. Once you do this, the only companies that can send you credit card offers are banks or financial institutions with which you have a pre-existing relationship.

"Just like people can do their own taxes for free, they can protect their own identity. Or they can hire an accountant to do their taxes and use LifeLock to help protect their identity."

What are some things a person should look for as clues of identity theft?

Todd Davis: "When you review your credit reports, look for trade lines that don't belong there, such as credit card accounts or loans that you never applied for or received. One way many people find out they've been victimized is that they'll begin to receive calls from a collection agency trying to collect money for an overdue account that doesn't belong to them and that they were not aware of.

"I also recommend checking your credit card, debit card, and banking statements carefully every month. Be on the lookout for items, purchases, or charges that don't belong to you and that you did not authorize.

"Another indicator is if you or your kids, for example, start receiving catalogs from companies that don't relate to your interests

Credit Tip

Once you can prove you have been a victim of identity theft or related fraud, you can place a fraud alert on each of your credit reports that will remain there for seven years, without you having to renew them every 90 days. To do this, however, you will typically need to provide copies of police reports and other documentation to the credit reporting agencies.

or buying habits. If your 5-year-old child or 90-year-old grandmother starts to receive catalogs for motorcycle replacement parts, for example, that could indicate that someone is using their name for fraudulent purposes and that their name has been added to a database as a result of someone else's fraudulent actions.

"Also, from the Social Security Administration, order a copy of your work history. This can help you determine if someone is posing as you to gain employment."

What is the biggest mistake people make that can put their identity in jeopardy?

Todd Davis: "You can do everything right and even take the added precaution of shredding your personal documents before throwing them in the garbage, but it's still possible that your personal data can be acquired by thieves and criminals. It's important to understand this.

"One of the biggest mistakes people make is giving out personal information about themselves when they reply to fraudulent offers via the internet. Criminals create emails that look like they're being sent by reputable and well-known companies and financial institutions, but the goal of these emails is to trick innocent and unsuspecting people into revealing their personal information, such as a credit card number or their Social Security number. Some of these online messages look very legitimate. Avoid being a victim of one of these scams. Don't respond to any of these requests, unless you have initiated the contact online. Also, when you shop online, make sure you're using a secure website. Look for the little lock symbol at the bottom of the web browser."

Thoughts About Bankruptcy from an Attorney

If you've gotten yourself into serious financial problems, declaring bankruptcy is not a magical solution that will make all of your problems and debts simply go away. As you've already learned, bankruptcy should be considered only as an absolutely last resort after you've consulted with a credit counselor or financial expert to determine if there are other ways out of your financial predicament.

In this final interview, you'll learn more about bankruptcy from Kimberly Pelkey Sdeo, a bankruptcy attorney from Maselli Warren, P.C. (www.maselliwarren.com) in New Jersey. Kimberly Pelkey Sdeo has been practicing bankruptcy law for more than five years. Her clients include individual consumer debtors and some individuals with failed or failing small businesses.

If someone is experiencing financial problems, at what point should they consider filing for bankruptcy?

Kimberly Pelkey Sdeo: "I feel it's always important to explore your options. Consulting with a bankruptcy attorney initially often costs no more than an hour of your time. Most attorneys offer consultations free of charge. I don't feel that it's my role to shove bankruptcy down people's throats. If it's not a good fit, I let them know. Just as with any decision, you have to weigh the costs and benefits. Filing for bankruptcy is no different."

What are some of the biggest benefits and pitfalls related to filing for bankruptcy?

Kimberly Pelkey Sdeo: "One of the most powerful tools built into the bankruptcy code is the automatic stay. The automatic stay prohibits creditors from taking collection action against debtors while in bankruptcy. This means the telephone calls, collection letters, and lawsuits stop the minute the bankruptcy petition is filed. A creditor cannot repossess a vehicle or continue with a foreclosure if the debtor files bankruptcy without seeking permission from the court to continue these actions.

"Most consumer debtors file for bankruptcy relief under Chapter 7, which is a liquidation, and most Chapter 7 cases filed are no asset cases. This means that the debtors receive a discharge, elimination of most, if not all, of their debts without repayment, and are able to keep all of their property."

What options should consumers consider before taking this route?

Kimberly Pelkey Sdeo: "Consumers should do their homework and explore their options. It is important to understand what bankruptcy is, how it works, and its limitations. It is not the right choice for everyone facing debt problems, although it can be an extremely powerful tool for some.

"I was meeting with a potential client recently, and he wasn't sure what to do. He had approximately $15,000 in credit card debt. He owned a home free and clear, and his only source of income was Social Security. While he was eligible to file a Chapter 7, he would have risked losing his home to pay off the debt.

"When we looked at a possible Chapter 13 and ran some sample calculations, the necessary payment plan was only nominally less than what it would take to pay off the credit cards on his own in three years.

"While bankruptcy would offer a cost savings of having the interest frozen as of the petition date and the potential that not all the creditors would file claims to be paid, he would be committed to a bankruptcy plan for three years and prohibited from using other credit during that time.

"In this circumstance, filing is a more nuanced decision. Other options included taking a home equity loan to pay off the credit cards and repay the debt at a lower interest rate, but that has its own set of risks, including turning unsecured debt into secured debt. If he defaults on the home equity loan in the future, he would risk losing his home through a foreclosure action."

At what point should someone seek out the assistance of a bankruptcy attorney?

Kimberly Pelkey Sdeo: "When they are feeling overwhelmed and feel that there is more money going out the door than coming in. Many will wait until they are served with a collection lawsuit, foreclosure complaint, or notice of a wage garnishment or bank levy."

What can someone expect from the experience of working with a bankruptcy attorney? What is the process like? How long does it take? Does it need to be done in person, or can it be handled on the phone or via email?

Kimberly Pelkey Sdeo: "My role is to walk my clients through the bankruptcy process step by step. I am there to explain their options and hold their hands through the process.

"The process of filing and receiving a discharge is fairly quick for debtors filing no asset Chapter 7 cases. The process from the date the petition is filed to the date they receive their discharge is often less than six months. Chapter 13 cases involve repayment plans and take between three and five years to complete.

"I meet with clients in person for the initial consultation, as well as to review and sign the petition, and for the court date relating to the meeting of creditors. The rest can be handled via email or phone calls. Sometimes, clients like to stop in and ask a question or drop off documents in person. I welcome that as well. This is a stressful time in their lives, and we are here to reassure them."

How much does it typically cost for someone to hire a bankruptcy attorney and file for bankruptcy? What if someone is in serious debt and doesn't have the money to pay legal fees?

Kimberly Pelkey Sdeo: "Bankruptcy costs less than most people think. The costs will depend upon the complexity of the case and type of bankruptcy to be filed. In general Chapter 7 cases are generally less expensive than Chapter 13 cases.

"The attorney's fees may also be capped by the court. In my district, attorneys cannot charge more than $3,500 for a standard Chapter 13 case. If they wish to charge more they need to explain why to the court.

"An attorney's fees for bankruptcies are often billed on a flat-fee basis. Most attorneys require fees for Chapter 7 cases to be paid in advance. If they're not collected before filing, the attorney becomes a creditor and cannot ask the client to repay. In Chapter 13 cases, attorney's fees can be paid through the plan. Attorney's fees for no-asset Chapter 7 cases are often a small fraction of the debt owed. For debtors eligible to file Chapter 7 who have few assets, there can be a significant cost savings.

"For the indigent debtor, there are pro bono programs that require only the payment of the court filing fees, which are around $300 for a Chapter 7. The court may allow a debtor to pay the filing fee in installments, or may waive the filing fee in certain circumstances."

How can someone go about finding a reputable attorney to work with?

Kimberly Pelkey Sdeo: "Word-of-mouth or the local bar association are great resources. A lawyer referral service is also a way to find an attorney who specializes in bankruptcies."

Before taking this route, what other options should someone pursue if they're in deep financial trouble?

Kimberly Pelkey Sdeo: "Calculate repayment options. Do research. Discover your options so you understand what can and cannot be accomplished, and call an attorney for a consult."

After someone files for bankruptcy, how will their financial life, credit rating, and credit scores be impacted?

Dirty Little Secrets

Kimberly Pelkey Sdeo: "Bankruptcy is a single event in a person's credit history. While the bankruptcy itself will be reported for seven to ten years, it is not a death sentence.

"Bankruptcy is often referred to as a 'fresh start.' After discharge, individuals have the opportunity to rebuild their credit. Their future behaviors will shape their credit future. For debtors coming out of bankruptcy with car loans and mortgages that they have been paying timely throughout the process, they may be able to have a faster credit rebound. Learning to use credit effectively and wisely coming out of bankruptcy will help in the rebuilding process."

What is the biggest misconception people have about bankruptcy?

Kimberly Pelkey Sdeo: "There are lots of misconceptions. Bankruptcy is embarrassing for a lot of people. I try to reassure them and hold their hand throughout the entire process. I remind them that many people who are considered successful have filed bankruptcy, including Walt Disney, President Grant, and Donald Trump, just to name a few.

"I focus on how bankruptcy provides a fresh start and is only one point in the time line of an individual's credit history. People have concerns that bankruptcy will destroy their credit forever, and that they will never be able to purchase a home or finance a car in the future.

"Sometimes, bankruptcy can improve a credit score by eliminating the 'bad debt.' The fresh start gives an individual the chance to start over and rebuild a new, positive credit history by using credit wisely. While the bankruptcy may be reported on a credit report for seven to ten years, it doesn't mean their credit will be shot for that entire time period.

"What an individual chooses to do after filing and receiving a discharge will have the greatest impact on their credit future. Many married couples think that they have to file bankruptcy together, which is also untrue. A spouse can file alone, and if there are no joint debts, the non-filing spouse remains wholly unaffected.

Dirty Little Secrets

"Many clients are concerned about others finding out about their bankruptcy. I remind them that overall bankruptcy is a private process. Your neighbors and relatives, unless they are your creditors, will not find out. They would have to go to the courthouse and search for you by name in order to gain any information about your bankruptcy filing."

What are the biggest mistakes people should avoid when filing for bankruptcy?

Kimberly Pelkey Sdeo: "Not doing their homework. Bankruptcy, like many other options, has both risks and rewards. People get caught up on the fact that bankruptcy will appear on their credit reports, but forget that they already have established a negative credit history from months or more often years of late or non-payment."

Based on your experience, can you offer any additional advice that will save people time, money, confusion, or frustration?

Kimberly Pelkey Sdeo: "Don't be afraid to reach out for help, and reach out for help early. It is much easier to handle debt problems in their infancy and maybe avoid a potential bankruptcy than to have a mad scramble to file once you have received a notice that your wages will be garnished in the next pay cycle or your home is about to be sold at sheriff's sale after a foreclosure."

What's Next?

In the final chapter of *Dirty Little Secrets*, we'll take a look at some of the tools you can use to help you manage your personal finances and ultimately protect or enhance your credit rating by being responsible with your credit cards and bank accounts. Whether you want to use an online-based service, computer software on your PC or Mac, or an app on your smartphone or tablet, a wide range of free and low-cost tools is at your disposal.

Managing Your Finances
There's an App For That

What's in This Chapter

- Tools to help you manage your personal finances and pay your bills

- Personal finance software, apps, and websites

By now you should know you'll need to properly manage your personal finances and pay all of your bills on time in order to protect or improve your credit rating and overall credit scores. The good news is that there are a variety of easy-to-use online tools, software for your computer, and/or apps for your smartphone or tablet that can make this process much easier.

Using the technological tools available to you to manage your finances, you can automatically be reminded to pay each of your bills before it's due. Plus, you can utilize online banking to either manually pay your bills or set it up so your important bills are paid automatically using funds from your checking account.

When it comes to managing your personal finances, credit cards, and other bills, you have a handful of options, including:

■ You can access the online banking services offered by your bank or financial institution to manage your checking and/or savings account, check balances, transfer funds between accounts, and pay your bills online, for example. Online banking is typically a free service offered by a bank.

⑤ Credit Tip

Assuming you have the funds available, you can set up autopayments for each of your credit card accounts so that the minimum payment for each is automatically made on or before it's due. This will help you avoid costly late-payment fees and maintain your credit rating.

You always have the option to manually pay more than your minimum payment each month, but having the auto-payment feature set up ensures that you'll continuously remain in good standing with each of your credit card accounts.

You can set up an auto-payment option from your credit card issuer's website or app, use an online personal finance tool (such as Mint.com), or use personal finance software that's installed on your computer (such as Quicken) to access and manage your checking, savings, credit card, and investment accounts.

■ You can access the online tools offered by your credit card issuer to manage your individual credit card accounts, check available credit, review recent transactions, view your monthly statements, make payments, or schedule automatic payments, for example. This is a more timely method of managing your accounts than reviewing monthly printed statements that are mailed to you.

■ You can access independent personal finance-related online tools, like Mint.com (www.mint.com), and manage your checking, savings, credit cards, and investment accounts from one centralized and secure service. Once set up, a service like Mint.com allows you to manage your personal finances, transfer money between your accounts, pay bills online, and handle other money-related tasks from one centralized service that links to your own bank, credit card issuers, and other finance-related companies you work with. The benefit to using this type of online service is that your financial data is secure but accessible from any computer or mobile device with internet access. This allows you to log in from home, work, or while on the go to check balances, pay bills, or handle a wide range of other tasks.

■ You can use personal finance software, such as Quicken from Intuit (www.intuit.com), to manage all aspects of your personal

Warning

If you set up auto-payments for your credit cards or other bills, make sure you have ample funds in your checking or savings account to cover the payments. Otherwise, your bank will charge you overdraft fees, plus the companies to which the automatic payments were supposed to go could charge you late fees.

Dirty Little Secrets

You Should Know . . .

Bank of America, Wells Fargo, Chase, Citibank, Capital One, PCN, Citizens Bank, TD, U.S. Bank, and SunTrust are among the many banks and financial institutions that offer free apps to account holders. Many credit card issuers, including American Express and Discover, as well as specific banks that issue credit cards, offer free apps for managing individual credit card accounts.

finances on your PC or Mac computer. The benefit to using this type of software is that your data gets stored securely on your computer, as opposed to online. However, you can then manage your finances only from the computer on which you have the software and related financial data stored, although you can back up your data to a USB thumb drive, which you can insert into another computer that has the correct software. If you work off of the thumb drive on another computer, you have to remember to copy it back to your home computer.

 *Warning*

When setting up accounts with your banks, credit card issuers, or other companies that you'll be accessing online, do not use the same user name and password for each. While doing this makes it easier to remember the log-in information for each website or account, it also puts you at greater risk if an unauthorized person gains access to your information.

Dirty Little Secrets

■ You can use personal finance apps from third parties or that are available for free from your bank and/or credit card issuers to manage your various accounts from your Apple iPhone, iPad, or Android-compatible smartphone, tablet, or mobile device. As you'll discover, there are apps that sync data with Quicken and other personal finance software, as well as Mint.com (and related online services).

Mint.com Is an Online and App Tool

If you want to manage your bank accounts, credit card accounts, and investment accounts using one centralized tool set, plus be able to transfer money between accounts, pay bills online, and track your spending, Mint.com (www.mint.com) offers a free, easy-to-use, but very powerful solution.

Mint.com is an online service that can be used from any PC or Mac that's connected to the internet. Free apps for the iPhone, iPad, or Android are also available, allowing you to access and manage all of your financial data remotely.

Mint.com first launched in September 2007 but since then has continued to evolve by adding a wide range of new features and functionality. The service is now owned and operated by Intuit, the makers of the popular Quicken and QuickBooks software.

Because the service is free, you will see subtle advertising messages that relate to your personal finances as you use the online service or app. These ads will often direct you to optional fee-based services you may find useful, such as ways to track your credit score and access credit reports, use a price comparison tool that can help you save money on your insurance, or tools for finding good deals on credit cards, auto loans, or other financial products. You always have the option to ignore these ads while still taking full advantage of the free aspects of the Mint.com service to manage your finances.

Once set up, Mint.com links to all of your various accounts, regardless of the bank, financial institution, or credit card issuer, and

Dirty Little Secrets

then provides you with real-time information about your accounts (including balances and recent transactions), as long as your computer, smartphone, or tablet has internet access.

In addition to manually paying your bills online (including your credit card payments, mortgage, and car payment) without having to write and mail checks, for example, you can schedule automatic bill reminders to be sent via email or text message to your smartphone.

Using Mint.com, you can also set up automatic payments for recurring monthly bills. Whether you're trying to rebuild your credit or protect your credit rating, using Mint.com will help to ensure that you pay all of your bills on time, plus keep close tabs on how you're spending and managing your money.

What's nice about Mint.com is that you don't need to be a financial wizard to understand how the service works. You can set up and learn to use Mint.com's online tools and smartphone/tablet app in less than 30

Mint.com Offers Several Useful Fee-Based Premium Services Too

Mint.com also offers an optional and fee-based credit monitoring service that allows you to access your credit scores and view changes to your credit reports as they happen. You can also research to apply for new credit cards that offer good deals to consumers.

Plus, Mint.com can be used to help you find and apply for many types of insurance, as well as choose investment opportunities. Click on the "Find Savings" option from the main Mint.com webpage to learn about the optional services it offers. While a few of these features are fee-based, using them through Mint.com allows you to manage all aspects of your finances from one centralized place.

minutes, and then use it to create, manage, and stick to a personalized budget with minimal effort moving forward.

This service is compatible with almost every major bank and financial institution, so you can seamlessly and automatically link your Mint.com account to your other accounts in minutes. As the service accesses your checking account, for example, it will automatically categorize many of your recurring expenses, such as car payments, mortgage payments, or insurance payments. For some expenses, you'll need to categorize them manually once, and then the Mint.com service will handle the categorization of those expenses in the future.

To get started using Mint.com on your PC or Mac, visit www.Mint.com. You can also visit Apple's App Store to download and install the free Mint.com iPhone/iPad app. As you get yourself up and running using Mint.com, access www.mint.com/community/videos to watch free how-to videos that cover a wide range of topics, from learning to use Mint.com to creating and sticking to a personalized budget.

Manage Your Credit Cards with a Smartphone App

Many credit card companies, banks, and financial institutions now offer their own proprietary iPhone/iPad and Android phone apps for managing credit cards issued by their institution (as well as checking or savings accounts).

One of the great things about using an app to manage your credit cards is that you can easily sign into your credit card account

You Should Know...

Proprietary Apple iPhone apps for managing credit cards also work with the iPad, while Android apps will work on most Android-compatible smartphones or tablets.

Dirty Little Secrets

($) *Credit Tip*

If your credit card offers some type of reward, such as cash back, the ability to earn airline frequent flier miles, or points redeemable for merchandise, these iPhone or Android apps can often be used to manage and/or redeem those rewards.

---

from anywhere, and then access your up-to-date balance information, determine your available credit, learn when your next payment is due, and discover what the minimum payment will be for that billing cycle. You can also access details about recent transactions and make online credit card payments directly from your checking account using one of these apps.

Using the app available from each of your credit card issuers for each of your credit cards can help you avoid late-payment and over-credit-limit fees, while making it convenient to make your monthly payments and track your credit card spending. If you have two or more credit cards from the same issuer, such as Capital One, you can manage those cards using the same Capital One app. Likewise, if you have a checking and/or savings account with that same financial institution, you can often manage those accounts as well from the app.

However, if you have credit cards from different banks or financial institutions, you will need to use separate apps for each of them (or use a service like Mint.com and a related app to handle everything from a single app).

On your iPhone or iPad, visit the App Store to determine if your credit card issuer has a proprietary app for managing your account. Within the search field, enter the name of your credit card issuer or bank, such as Bank of America or Capital One. If you use an Android-based phone or tablet, the bank or credit card issuer's website will direct you to where you can download and install the app.

Dirty Little Secrets

You Should Know . . .

For the iPhone and iPad, American Express and Discover both have their own proprietary and feature-packed apps that can be used for managing those credit cards. Both apps are available from the App Store for free, but are only useful to American Express or Discover cardholders.

Just like performing online banking tasks from your primary computer, managing a credit card account from your mobile device is a secure process. When you first install the app, you'll be required to create a user name and password for accessing your account via the app.

Depending on the app, one popular feature is the ability to set up automated alerts that remind you when to make payments, when specific transactions are cleared, when pre-set automatic monthly payments are made, and/or when you're about to reach your credit limit.

The various types of alerts the app is capable of generating can be set up from within the app and then sent to your mobile device via email, text message, or through messages within the app that on an iPhone or iPad can be displayed within Notification Center.

For the iPhone and iPad, there are a handful of apps from third parties that can be used to help you manage one or more credit card accounts, regardless of the issuer. These apps, available from the App Store, include:

■ *Credit Card Expense Manager* ($14.99). This app is designed to simultaneously manage all of your credit card accounts from one app. Use this app to view your overall credit situation on one screen and determine how much credit is available on each card, while simultaneously viewing your overall credit utilization. The app will automatically download account-specific information for each credit card account, so you can also view detailed transaction summaries. You will need internet access.

Dirty Little Secrets

> **($) Credit Tip**
>
> Using the calculators that are built into many of the apps designed for managing credit card accounts, you can figure out how much a particular purchase will ultimately cost you, including interest, if you pay for it using a specific credit card and plan to pay off the balance over time, based on the interest rate and specific credit card charges.

- *Debt Manager* ($1.99). This app utilizes the "debt snowball" method to show you exactly how to efficiently pay off your credit card debts in the fastest and least expensive way possible, whether you want to pay off the lowest or highest balances first or focus on first paying off your highest interest credit cards.
- *Credit Card Calc* (Free). By entering information about your credit card debt into this easy-to-use app, it's possible to quickly calculate how long and how much it will cost to pay off your debt if you only pay the minimum payment due each month, or if you pay a fixed amount each month that's above the minimum payment. You also have the option to select a payoff period and then calculate what your monthly payments will need to be, based on the interest rate and other fees associated with each credit card account.

To find other iPhone or iPad apps designed to help you manage your personal finances, create and manage a budget, or manage your credit card accounts, visit the App Store. Within the search field, enter the keyword "bank" to find proprietary apps from specific banks. You can also enter the name of your specific bank, such as Capital One, Chase, Bank of America, or Citibank, to find specialized apps offered by those financial institutions.

Use the phrase "credit cards" to find apps ideal for managing multiple credit card accounts, or use the keywords "budget" or

Dirty Little Secrets

"personal finance" to help you find apps that can be used to manage your personal finances.

If you're good at using spreadsheets, the Numbers app for the iPhone or iPad has several templates that are ideal for managing budgets and/or specific types of accounts.

Once search results are displayed within the App Store, pay attention to an app's description, price, and the ratings and reviews it's received. It's these ratings that will help you determine if the app functions as it's described by the developer. For example, an app with a bunch of four- or five-star ratings is apt to be much higher quality than an app with just a few two- or three-star ratings.

As of late September 2012, the Mint.com Personal Finance app for the iPhone/iPad had received more than 10,480 star-based ratings, and its average rating was 4.5 out of 5 stars, which is a really good indication that this is a top-quality app that functions as described by its developer. By then reading the text-based reviews related to the app, which are written by fellow iPhone or iPad users, you can get a good idea about what people like or dislike about it.

Using smartphone or tablet apps to manage your personal finances and credit card accounts makes the process easy. Plus, you can keep tabs on your accounts any time and virtually anywhere, as long as an internet connection is available. Assuming you have the available funds, using apps eliminates many excuses people use to avoid paying bills and making credit card payments in a timely manner.

Now It's Your Turn . . .

If you're experiencing financial problems or have developed a poor credit rating, it's easy to make excuses, blame the economy and/or the government, and convince yourself that your situation is hopeless. While the poor U.S. economy probably has not helped your financial situation, chances are if you follow even some of the advice offered within this book, you have it within your power, starting right now, to begin turning your situation around.

Dirty Little Secrets

Repairing your credit rating and boosting your credit scores is going to take time, persistence, and patience. However, if you make the commitment to take the steps necessary, and then stick to your plan, you will begin seeing at least some positive results within just a few months.

Take responsibility for any mistakes you've made in the past. Learn from those mistakes, and move forward with a detailed plan for improving the situation, keeping in mind that your plan can and should include seeking out the advice you need from financial professionals.

Simply understanding how your credit rating, credit scores and credit reports work, however, puts you at a definite advantage. Now, take the knowledge and understanding you've acquired, and put it to good use on an ongoing basis.

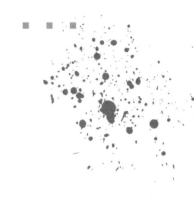

Glossary

Understanding the following credit-related terms will help you better build, manage, and protect your credit rating.

Annual Credit Report Request Service: A centralized service operated by the three credit reporting agencies (credit bureaus) that processes all requests from consumers who wish to receive their free credit reports from each agency. This can be done online, by phone, or by mail.

Annual Fee: Related to credit cards, this is a fee that's charged to the consumer every year for the privilege of having a specific credit card. Depending on the card, the annual fees range from free to $150 per year. If the card has some type of reward for usage (such as airline miles) or a cash-back bonus tied to it, an annual fee will often apply. Ideally, you want a credit card with no annual fee.

Annual Percentage Rate (APR): This is a measure of the cost of credit, expressed as a yearly interest rate.

Average Daily Balance: This is the method the credit card issuer uses to calculate your payment due. Your average daily balance is determined by adding each day's balance and then dividing that total by the number of days in a billing cycle. Your average daily balance is then multiplied by a card's monthly periodic rate, which is calculated by dividing the APR by 12.

Balance Transfer and **Balance Transfer Rate**: A balance transfer involves moving an outstanding balance from one credit card presumably to a lower interest credit card to save money. (The balance would remain the same, but you'd then be paying a lower interest rate.) In order to entice consumers to utilize this, many credit card issuers offer a special incentive or teaser rate on balance transfers. Keep in mind, however, there can also be an additional fee associated with balance transfers, so understand the terms and conditions on both credit cards. The Balance Transfer Rate is the APR you'll receive on the amount of money you transfer to the new card. If you're being offered a special teaser rate, determine what the APR will be when that teaser rate expires. Read the Card Holder Agreement carefully.

Cardholder Agreement: This is the "fine print" associated with each credit card. It lists all of the terms and conditions, fees, and other information a cardholder should know pertaining to the use of that card. All fees, for example, will be listed within the Cardholder Agreement.

Cash Advance Fee: Many credit cards are accompanied by an ATM PIN (Personal Identification Number) that allows you to obtain cash advances using that credit card. Depending on the credit card issuer, there might be a flat fee associated with each ATM transaction, or you could be charged a percentage of the amount withdrawn (and possibly a flat fee as well). Withdrawing money from an ATM using a credit card is referred to as a "cash advance."

Credit: When someone borrows money with the understanding it will be repaid, that person is given credit. Obtaining credit from a creditor has costs associated with it. The cost is incurred based on the interest rate and fees you'll be required to pay over time, in addition to the principal. Although the interest rate can be pre-set or variable, how much you ultimately pay will also be determined by the amount of time it takes you to fully repay the loan, whether it's a mortgage, credit card, car loan, or any other type of loan. There are many forms of loans and credit and each works slightly differently.

Credit Card Transaction Fees: These are extra fees you'll need to pay to use your credit card for certain types of transactions, such as ATM (cash advance) withdrawals, making a late payment, or going over your credit limit.

Credit Counseling: A service that teaches you how to better manage your finances and that can negotiate with your creditors on your behalf to help you regain your financial stability and rebuild your credit. There are often fees associated with credit counseling services, even if the organization you work with is a nonprofit corporation.

Credit Rating: From a potential lender's standpoint, a consumer's credit rating is a summary of his or her credit history and an estimate or educated guess relating to credit worthiness: whether he or she will repay debts on time, with the appropriate interest.

Credit Report: Compiled by one of the credit reporting agencies, such as Equifax, Experian, or TransUnion, a credit report contains personal and financial information about you, including your name, address, phone number, Social Security number, date of birth, past addresses, current and past employers, a listing of companies that have issued you credit (including credit cards, charge cards, car loans, mortgages, student loans, home equity loans, etc.), and details about your credit history (whether or not you pay your bills on time). Each of the major credit reporting agencies compiles a separate credit report for every individual. However, much of the information on each report should be identical or similar.

Credit Reporting Agency (aka Credit Bureau): The three national bureaus that maintain credit reports on virtually all Americans with any type of credit history are Equifax, Experian, and TransUnion. These agencies maintain vast databases that are updated regularly. Their purpose is to supply creditors with timely and reliable financial information about individual consumers. It's important to understand that a credit reporting agency does not decide whether an individual qualifies for credit or not. Credit reporting agencies simply collect information that is relevant to a person's credit history and habits and then provides that information (for a fee), in the form of a credit report, to creditors and lenders.

Credit Score: Using a complex formula that's calculated based on many criteria related to your current financial situation and credit history, the credit reporting agencies, individual creditors and lenders, and third-party companies (including Fair Isaac Corporation) can calculate and regularly determine and update your credit scores. According to the Federal Trade Commission, "Most creditors use credit scoring to evaluate your credit record. This involves using your credit application and report to get information about you, such as your annual income, outstanding debt, bill-paying history, and the number and types of accounts you have and how long you have had them. Potential lenders use your credit score to help predict whether you are a good risk to repay a loan and make payments on time." TransUnion reports someone's credit score is "a mathematical calculation that reflects a consumer's credit worthiness. The score is an assessment of how likely a consumer is to pay his or her debts."

Debt Consolidation: This involves taking out a new, larger loan at one pre-determined interest rate, so that you can pay off multiple outstanding debts that are overdue and/or that potentially are charging much higher interest rates.

Dirty Little Secrets

Debt Management Plan (DMP): A formal and personalized plan used to systematically pay off debt over an extended period of time.

Debt Negotiation Service: Like a credit counseling company, a debt negotiation service will help you make contact with your specific creditors and negotiate on your behalf to help you pay off or settle your debt, depending on the circumstances.

Dispute: To question the truth or validity of information in your credit report with a creditor and/or credit reporting agency. If you find an error in the information listed within your credit reports, you have a right to initiate a dispute. By law, a dispute must be investigated within 30 days. If the information is, in fact, inaccurate, it must then be corrected, causing your credit report and potentially your credit scores to be revised.

Fair Debt Collection Practices Act: Legislation passed by the federal government that outlines the legal rights of consumers, lenders, creditors, and collection agencies; it prohibits debt collectors from engaging in unfair, deceptive, or abusive practices, including over-charging, harassment, and disclosing consumers' debt to third parties.

Federal Trade Commission (FTC): This branch of the U.S. government deals with issues that relate directly to the economic lives of most Americans. The Bureau of Consumer Protection, which operates under the FTC, is responsible for protecting consumers against unfair, deceptive, or fraudulent practices. The Bureau enforces a variety of consumer protection laws enacted by Congress, as well as trade regulation rules issued by the Commission. The FTC is in charge of enforcing the Fair Debt Collection Practices Act.

Grace Period: The time between the day credit card purchases are made and when finance charges (interest, etc.) will start being added to the new balance; typically between 15 and 30 days. If no grace period is offered, finance charges will accrue starting the moment a purchase is made with the credit card.

Identity Theft: The unauthorized use of personal identification information to commit fraud or other crimes. This could include someone using your credit card(s) to make unauthorized purchases or using your identity to take out loans or establish credit in your name.

Minimum Payment: The lowest amount a credit card holder must pay to keep his or her credit card account from going into default (and being reported negatively to the credit reporting agencies). The minimum payment is typically about 2 percent of the outstanding balance.

Mortgage: A long-term loan that is secured by the collateral of a specific real estate property. The borrower is obliged to make a predetermined series of payments to cover the principal, interest, and any related fees.

National Foundation for Credit Counseling (NFCC): The largest and longest-serving national nonprofit credit counseling organization in the U.S. The NFCC's mission is to set the national standard for quality credit counseling, debt reduction services, and education for financial wellness through its member agencies.

Over-the-Limit Fee: A fee charged by your credit card company if you exceed your credit limit in any given billing cycle. Many credit card issuers charge a $38 over-the-limit fee.

Trade Line: Each item listed on your credit report, including mortgage, car loan, student loan, credit card, charge card, or other type of loan. For each Trade Line, you will see detailed information with your credit reports.

Index

Dirty Little Secrets